DISRUPTIVE STORIES

Disruptive Stories

Amplifying Voices from the Writing Center Margins

EDITED BY
Elizabeth Kleinfeld, Sohui Lee, and Julie Prebel

UTAH STATE UNIVERSITY PRESS
Logan

© 2024 by University Press of Colorado

Published by Utah State University Press
An imprint of University Press of Colorado
1580 North Logan Street, Suite 660
PMB 39883
Denver, Colorado 80203-1942

All rights reserved

 The University Press of Colorado is a proud member of Association of University Presses.

The University Press of Colorado is a cooperative publishing enterprise supported, in part, by Adams State University, Colorado State University, Fort Lewis College, Metropolitan State University of Denver, University of Alaska Fairbanks, University of Colorado, University of Denver, University of Northern Colorado, University of Wyoming, Utah State University, and Western Colorado University.

ISBN: 978-1-64642-609-6 (hardcover)
ISBN: 978-1-64642-610-2 (paperback)
ISBN: 978-1-64642-611-9 (ebook)
https://doi.org/10.7330/9781646426119

Library of Congress Cataloging-in-Publication Data

Names: Kleinfeld, Elizabeth, editor. | Lee, Sohui, editor. | Prebel, Julie, editor.
Title: Disruptive stories : amplifying voices from the writing center margins / edited by Elizabeth Kleinfeld, Sohui Lee, and Julie Prebel.
Description: Logan : Utah State University Press, [2024] | Includes bibliographical references and index.
Identifiers: LCCN 2024002517 (print) | LCCN 2024002518 (ebook) | ISBN 9781646426096 (hardcover) | ISBN 9781646426102 (paperback) | ISBN 9781646426119 (ebook)
Subjects: LCSH: Writing centers—Social aspects. | Writing centers—Administration. | English language—Rhetoric—Study and teaching (Higher)—Social aspects. | Academic writing—Study and teaching (Higher)—Social aspects. | Report writing—Study and teaching (Higher)—Social aspects. | Writing centers—Anecdotes. | Tutors and tutoring—Anecdotes.
Classification: LCC PE1404 .D58 2024 (print) | LCC PE1404 (ebook) | DDC 808/.042—dc23/eng/20240223
LC record available at https://lccn.loc.gov/2024002517
LC ebook record available at https://lccn.loc.gov/2024002518

The editors of this collection would like to thank California State University Channel Islands for the Provost's Direct Costs Grant for Research and Creative Activities, which covered the cost of proofreading and indexing of this project.

Cover photograph by Aida L. on Unsplash

Contents

List of Illustrations vii

Introduction: Narratives of Marginalization and Activist Editing Practices
Elizabeth Kleinfeld, Sohui Lee, and Julie Prebel 3

Section One: Structural Marginalization

1. Of Budgets and Institutional Bumbling: New Writing Center Directors Reflect on Their First Year
   Enrique Paz and Elise Dixon 33

2. A Tale of Two Writing Centers: Navigating Fraught Institutional Legacies
   Joshua Botvin and Elisabeth H. Buck 49

3. Belonging in the Center
   Wendy Rider 66

4. Hidden in Plain Sight: Professional Tutors in the Writing Center
   Shareen Grogan, Pam Bromley, and Denise Stephenson 71

5. From Pieces to Whole: Professional Tutors and Instability in the College Writing Center
   Aja Gorham 88

   Response to Section One: Structural Marginalization
   Kerri Rinaldi 103

Section Two: Globalization and Marginalization

6. Becoming a Writing Center Administrator: A Transnational Counterstory
   Nancy Henaku 109

7. Harnessing the Periphery: A Community of Practice in México
   Abigail Villagrán Mora 127

   Response to Section Two: Globalization and Marginalization—Nuancing Narratives of Marginalization in the Writing Center: Reflecting on Identity, Language, and Literacy
   Weijia Li and Esther R. Namubiru 144

Section Three: Embodied Marginalization

8. Tutors/Tutees Tango: Cross-Stepping [Dis]Abilities in Writing Centers
   Myra Tatum Salcedo 149

9. Cripping Marginality: Disability and Directing a Writing Center
   Karen Moroski-Rigney 154

10. Please! Stop Doing More with Less
    Elena Garcia 172

11. Sign of the Cross: A Case Study of a First-Gen Latina's Experience of Marginalization at an Evangelical Christian University
    Deborah Escalante 177

12. Is the Writing Center Safe Yet? Narrative Vignettes of Women's Bodily Security in Our "Cozy Homes"
    Sarah Fischer 194

13. Womanist Way-Making in Writing Center Administration: Reflections on Marginalization, Misogynoir, and Resistance
    Zandra Jordan 199

    Response to Section Three: Embodied Marginalization
    Rachel Azima 215

Afterword: Imagining—and Enacting—Inclusive Writing Center (Scholarly) Practices
   Elizabeth Kleinfeld, Sohui Lee, and Julie Prebel 219

Index 227
About the Editors 237

Illustrations

Figures

0.1. Traditional double-anonymous publishing process in peer-reviewed journals   13
7.1. The three segments of a semi-structured interview   134
7.2. Coding for the specific elements of a KI within three types of practice: tutoring, collaborative projects, and current professional activities   136

Tables

4.1. Types of tutors working in US writing centers   77
4.2. Types of tutors mentioned in *WCJ* articles, 2005–2019, by percentage   80
5.1. Participant information anonymized   92
6.1. Notes from administrator's meeting   123
7.1. Data collection from the online questionnaire   135
7.2. Data collection from the semi-structured interview   135

DISRUPTIVE STORIES

INTRODUCTION

Narratives of Marginalization and Activist Editing Practices

ELIZABETH KLEINFELD, SOHUI LEE, AND JULIE PREBEL

Working and writing in a time of heightened social justice and advocacy movements that recognize and amplify unheard, silenced, and marginalized voices, writing center practitioners and scholars are compelled to reckon with the stories we tell that may, whether overtly or inadvertently, reify discourses of marginalization. Turning a lens on the narratives we disseminate in the articles and books we publish, the editors of this collection ask: What stories and voices are left out when we perpetuate the writing center grand narratives? In *Peripheral Visions for Writing Centers*, Jackie Grutsch McKinney points to the tendency in writing center studies to subscribe to "grand narratives," common (and often experience-based) stories that highlight our shared beliefs about the work we do (2013). While the problem of grand narratives—what some scholars call "orthodoxy" (Santa 2002) or "lore bias" (Kjesrud 2015)—has been examined before and through a variety of lenses including the way we collect data and relay information (Lerner 2014), Grutsch McKinney delves into why orthodox discourse may be so attractive, even though communities like writing centers can be vastly different in administrator's status, organizational structure, services, and practices. Our professional community is drawn to grand narratives because these are simultaneously "beneficial and constraining": writing center grand narratives create a sense of belonging within an imagined, unified community of practice but can also be limiting in delineating theories and practices that conflict with the experiences of writing center practitioners in disparate institutions within and outside the US. Not surprisingly, writing center grand narratives carry assumptions about practices and theories that are, in fact, culturally based and situated in US higher education. The grand narratives of writing center work create a "collective tunnel vision" (2013, 5) that may overlook underrepresented labor and iron out the messy pluralities of experiences and realities in writing center work that do not fit neatly in our lore.

One main objective of this collection is to scrutinize and disrupt writing center grand narratives by giving center stage to voices that have been marginalized in our scholarly conversations. The authors in this collection shine the spotlight on often-overlooked writing center work experiences that are not often represented in our scholarship. However, as we explain later when describing our methodology, the process of finding and providing support for overlooked voices is as critical as the voices themselves. As we argue, the publishing of marginalized voices requires a radical shift in how we practice writing center scholarship so that it is intentionally more inclusive (Blewett et al. 2019; Kleinfeld, Lee, and Prebel 2021a; Webster 2021). Thus, with this collection, we both highlight perspectives and topics not explicitly or often enough addressed in writing center scholarship and, at the same time, disrupt our field's scholarly pathways through an editorial process that creates the space for more diverse voices.

We are certainly not the first to be interested in amplifying marginalized voices. The work in this collection emerges from and alongside ongoing conversations in writing centers and composition studies focused on antiracist, anti-ableist, queer, and inclusive pedagogies. Anne Geller, Michele Eodice, Frankie Condon, Meg Caroll, and Elizabeth Boquet, for instance, push writing center practitioners to be more self-conscious in the shaping of writing centers by recognizing and actively dismantling racist pedagogical practices and structures embedded in academe (Condon 2007; Geller et al. 2007). Reminding us that writing centers are complicit in oppressive literacy practices, Vershawn Ashanti Young calls for a reconsideration of translingualism as an antiracist writing center responsibility (2010; Young and Martinez 2011). In *Writing Centers and the New Racism: A Call for Sustainable Dialogue and Change*, Laura Greenfield and Karen Rowan bring these and other scholars together in what has become a foundational collection examining white privilege and the "whiteliness" (Inoue 2016) of writing center practices (Greenfield and Rowan

2011). In their literature review, Greenfield and Rowan note the "paucity of explicit and critical dialogue about race" in writing center scholarship (9) and call for more diverse voices to contribute to our field's research and scholarship. Extending this previous work, scholarship has increasingly examined how racialized spaces of writing centers have reproduced systemic inequities (Faison 2018; Lee 2019; Lockett 2019). Wonderful Faison, for example, interrogates an element common in our grand narratives: the racialized connotations of writing centers as cozy or safe(r) spaces that purport to provide comfort for clients and staff. By focusing on the experiences of Black tutors who may be forced to perform aspects of their identities in their writing center work and whose voices are "historically marginalized," Faison reveals how norms of whiteness inevitably shape our practices—and our scholarship (2018). Alexandria Lockett similarly highlights the "racial significance of [their] lived experience performing [the] conventions" of writing center work as a "black queer tutor" to interrogate the labor conditions in a graduate writing center and broaden our field's racial perspectives (2019, 20). Lockett, like Faison and others, identifies an urgent need in our field to increase scholarship "that explicitly addresses race and racism" and to publish marginalized voices (28).

Just as these and other scholars have argued how writing centers are racialized spaces—and offered concrete ways for our centers and scholarship to become antiracist—Harry Denny writes of the heteronormative origins of writing centers and defines the queer writing center as a space that supports the diverse identities of student writers. In the landmark article "Queering the Writing Center," Denny acknowledges that "writing centers are sites around which folklore circulates," extending our field's understanding of the importance and relevance of embodied experiences of identity in shaping the stories we tell (2010a, 95). Denny widens this focus on how the stories we tell highlight a tension between experiences of "margin" and "center" wherein it is not only the "absence of experiences and voices of Others" that are "conspicuous [and] jarring" but also the "complicity in silencing and failing to listen to" marginalized voices that are ubiquitous in our scholarship (*Facing the Center*: Denny 2010b, 5–6). Denny situates the embodied experiences of oppression and marginalization in writing center work within the cultural and historical contexts of identity social movements, laying a pathway for scholarship focused on the inextricable links between the work we do and the possibilities of social action. In a more recent collection, Denny and coeditors Robert Mundy, Liliana Naydan, Richard Sévère, and Anna Sicari build on this social activist work in writing center research by bringing together a "diverse collection of voices" representing the intersecting experiences of identity of writing center practitioners (*Out in the Center*: Denny et al. 2019). Our collection extends this focus on the social and cultural politics that shape writing center work as we emphasize how the scholarly practices of our field have tended to reify inequities. We recognize that writing center scholarship has focused on concerns of equity and access for many years, and this work continues to be pertinent as shown in special issues of the *Dangling Modifier* (spring and fall 2020), which address underrepresentation in the professional and lived experiences of writing center consultants, and in the two-part special issue of *Praxis* (2019, 2020) focused on queer invisibility and marginalization in writing centers and writing center discourse.

As this scholarship in racial and gender marginalization makes clear, it is important that we continue to understand and talk about the interactions of our identities with our administrative labor. As Travis Webster notes, the stories of marginalized writing center practitioners are often drowned out by the dominant lore circulated in our professional conversations and scholarship (2021, 6). Webster's recent International Writing Centers Association (IWCA)–award-winning book, *Queerly Centered: LGBTQA Writing Center Directors Navigate the Workplace*, which focuses on queer discomfort and invisibility in writing center work, is a timely contribution to research in our field that examines how the labor of a marginalized writing center administrator (WCA) might not fit easily into our commonly told practices. Webster's book explores both the "discomfort and rewards" of queer labor in writing center work through an empirically driven study of queer writing center practitioners (5). Through this research, Webster provides a call to action for all writing center administrators and advances claims we find especially resonant with our collection. First, Webster concludes that examining writing center administration through a queer lens both "aligns and departs from current conversations in writing center administrative labor" (5). Webster resists the "lore and hearsay" (5) of writing center labor practices—what we refer to as the grand narratives—in order to situate intersectional experiences of laboring in our practices and our scholarship. Second, Webster turns the lens to focus on the "invisible labor" of the book's participants, revealing stories and discussions of marginalization that amplify experiences and concerns that writing center scholarship has not "explicitly addressed" (11). This collection is aligned with Webster's project, and we reach similar conclusions about how the administrative labor of writing center work is often rendered invisible. Whereas *Queerly Centered* makes visible the work writing center administration entails through the narratives of queer practitioners, our collection emerges alongside Webster's and broadens the scope by including a range of experiences of marginalization.

We have cited only a fraction of the scholars whose work has shaped our own and that of the authors in this collection. This scholarship prompts us to look deeply at how we experience marginalization in our work and how we might perpetuate experiences of marginalization in our scholarly practices. We recognize too that marginality is not a new topic for writing centers. Marginality in and of writing centers in academe has been both bemoaned and embraced in writing center scholarship (Delli Carpini and Crimmins 2001; Macauley and Mauriello 2007; Shelly 2014; Denny et al. 2019; Mackiewicz and Babcock 2019). Rebecca Hallman Martini (2002), for example, discusses the challenges of opening or keeping open a writing center when administrative decisions point to a devaluing of our work and the people doing this work. Hallman Martini's solution (2002) to the effects of marginalization experienced by many writing centers and WCAs is to build strategic partnerships forged through shared commitments to the importance of writing in higher education. Hallman Martini (2002) reminds us too that the crisis moments that contribute to our experiences of marginalization may open up possibilities of change and help us envision ways to disrupt the status quo by responding innovatively and—we would add—agentively. As such, while not a new topic, marginalization continues to be relevant in the experiences of many WCAs and necessary for us to examine and respond to as a field.

Our focus—and the focus of the authors in this collection—on experiences of marginalization is also kairotic given the oppressive and violent discourse and actions (cultural, political, legislative) that continue to perpetuate discrimination, inequalities, and injustices directed especially at people of color, disabled people, and queer and trans people. Following the murder of George Floyd in the summer of 2020, soon after the killing of Breonna Taylor earlier that spring, many writing centers created solidarity statements, which were shared widely through our professional mailing lists. These statements recognized the systemic marginalization of Black people in particular and people of color, queer, and trans people more broadly as writing centers (re)committed themselves to actions that actively promote antiracism and justice, equity, and inclusion. Writing center scholarship too turned a critical lens to examine, as Faison and Condon assert, the legacy of white supremacy and how this "legacy has been made manifest in writing centre scholarship, practice, tutor education, and writing centre design and management" (Faison and Condon

2022, 5). The chapters in Faison and Condon's collection, similar to those in ours, which narrate the lived experiences of WCAs, provide resistant counterstories to the dominant racial ideology that infuses all aspects of writing center work. As Aja Martinez explains, counterstory can be understood as a rhetorical method informed by scholarship in critical race theory and when practiced provides a way to tell the "stories of . . . people whose experiences are often not told" (2020, 26). With these social and disciplinary frameworks in mind, this collection is thus situated within discourses and surrounding activism focused on recentering historically marginalized voices and making those voices heard.

We are also aware that our collection is far from being comprehensive. When reviewing submissions for the collection, we found some of the omissions were obvious. For example, we noticed the lack of submissions from writing center practitioners representing tribal colleges or Historically Black Colleges and Universities (HBCUs). There are contributors in this collection who have attended or worked in HBCUs, but we recognize that race, racialization, and writing center administration need deeper exploration within this collection and in writing center scholarship more broadly. In the case of tribal colleges, we made serious attempts to contact administrators, faculty, and tutors in tribal writing centers, creating a spreadsheet of thirty-seven tribal colleges after researching contact information for their student support services. We emailed their administrators or writing tutors multiple times, but we received no responses. The silence, though, may not be due to lack of interest. Considering the narratives conveyed by our own authors in this collection, the silence may speak to how writing tutoring is positioned institutionally, how employees are rewarded or recognized (or not) for particular activities, and whether administrators/tutors see themselves as part of a larger writing center community. These structural, material, and perceptual realities—also voiced by our authors in this collection—may be barriers to participation and publication.

Another barrier to publication may be our field's emphasis in the last few decades on validating writing center experiences through research that is replicable, aggregable, and data-supported (RAD). First proposed by Richard H. Haswell (2005), RAD research aligned with research principles in the sciences and social sciences and thus offered a way to reach wider audiences and legitimize writing center work (Driscoll and Powell 2015). Following Haswell, RAD research has become more than just a way to (re)conceptualize writing center work as something other than social interactions and observations; RAD has been defined as a "process that shapes our inquiry, strengthens our credibility, and positions us to speak with authority" (Driscoll and Powell 2015). While scholars emphasize that RAD research is not only about quantitative data collection, there has been a notable turn to writing center scholarship that is less "lore-based" and more grounded in methods of handling data using systematic practices such as qualitative coding strategies or other ways of measuring writing center phenomena (Driscoll and Wynn Purdue 2014; Lerner 2014; Driscoll and Powell 2015; Mackiewicz and Thompson 2015). However, with increased focus on antiracist and inclusive writing center practices in recent years, some scholars have pushed back on the assumptions that RAD research is the primary way our field can be recognized as a "respectable intellectual discipline" and no longer compared to an "academic ghetto" (Lockett 2019, 23). With this collection, we aim to demonstrate that the experiences of WCAs shared here may in themselves be worth examining; some of the contributors do employ RAD practices in their chapters. However, we also include embodied narratives of writing center tutors and administrators for two reasons: first, because the perspectives of those who are marginalized are still "overwhelmingly absent from [our] scholarship" (Lockett 2019, 21). Second, conducting and publishing RAD research may not be possible within the constraints of the positions of some authors, who are not provided the affordances of time, support, or training necessary to conduct research "both within and beyond writing centers": a central tenet of RAD research (Lerner 2014; Driscoll and Powell 2015).

Finally, with research-based studies and narratives, we attempt to move writing center scholarly conversations forward by not only exploring topics of marginalization but also assembling this collection through what we call an activist editorial methodology. Through the chapters, the contributors provide an important and, for some topics, still undertheorized look into the experiences of writing center professionals in a range of positions: faculty tenure-track, full- and part-time staff, contingent faculty or staff, and professional tutors. As a whole, this collection asks readers to reflect on and question how current writing center scholarly practices remain invested in dominant narratives and traditional publishing methods that fundamentally contradict our field-wide values of inclusivity, diversity, and multivocality.

Whose Narrative Is It Anyway?

One way to study "grand narratives" is by examining who is writing the narrative in the first place. This collection emerges from an earlier study we conducted drawn from our interests in understanding who is speaking (i.e., publishing) and whether the "collective" voices were representative of the diverse community it sought to represent. In "Whose Voices Are Heard? A Demographic Comparison of Authors Published in *WLN* 2005–2017 and Writers Interested in Publishing" (Kleinfeld, Lee, and Prebel 2021a), we wanted to know whose voices are actually being heard in writing center scholarship and therefore shaping the grand narrative. Consequently, we examined authors who published in *Writing Lab Newsletter* (*WLN*), the oldest peer-reviewed journal in writing center studies and, arguably, the most well read and influential among writing center practitioners both in the United States and around the globe.

For our study, we conducted two surveys. The first one (which we called the "Author Survey") focused on *WLN* authors spanning more than a decade. For comparison, we also conducted an "Interest Survey" of those who wanted to publish. The Author Survey involved creating a list of all *WLN* authors from 2005 to 2017. The Interest Survey was conducted in 2018 through several writing center list services in the US, Europe, and Asia. We had the following three major findings. First, we found that people from comprehensive institutions with graduate programs were heavily represented in authors who published in *WLN*; they exceeded the percentage of those in the Interest Survey by 10 percent. By contrast, community colleges were dramatically underrepresented: only 0.7 percent of *WLN* authors were authors from community colleges, compared to 10.6 percent of those in the Interest Survey who work in community colleges. In addition, we discovered that respondents held a wider range of positions in our Interest Survey than in the Authors Survey. Many more occupied part- and full-time non-tenure-track positions. Finally, our last important finding indicates that an overwhelming majority of published authors were self-identified as white. Interestingly, by comparison, our Interest Survey showed that there is a higher percentage of people of color who want to be published.

Our three findings may not be surprising, considering the demographic studies done by Sarah Banschbach Valles, Rebecca Day Babcock, and Karen Keaton Jackson (2017) on writing center professionals (see also Olson and Ashton-Jones 1988; Healy 1995), but we thought it was important to qualitatively mark how writing center scholarship remains largely represented by tenure-line white faculty in comprehensive universities. Our findings reinforce what others discovered about our problematic system of academic publishing. Elisabeth Buck (2018), for example, in analyzing writing center publishing sites and those who publish in them, sees publishing as deeply embedded in the old guard ethos and methods of getting writing center scholarship into print. In surveying more than 200 writing center scholars, Buck (2018) brings our attention to issues of access—the ease with which one can locate and engage with articles in the top writing center journals—and connects access to labor. Our findings support this connection, as we recognize that because of how writing center positions are structured, we are *least likely* to hear stories from people in positions that are insecure and low paying. Moreover, our publication survey mirrors a glaring absence of diversity in writing center leadership in general. All of these factors make it even harder for alternative voices to break the grand narratives that are shaped by scholarship.

The findings of our study indicated clear publication trends on white authorship (and most often authors with higher institutional status) and suggested white authorship's connections with the current and most common process for evaluation of manuscripts: the double-anonymous peer review. Currents of underlying assumptions and thoughts—that writing center directors are faculty, that writing center directors are white (though tutors are diverse), that writing centers serve (but don't employ) people with disabilities, that writing center tutors should be peer tutors, and that the US writing center model is the default writing center model—ripple through the grand narratives circulating in and through writing center scholarship. Jaqueline Jones Royster reminds us that "disciplinary practices have built up a high intolerance to the assigning of value and credibility to any site, focal point, theory, or practice other than those whose contours are already sanctioned historically within the circle of understanding" (2003, 150). Thus, as Royster explains, a barrier to even noticing so-called writing center outliers is the lack of scholarship on them, which creates a closed circle versus space for inclusion.

When the entire picture of who works in writing centers, how their positions are structured, and what models of writing center work they enact in their centers is shaped by a demographically narrow group of scholars, it is harder to imagine writing center work, scholarship, and models that look different from what is established as "normal" or expected. Writing about similar concerns about scholarship in geography, Carrie Mott and Daniel Cockayne connect a discipline's citation practices to knowledge production. Looking at citation in geography through an antiracist feminist lens, they note that "citation is equally a technology for reproducing sameness and excluding difference" (Mott and Cockayne 2017, 960), echoing Royster's comments that the status quo reproduces itself (2003).

This collection makes an intentional effort, then, to counteract and disrupt the reproduction of "sameness and excluding difference" both by the selection of our theme on marginalized writing center professionals and the practice of activist editing.

Enacting an Activist Editing Methodology

For us, activist editing means to openly acknowledge how traditional publishing practices favor high-status white authorship and to adjust practices that help diversify authorship in scholarly publication. Activist publishing has been growing in the writing field. Kelly Blewett, Christina LaVecchia, Laura Micciche, and Janine Morris describe work they have done as editors of the journal *Composition Studies* to resist and push back against structural inequality by practicing antioppressive work as editors (Blewett et al. 2019). They outline specific steps they take to diversify the authors featured in the journal, including moving beyond the traditional genre of the scholarly article and working closely with authors who received revise-and-resubmit requests to increase the likelihood of publication. Moreover, the University Press of Colorado recently added to their website a document called "Our Publication Processes and Timelines" (2022), which aims to make explicit publication processes that often are shrouded in secrecy; that secrecy functions to maintain the dominance of the established voices who have already made it through the system and thus understand it. In the writing center field, the editors of *Writing Center Journal*—Anna Sicari, Harry Denny, and Romeo Garcia—released an "Editorial Philosophy and Vision" (2021), which proclaimed a commitment to enacting the ideas put forth in "Anti-Racist Scholarly Reviewing Practices" and an intention to mentor and publish "voices that remain on the margins" (Sicari, Denny, and Garcia 2021).

As activist editors, we aim to practice and reimagine a publication process that is intentionally inclusive and supportive of difference. Traditional publishing practices for peer-reviewed journals go through a process of double-anonymous peer review, and this practice has its roots in a history of peer reviewing that dates back to the 1600s and 1700s. The double-anonymous peer-review process emerged to validate emerging scientific findings and disseminate these findings through some of the first scientific scholarly journals. This process became the preferred method for determining the legitimacy of an author's data, quickly creating a system for evaluating or ranking the prestige of an academic journal. Figure 0.1 is a simplified diagram of the

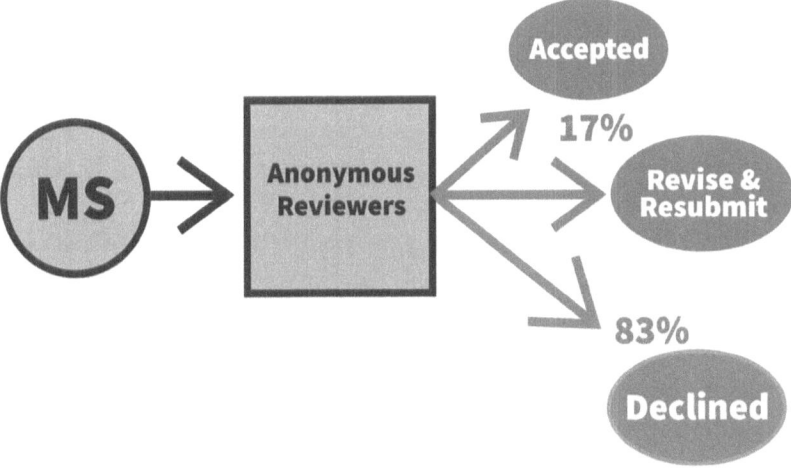

FIGURE 0.1. Traditional double-anonymous publishing process in peer-reviewed journals.

typical process where the anonymized manuscripts, after being considered by the journal editors, are evaluated and recommended by anonymous reviewers and then returned to the journal editorial team for the final decision.

This is what we call "double-anonymous": authors do not know who is reviewing their manuscript, and peer reviewers do not know whose manuscript they are reading. The argument for this process is that it ensures fairness and minimizes bias (or prejudice). In peer-reviewed journals like *WLN* or *Writing Center Journal* (*WCJ*), less than 20 percent of manuscripts are either accepted or recommended to be "revised and resubmitted." At *WCJ* the acceptance rate is 17 percent of all submitted manuscripts; *WLN*'s acceptance rate is even lower at 12 percent. Reviewers recommend manuscripts based on factors of its innovative argument, quality of writing, and appeal to the audience.

Although double-anonymous peer review is widely considered to be an objective means for assessing scholarly work, both by peers in disciplinary fields and for tenure and promotion, the review process's objectivity has been questioned. Notably, one study found that reviewers using the double-anonymous method are more likely to recommend for acceptance submissions from already-known authors and those from top universities (Tomkins, Zhang, and Heavlin 2017). In our study of the publication trends in *WLN*, for example, we found much the same (Kleinfeld, Lee, and Prebel 2021a); peer-reviewed journals following the double-anonymous process tend to publish authors who are more likely to represent full-time tenure-track directors (44%), work at four-year comprehensive institutions (67%), and who are primarily white (90%). Our study's published author profile mirrors Valles, Babcock, and Jackson's (2017) demographic finding of writing center directors: 57 percent identified as faculty, 77 percent worked at four-year institutions, and 91 percent identified as white. Some important limitations acknowledged in Valles, Babcock, and Jackson's study are that their data missed Minority Serving Institutions (MSIs) and that their data on Hispanic Serving Institutions (HSIs) are "not entirely representative" (Valles, Babcock, Jackson 2017). Overall, the comparable data gathered on the percentages of those who represent the director roles (Valles, Babcock, and Jackson 2017) and those who are published (Kleinfeld, Lee, and Prebel 2021a) in writing centers suggest a dire lack of diversity in writing center work relative to the national population, which is increasingly more racially and ethnically diverse. In other words, writing center leadership (directors and coordinators) as well as writing center scholarship are not reflective of the current US population. According to the 2020 US Census, only 63.7 percent of the US population identifies as white alone (Jensen et al. 2021). And while our study on publishing authors showed that no Hispanic or Latinx authors have published in *WLN* between 2005 and 2017, Hispanic or Latinx groups now comprise 18.7 percent of the US population.

For writing centers, known for their wide range of institutional contexts and administrative roles, this fact should be unsettling. Focusing on published authors specifically, we realize how current publishing practices tend to magnify stories by particular populations in the writing center field and synecdochically distribute stories of this group as stories of the whole. One goal of this collection was to explore how we might disrupt the traditional publishing process. As editors we asked ourselves: What stories and voices of writing centers can we feature through our activist editing practices that haven't been heard? How do we find and support these stories through a process that traditionally filtered them out?

Like Blewett, LaVecchia, Micciche, and Morris (2019), we believed that part of our role as editors of this collection included the responsibility of identifying and supporting underrepresented writers and scholars through an editorial process that increased the likelihood of publication. Our activist editor methodology included first designing a survey to intentionally collect (rather than hide) demographic information of authors and using this information to help inform our selection, and second, scaffolding of extensive support for authors in the editing process. We started by creating a submission survey that asked authors to provide information that is traditionally hidden in the double-anonymous process: name, race/ethnicity, disability, degree, status of position, institution, and even publication history. With our collection, the editors then collected all submissions and created a spreadsheet with these demographic identifiers. We discussed each submission and considered them for inclusion in our collection based on how well the proposal addressed our call for papers (CFP), the type of proposal submission (narrative chapter or research-based chapter), and the contributor demographic representation. We spent significant time discussing why having both types of chapter proposals was important: narrative articles, in particular, were designed to be short (no more than 1,500 words) to accommodate authors who may not have training, experience, or resources to write research-based or theoretical chapters, which were between 5,000 and 6,000 words. In other words, our selection process aimed to balance ideas proposed with the perspectives and proposal types so that we could recruit authors from a range of backgrounds, positions, abilities, and national affiliations. After receiving the submissions and inputting the demographic and publishing data into a spreadsheet, each of the three editors were also readers: we read all submissions, provided a column for comments, and provided another column where we made one of three recommendations (Yes, No, Maybe). Whenever there were disagreements on a submission, we discussed the work at length until we arrived at consensus. The following example of review comments illustrates how editors considered one author's underrepresented role in writing center discourse and the proposal's fit for the collection:

> EDITOR 1: Yes. She's both "deeply immersed" and "adjunct"—what an interesting tension.
>
> EDITOR 2: I think this is a very solid proposal as a short narrative that I could see fitting into a section of the book that looks at marginality and contingent faculty/staff.
>
> EDITOR 3: I was really drawn to her story, and I believe she is right—Writing Center talk about adjunct status is not explored deeply, especially in terms of how they collaborate and maintain professionalism.

This process for submission ranking allowed us to identify and accept eleven submissions that all three editors agreed upon quickly and discuss eight submissions that generated mixed responses. Those with mixed responses were considered based on how many submissions covered similar topics, originality of idea explored, appropriateness for the collection, and type of chapter proposed. Race and ethnicity as well as disability were on our minds, and these categories were highlighted on our spreadsheet, but this factor was not necessarily a deciding one. Proposals by underrepresented perspectives were prioritized over the writing quality of a proposal, as we assumed that we would be providing extensive feedback and support for the authors. Ultimately, our selection process resulted in the following:

- 13 out of 28 submissions were accepted (46% acceptance rate);
- 7 out of 16 (43%) of total authors (including all coauthors) were authors of color (5, or 31%, of accepted authors self-identified as Hispanic/Latinx; 2, or 12.5%, were Black/African);
- 8 out of 16 (50%) were authors who did not have faculty status;
- 6 out of 16 (38%) were authors who identified as being a person with disabilities;
- 5 out of 16 (31%) had never published before.

After the selection process, the second part of our activist editing process was in providing feedback for our authors. Our feedback process was more extensive than most editorial feedback practices, as we needed to consider our authors' particular positionalities within writing center communities and their experience. Authors submitted their first draft on July 1, 2021. They received responses from two editors as first reader and second reader and were asked to provide their first revision. As readers, we rotated with each round so that each of us (Julie, Sohui, and Elizabeth) read all chapters at different stages of the revision process multiple times. Between July 2021 and June 2022, we provided authors four rounds of feedback and multiple one-on-one Zoom conferences to help them prepare their chapters for the collection. The meetings with authors helped editors improve their understanding of the author's perspective and approaches while also aiding in communicating more substantial revisions that needed to be done. Zoom meetings also improved interpersonal communication between editors and authors: seeing one another helped establish trust that strengthened communication and timely completion of tasks.

Finally, we invited established writing center scholars to provide a response to the chapter essays organized in three thematic sections of our collection, which we explain in the next sections. Kerri Rinaldi responded to section one, "Structural Marginalization"; Weijia Li and Ester R. Namubiru on "Globalization and Marginalization"; and Rachel Azima on "Embodied Marginalization." We found each respondent's work to be critical to this collection in three ways: first, they provide unity, threading chapter narratives and research together and helping readers make thematic connections. Second, they provide new insights in reading these stories together. For instance, Li and Namubiru remind us that the "foundation of writing center work" is literacy, and the two chapters in the section "Globalization and Marginalization" demonstrate that this literacy work is not always in English. Finally, the section responses allow for the work of our authors (a third of whom have never published) to be folded in dialogue with established scholars from the onset that set up future conversations.

Organization of the Collection

This collection, through its activist editorship, presents narratives and quantitative research studies by diverse authors ranging in race and ethnicity, abilities, experiences in publication, and professional roles in writing center work. The majority of the authors in this collection are not tenure-line faculty, and some are staff or professional tutors. As noted in the previous section, manuscripts were selected based on a range of factors, but one of the critical selection criteria was how proposed topics investigate or challenge some important assumptions carried in writing center grand narratives; others provide valuable qualitative perspectives that are often overlooked or missing in writing center discussions. Through these chapters, authors seek to help readers complicate their engagement with writing center grand narratives in three thematic categories of marginalization experiences: structural, global, and embodied.

STRUCTURAL MARGINALIZATION

The structural marginalization of writing centers has often been tied to physical location in basements or less visible spaces, or where centers are housed administratively as adjunct to departments or other services (Perdue, Driscoll, and Petrykowski 2017). Just as significant, WCAs may experience marginalization within their institutions because it is unclear where they fit in, often finding themselves "positioned as substrata of writing program administration, even further removed from the academic scholarship and intellectual inquiry of English studies" (Geller and Denny 2013). In this collection, the theme of structural marginalization in academe expands on the peripheral and ambivalent role of writing center administrators by exploring how writing studies graduate programs do not adequately prepare future WCAs for their work, how job descriptions perpetuate such ambivalence, and how marginalization is systemically reinforced in contingent labor practices.

GLOBALIZATION AND MARGINALIZATION

Although writing centers' marginalization in the academe is familiar to most readers, globalization of writing center work is a topic that is less explored and exposes the assumptions of US-based scholarly discourse. Early on, Joan Mullin (2000) noted the impact of "local conversations" of writing center work on "other countries" and lauded the "increased visibility of colleagues in journals" like *Writing Lab Newsletter* (*WLN*) and *Writing Center Journal* (*WCJ*) (3). But even as we began to see the emergence of US-style writing centers in countries around the world, concerns immediately popped up: Tracy Santa (2002) and John Harbord (2003), publishing in *WCJ* and *WLN* respectively, questioned the unseen application of writing center theory, shaped by writing center scholarship, which was primarily written by US authors for US institutions. Underlying the writing center's grand narratives, then, are assumptions of the US-based tutoring system and the assertions of Western academic practices. As writing centers appear across numerous other countries with different roles and missions, there is an obligation of scholars to increase our awareness of the global writing center audience and incorporate language that recognizes these differences (just as we now recognize different Englishes); or, as Santa put it, writing center scholars need to acknowledge they also write to "an international community of writing centers" and situate their various environments and cultures into "professional conversation on local levels and . . . global [levels]" (2002, 37). As of 2022, twenty years since Santa's call for professional conversations that recognize and invite conversations involving global writing center practices, we have identified only fifteen articles or chapters that examine writing center studies in counties outside the United States: 60 percent (nine) of these works are not published in recognized writing center journals and thereby have diminished impact in professional discussion among writing center professionals. To revisit this conversation in this collection, two directors of writing centers, in México and Ghana, explore US writing center practices through a transnational, postcolonial lens, exploring their cultural contexts and the limits of US writing center theories and practices in their country.

EMBODIED MARGINALIZATION

Finally, under the theme of embodied marginalization, the collection explores how WCAs experience marginalization because of their lived experiences within institutional structures of hegemony (Faison and Condon 2022) or social expectations of ableness. In a field where white people—and more specifically, white abled women—occupy the majority of WCA positions (Valles, Babcock, and Jackson 2017), Black, Indigenous, and people of color (BIPOC) WCAs and WCAs with disabilities experience intersectional forms of marginalization. Racial hierarchies and power structures within academic institutions and in writing center scholarship more broadly are additional barriers that impact the labor experiences of racially marginalized WCAs (Jackson 2018).

Covering these three themes, this collection explores how marginality impacts writing centers, the people who work in them, and the scholarship generated from them. The collection examines the consequences, both positive and negative, of marginalization through a mix of narratives and research. It is unique in providing perspectives ranging in status, role, nationality, race, and ability that have been absent or little explored in writing center conversations. This collection will be important to those who are training to be writing center administrators, current administrators, and scholars who want a more complex picture of the varied challenges of writing center work and those who provide it.

Overview of Chapters

While this collection is arranged into three sections exploring common themes of marginalization, the chapters connect across sections with authors echoing one another in their experiences, research topics, and recommendations. As part of our inclusive, collaborative revision and editorial process, we asked authors to read and refer to each other's chapters, even if briefly, to deepen or extend these connections. Moreover, instead of introductions to each section, we include respondents' reflections on the common themes highlighted in the chapters (and the respondents' own similar experiences of marginalization in writing center work), which amplifies the connections. Our approach to creating cohesion in the collection thus affirms our intentionality in bringing more voices into the conversation about writing center administration and in forging new conversations among writing center professionals.

The chapters in the first section of the collection explore experiences of what we term structural marginalization in the form of lack of professional preparation, knowledge of often-ambiguous writing center expectations, and managing writing centers while laboring in contingent or underrecognized roles. Together these chapters not only point to the effects of such marginalization but also propose solutions to mitigating or eliminating systemic, structural barriers to meaningful writing center work.

In chapter 1, "Of Budgets and Institutional Bumbling: New Writing Center Directors Reflect on Their First Year," Enrique Paz and Elise Dixon interrogate the discourse of the grand narrative passed down through stories or lore of what to expect when taking on a new role as a writing center director. They argue that the quotidian practical labors of writing center work result in the perpetual marginalization of writing center directors and undermine their professionalization. This chapter explores narratives of marginalization of writing center administrators, focusing on the material realities of writing centers and WCA positions for new WCAs, assessing how narratives of marginality have shaped graduate training and professional development. The authors ultimately argue that attention to the practicalities of writing center administration, such as budgeting and maintaining spaces, is critical to transitioning out of marginality and must be included in writing graduate program curriculum and training.

Joshua Botvin and Elisabeth H. Buck similarly examine how the structure of WCA positions can impact the marginality of both writing centers and the people who run them in chapter 2, "A Tale of Two Writing Centers: Navigating Fraught Institutional Legacies." Botvin and Buck examine how the structure of WCA positions can impact the marginality of both writing centers and the people who run them, and they offer guidance to job seekers about questions to ask when accepting a new role managing a writing center. The authors argue that when hired to work in a center, a new director is often expected to navigate a set of "lived realities" that are far different from the job as outlined on paper. They point out that WCAs often are expected to make changes to the status quo but given little support to succeed in enacting such changes, which can result in tensions within existing center and administrative structures that contribute to WCA experiences of marginality. Picking up on the recommendations posed by Paz and Dixon, Botvin and Buck offer concrete questions newly hired writing center directors or assistant directors might ask to help address such tensions between new expectations and previous practices and structures.

In the narrative of chapter 3, "Belonging in the Center," Wendy Rider approaches structural marginalization through the experience as an adjunct faculty member who may be unrecognized in the grand narrative despite having a leadership role in her center. Rider examines the institutional structure that simultaneously allows adjunct faculty to contribute to the work of supporting and educating students and denies them the full privileges of the academy. Rider argues that despite the challenges that come with adjunct status in the academy, she has been able to develop her identity as a writing center professional through mentorship and involvement in regional writing center associations. Rider's chapter thus points to ways to mitigate the effects of not being included in the grand narrative or being marginalized in the profession.

Shareen Grogan, Pam Bromley, and Denise Stephenson point to another facet of structural marginalization and invisibility in writing centers and writing center scholarship in chapter 4, "Hidden in Plain Sight: Professional Tutors in the Writing Center." These authors challenge the grand narrative that peerness is a prerequisite for collaboration, arguing that professional tutors should be made visible, their contributions explored, and their presence celebrated in writing center scholarship. They argue that professional tutors are made invisible both in writing center scholarship and in the field more broadly by the focus on the centrality of undergraduate peer tutoring and idealized notions of what constitutes peerness and collaboration. As they show, tutor identity has been defined largely as representative of undergraduate peer tutoring, which results in the marginalization of graduate and professional tutors, whose expertise is often diminished in the writing center grand narrative.

Writing from the perspective of both an adjunct faculty member and professional tutor in chapter 5, "From Pieces to Whole: Professional Tutors and Instability in the College Writing Center," Aja Gorham argues that the "labor instability" of contingent faculty and writing center staff has an impact on students' writing center experiences. Gorham's research utilizes interviews with professional tutors at a community college writing center to examine the intersection of contingent labor and the tutors' ability to contribute meaningfully to the writing center. Citing factors such as work exhaustion, feelings of underappreciation, and stress (both emotional and financial), Gorham's interviews reveal ways that the marginalization of contingent writing center professionals can result in detachment from students and negative effects on a student-centered writing center mission. Like Grogan, Bromley, and Stephenson, Gorham calls for more accountability to professional tutors in both writing center theory and practice.

In responding to this first section Kerri Rinaldi recognizes their own professional journey in the stories of the chapters' authors, noting that this pathway began by cobbling together a living through an "assemblage" of contingent positions (like those described in the chapters). Rinaldi identifies a profound sense of "powerlessness" in the effects of structural marginalization and highlights the implications of working in contingent, staff, and other non-tenure-line writing center positions, especially the lack of institutional support, which often results in experiences of invisible labor, a devaluation of that labor, and the ways that the "grand narrative" reinforces individual versus structural responsibility for these experiences of marginalization. Of importance, Rinaldi calls for an "ethic of responsibility" both institutionally in the ways we structure our writing center laboring practices and in our scholarship, which needs to recognize and promote critiques of our laboring conditions.

In the second section of the collection, we turn to the intersections between marginalization and the increasing globalization of writing centers. The chapters in this section examine and critique the pedagogical assumptions and narratives in writing center scholarship that tend to focus on US-based models and practices. In this section, two directors of writing centers, in México and Ghana, explore the challenges of adopting US writing center structures and the tensions between practices supported in the grand narrative and those rooted in the locality of global contexts.

In chapter 6, "Becoming a Writing Center Administrator: A Transnational Counterstory," Nancy Henaku interrogates the stories told in writing center scholarship as dominated by North American experiences and thus lacking the diversity of practitioners working in international centers or with international students. Henaku explores the challenges of both being an international student in a US writing center, as a non-native English speaker from sub-Saharan Africa, and of co-directing a newly created writing center in Ghana. Using a transnational lens and the methodology of counterstory, Henaku exposes the invisible cultural markings and assumptions that frame the structures of US writing centers.

Echoing Henaku's focus on the challenges of establishing a writing center outside the US, in chapter 7, "Harnessing the Periphery: A Community of Practice in México," Abigail Villagrán Mora argues that internationalizing writing centers means looking beyond preparing tutors to serve multilingual writers. Villagrán Mora points to the material and systemic realities that separate academic communities from each other and prevent a community from coalescing, particularly in writing centers in the Western periphery. The author shares research from the writing center she directs in Puebla, México, which indicates that a focus on fostering the learning culture in the community of peer tutors can sustain a knowledge initiative regardless of the ever-changing nature of our learning ecology.

Li and Namubiru point out that the majority of writing center scholarship shows an investment in a central "grand narrative": the "Western-dominated stories about writing center work." In their response to the section on the intersections of globalization and marginalization, Li and Namubiru amplify Henaku's and Villagrán Mora's focus on the "unique characteristics, experiences, and backgrounds" of writing center work in non-Western locations. They situate their own experiences alongside Henaku and Villagrán Mora, noting that they have been both placed at the margins as international scholars and have also resisted this marginalization by centering their multifaceted experiences and identities through their work as writing center practitioners, scholars, and journal editors. Li and Namubiru remind us that there is "no single story about writing center" work and call for an "interrogation" of literacies of writing center lore.

In the third section of the collection, the authors examine and challenge commonly held beliefs about writing centers as inclusive spaces through a focus on embodiment. The chapters in this section explore many ways writing center practitioners are marginalized through narratives about bodies and mind-bodies. As the chapters show, even as writing center practitioners look for ways to make writing centers safe(r) for diverse students, the safety of writing center staff, tutors, and administrators often gets overlooked. These chapters explore how embodied experiences of marginalization intersect with disability studies, and critical race, gender, and sexuality studies, as they pose challenges to the hegemony of the writing center grand narrative.

In chapter 8, "Tutors/Tutees Tango: Cross-Stepping [Dis]Abilities in Writing Centers," Myra Tatum Salcedo shares what it is like to have to constantly "come out" as a hearing-impaired tutor and the challenges of confronting negative perceptions and stereotypes about hearing impairment. Salcedo sheds light on an underdeveloped topic in writing center literature: the experience of being a tutor with a disability. Exploring how some disabilities are rendered invisible through common writing center practices, Salcedo's narrative shows the devaluing of tutors' embodied experiences that occurs when centers prioritize ableist concepts of "good" tutoring as she offers concrete ways to bring disability out of the writing center margins.

Karen Moroski-Rigney similarly engages writing center best practices from her position as a neurodivergent (autism spectrum disorder [ASD] and attention deficit hyperactivity disorder [ADHD]) WCA to interrogate the silence surrounding disabled writing center professionals in chapter 9, "Cripping Marginality: Disability and Directing a Writing Center." Moroski-Rigney weaves together disability studies—the work of Margaret Price, Catherine Prendergast, Allison Harper Hitt, Jay Dolmage, and others—with writing center theory to engage questions about why disabled people are underrepresented in writing center work, what aspects of writing center work pose particular challenges to disabled persons, and how disability interfaces with the marginality of writing center work to create a unique nexus of career challenges. Moroski-Rigney offers concrete ideas for how to transform our writing center practices, and their chapter represents an important contribution to disability justice in writing center scholarship.

Elena Garcia shares the experience of embodied marginalization in the tension between living with a chronic illness and the expectation to work oneself to exhaustion in writing center practice. In chapter 10, "Please! Stop Doing More with Less," Garcia frames the tendency, which is often affirmed in the narratives of writing center scholarship and practice, to do whatever is asked of us as an ableist position that negatively impacts our bodies and our field. Contributing to the focus on disability justice in writing center scholarship, like Moroski-Rigney, Garcia argues that resisting such expectations constitutes an act of care for ourselves and each other.

In chapter 11, "Sign of the Cross: A Case Study of a First-Gen Latina's Experience of Marginalization at an Evangelical Christian University," Deborah Escalante shifts our focus to the "white habitus" (Inoue 2016) of our academic institutions and the writing centers within. Escalante explores the embodied experiences of racial microaggressions and the impact on her writing center work. She uses her experience as a case study for better identifying and responding to microaggressions that are psychologically and emotionally harmful—and which contribute to a toxic working environment for many writing center tutors, staff, and administrators. Ultimately, Escalante posits that one of the major barriers to diversity in writing center administration may be academe itself, which builds and reinforces structures of marginalization.

Echoing Escalante's focus on the institutional structures of marginalization that have an impact on embodied experiences, in chapter 12, "Is the Writing Center Safe Yet? Narrative Vignettes of Women's Bodily Security in Our 'Cozy Homes,'" Sarah Fischer unpacks the patriarchal frameworks in canonical best practices for writing center tutoring. Fischer argues that writing center scholarship would benefit from a more explicit acknowledgment of the ways in which women, including but not limited to those who have experienced sexual assault and harassment, often find the "cozy home" narrative challenging to their sense of personal safety and comfort when working in close proximity to students. Fischer's chapter underscores how valuing the lived experiences of tutors (undergraduate and professional) can help make our spaces safer and mitigate experiences of marginalization in the writing center.

In the final chapter of this collection, chapter 13, "Womanist Way-Making in Writing Center Administration: Reflections on Marginalization, Misogynoir, and Resistance," Zandra Jordan acknowledges, as do the authors of all of the preceding chapters, that misperceptions of writing center work have resulted in the devaluation and marginalization of writing center practitioners. Jordan describes, more specifically, the marginalization she encountered as a Black woman, non-tenure-track, writing center director in two contexts: first as founding director of a center at a small, private, predominantly white theological institution in the US South offering masters and doctoral degrees and currently as director of a center at a large, private, predominantly white research institution in the US West serving undergraduate and graduate students across the disciplines. Drawing on misogynoir and womanist ethics, this chapter theorizes both Jordan's lived experience and her approach to writing center administration. Jordan's conceptualization of "womanist way-making," with specific strategies for recognizing and valuing Black women's embodiment, offers the means to disrupt normative expectations and marginalization toward the creation of more equitable writing center practices and inclusive scholarship.

As Rachel Azima points out in the response to this section on embodied marginalization, all of the chapters "uncover deep fault lines in the 'cozy homes' grand narrative" by exposing assumptions about what constitutes a writing center safe space. Azima underscores how the chapters' authors recognize the oppressions that occur in writing center work through the harms of assuming and reifying white, able-bodied norms. Disclosure of embodied experiences and histories can itself be harmful, and telling our stories does not necessarily result in catharsis or equity. We must, as Azima reminds us, be vigilant in recognizing the oppressions we might inadvertently or knowingly perpetuate as we reexamine our writing center practices and the scholarship produced in response to our work.

Looking Ahead

We hope that this collection will inspire writing center practitioners to think more expansively about what writing centers do, who works in them, and how those nuances are represented or overlooked in writing center scholarship. We anticipate that this collection will raise more questions than it answers and some of these questions might be uncomfortable. Perhaps the questions that get asked can be reformed to take another point of view into account.

As we worked on this collection, for example, we examined our own positions within our institutions and in the field more broadly. In our afterword, we discuss how our pathways to writing center work invariably shaped our perspectives and interests in this collection, and we note that at times we have experienced aspects of marginalization in this work. While we may have experienced marginalization as academics or writing center administrators, we also recognize that we, unlike many of the contributors to this collection, benefit from having positions that are stable, tenured, and afforded opportunities for professional growth and development. Examining our privileges helped us to recognize the white supremacist academic values and experiences that have shaped and inhibited our perspectives and thinking. In many ways, ours are the voices that are already heard in the "institutional pathways" (Inoue 2016) where writing centers and writing center scholarship exist. With this collection, we seek to disrupt those pathways.

Our attempt at such disruption includes turning a critical lens on our own assumptions as directors of writing centers and as editors of this collection. In our afterword, we consider how the contributors' experiences of marginalization within their institutions might help us transform our writing center practices and make our work responsive to the critiques raised in the chapters. We recognize too that the chapters in this collection narrate experiences of marginalization on people's lives—and not only their work lives. As we discuss in the afterword, in working on this collection we found that their stories and the themes or topics they explore resonated with us and, at times, uncomfortably. Part of our commitment to making space in this collection for more voices to be heard meant acknowledging our implicit biases, which inevitably surfaced especially in the process of selecting essays for this collection and working closely with the authors in the revision process we describe above. In the afterword, we thus resist offering firm conclusions or suggestions for readers and instead generate questions for reflection that we hope lead to further discussion.

This is not a collection that will lend itself to a list of best practices, although we have discovered takeaways through discussions with colleagues at IWCA (Kleinfeld, Lee, and Prebel 2021b) and through the experience of working with our authors and publishing this book. In fact, we hope the pieces in this collection will lead writing center practitioners to question: Who are best practices best for? Who determined they were the best practices? Who is not served by those practices? What is obscured by those practices? Paying closer attention to the voices from the margins enables us to get a fuller understanding of writing centers and writing center work and also provides lenses through which to recalibrate how we interpret what it means to be inclusive. As inclusivity and social justice become more central to the work we do in writing centers, now is the time for us to problematize whose voices have dominated our scholarly discussions and whose have been silenced or ignored.

References

Blewett, Karen, Christine M. LaVecchia, Laura R. Micciche, and Janine Morris. 2019. "Editing as Inclusion Activism." *College English* 81 (4): 273–296.

Buck, Elisabeth. 2018. *Open-Access, Multimodality, and Writing Center Studies*. Cham, Switzerland: Palgrave Macmillan.

Condon, Frankie. 2007. "Beyond the Known: Writing Centers and the Work of Anti-racism." *Writing Center Journal* 27 (2): 19–38. https://www.jstor.org/stable/43442270.

Dangling Modifier, The. 2020. Edited by Sarah G. Huerta and Luke A. Iantorno. (spring and fall).

Delli Carpini, Dominic, and Cynthia Crimmins. 2001. "From the Margins to the (Writing) Center: Collaborative Efforts in Writing Center and Composition Program Activities." *WLN: Writing Lab Newsletter* 26 (3): 1–5. https://wac.colostate.edu/docs/wln/v26/26.3.pdf.

Denny, Harry. 2010a. "Queering the Writing Center." *Writing Center Journal* 30 (1): 95–124.

Denny, Harry. 2010b. *Facing the Center: Toward an Identity Politics of One-to-One Mentoring*. All USU Press Publications. https://digitalcommons.usu.edu/usupress_pubs/168.

Denny, Harry, Robert Mundy, Liliana Naydan, Richard Sévère, and Anna Sicari. 2019. *Out in the Center: Public Controversies and Private Struggles*. Logan: Utah State University Press.

Driscoll, Dana Lynn, and Roger Powell. 2015. "Conducting and Composing RAD Research in the Writing Center: A New Guide for Authors." *Peer Review*. https://thepeerreview-iwca.org/issues/issue-0/conducting-and-composing-rad-research-in-the-writing-center-a-guide-for-new-authors/.

Driscoll, Dana Lynn, and Sherry Wynn Purdue. 2014. "RAD Research as a Framework for Writing Center Inquiry: Survey and Interview Data on Writing Center Directors' Beliefs about Research and Research Practices." *Writing Center Journal* 34 (1): 105–134.

Faison, Wonderful. 2018. "Black Bodies, Black Language: Exploring the Use of Black Language as a Tool of Survival in the Writing Center." *Peer Review* 2 (1). https://thepeerreview-iwca.org/issues/relationality-si/black-bodies-black-language-exploring-the-use-of-black-language-as-a-tool-of-survival-in-the-writing-center/.

Faison, Wonderful, and Frankie Condon, eds. 2022. *Counterstories from the Writing Center*. Logan: Utah State University Press.

Geller, Anne Ellen, and Harry Denny. 2013. "Of Ladybugs, Low Status, and Loving the Job: Writing Center Professionals Navigating Their Careers." *Writing Center Journal* 33 (1): 96–129. https://scholar.stjohns.edu/english_facpubs/7.

Geller, Anne Ellen, Michele Eodice, Frankie Condon, Meg Carroll, and Elizabeth Boquet. 2007. *The Everyday Writing Center: A Community of Practice*. Logan: Utah State University Press.

Greenfield, Laura, and Karen Rowan. 2011. *Writing Centers and the New Racism: A Call for Sustainable Dialogue and Change*. Logan: Utah State University Press.

Grutsch McKinney, Jackie. 2013. *Peripheral Visions for Writing Centers*. Logan: Utah State University Press.

Hallman Martini, Rebecca. 2022. *Disrupting the Center: A Partnership Approach to Writing across the University*. Logan: Utah State University Press.

Harbord, John. 2003. "Minimalist Tutoring: An Exportable Model?" *Writing Lab Newsletter* 28 (4): 1–5. https://wac.colostate.edu/docs/wln/v28/28.4.pdf.

Haswell, Richard H. 2005. "NCTE/CCCC's Recent War on Scholarship." *Written Communication* 22 (2): 198–223.

Healy, Dave. 1995. "Writing Center Directors: An Emerging Portrait of the Profession." *WPA: Writing Program Administration* 18 (3): 26–43.

Inoue, Asao. 2016. "Afterword: Narratives That Determine Writers and Social Justice Writing Center Work." *Praxis* 14 (1): 94–99. https://www.praxisuwc.com/141-final.

Jackson, Karen Keaton. 2018. "A State of Permanent Transition: Strategies for WPA Survival in the Ever-Present Marginal Space of HBCUs." In *WPAs in Transition: Navigating Educational Leadership Positions*, edited by Courtney Adams Wooten, Jacob Babb, and Brian Ray, 25–36. Logan: Utah State University Press.

Jensen, Eric, Nicholas Jones, Kimberly Orozco, Lauren Medina, Mark Perry, Ben Bolender, and Karen Battle. 2021. "Measuring Racial and Ethnic Diversity for the 2020 Census." United States Census Bureau, August 4, 2021. https://www.census.gov/newsroom/blogs/random-samplings/2021/08/measuring-racial-ethnic-diversity-2020-census.html#:~:text=The%20White%20alone%2C%20non%2DHispanic,third%2Dlargest%20at%2012.2%25.

Kleinfeld, Elizabeth, Sohui Lee, and Julie Prebel. 2021a. "Whose Voices Are Heard? A Demographic Comparison of Authors Published in WLN 2005–2017 and Writers Interested in Publishing." *WLN: A Journal of Writing Center Scholarship* 45 (7–8). https://wac.colostate.edu/docs/wln/v45/45.7-8.pdf.

Kleinfeld, Elizabeth, Sohui Lee, and Julie Prebel. 2021b. "Imagining an Anti-Racist, Decolonial, and Anti-Ableist Writing Center Studies Publishing Model." International Writing Centers Association (IWCA) Conference, October 20–23.

Kjesrud, Roberta D. 2015. "Lessons from Data: Avoiding Lore Bias in Research Paradigms." *Writing Center Journal* 34 (2): 33–58. http://www.jstor.org/stable/43442805.

Lee, Kiara. 2019. *Black in the Writing Center: Race, Representation, and the Post-racial Lie*. New York: Routledge.

Lerner, Neal. 2014. "The Unpromising Present of Writing Center Studies: Author and Citation Patterns in *The Writing Center Journal*, 1980 to 2009." *Writing Center Journal* 32 (1): 67–104.

Lockett, Alexandria. 2019. "Why I Call It the Academic Ghetto: A Critical Examination of Race, Place, and Writing Centers." *Praxis: A Writing Center Journal* 16 (2): 20–33. http://www.praxisuwc.com/162-lockett.

Macauley, William J., and Nicolas Mauriello, eds. *Marginal Words, Marginal Works? Tutoring the Academy in the Work of Writing Centers*. 2007. Cresskill, NJ: Hampton Press.

Mackiewicz, Jo, and Rebecca Day Babcock, eds. 2019. *Theories and Methods of Writing Center Studies: A Practical Guide*. 1st ed. New York: Routledge. https://doi.org/10.4324/9780429198755.

Mackiewicz, Jo, and Isabelle Thompson. 2014. *Talk about Writing: Tutoring Strategies of Advanced Writing Tutors*. New York: Routledge.

Martinez, Aja Y. 2020. *Counterstory: The Rhetoric and Writing of Critical Race Theory*. Champaign, IL: National Council of Teachers of English.

Mott, Carrie, and Daniel Cockayne. 2017. "Citation Matters: Mobilizing the Politics of Citation toward a Practice of 'Conscientious Engagement.'" *Gender, Place, and Culture* 24 (7): 954–973. https://doi.org/10.1080/0966369X.2017.1339022.

Mullin, Joan. 2000. "What Hath Writing Centers Wrought? A Fifteen-Year Reflection on Communication, Community, and Change." *Writing Lab Newsletter* 25 (1): 1–3. https://wac.colostate.edu/docs/wln/v25/25.1.pdf.

Olson, Gary A., and Evelyn Ashton-Jones. 1988. "Writing Center Directors: The Search for Professional Status." *WPA: Writing Program Administration* 12: 19–28.

Perdue, Sherry Wynn, Dana Lynn Driscoll, and Andrew Petrykowski. 2017. "Centering Institutional Status and Scholarly Identity: An Analysis of Writing Center Administration Position Advertisements, 2004–2014." *Writing Center Journal* 36 (2), article 12. https://docs.lib.purdue.edu/wcj/vol36/iss2/12.

Praxis: A Writing Center Journal. 2019. *Special Issue: Race and the Writing Center* 16 (2). https://www.praxisuwc.com/162-full-back-issue.

Praxis: A Writing Center Journal. 2020. *Special Issue: Inclusion in the Writing Center* 18 (1). https://www.praxisuwc.com/181-full-back-issue.

Royster, Jacqueline Jones. 2003. "Disciplinary Landscaping, or Contemporary Challenges in the History of Rhetoric." *Philosophy and Rhetoric* 36 (2): 148–167.

Santa, Tracy. 2002. "Writing Center Orthodoxies as Damocles' Sword: An International Perspective." *Writing Center Journal* 22 (2): 29–38, article 4.

Shelly, Lynn. 2014. "'You Can't Get Anywhere without Relationships': Marginality and Mattering in the Writing Center." *WLN: Writing Lab Newsletter* 39: 3–4.

Sicari, Anna, Harry Denny, and Romeo Garcia. 2021. "WCJ Philosophy and Vision." https://docs.google.com/document/d/10ICef7cpnchP5DcoAjOrMZsqIJp0F0yeZtLM9O-0zvE/edit.

Tomkins, Andrew, Min Zhang, and William D. Heavlin. 2017. "Reviewer Bias in Single-versus Double-Blind Peer Review." *Proceedings of the National Academy of Sciences (PNAS)* 114: 48. https://doi.org/10.1073/pnas.1707323114.

University Press of Colorado. 2022. "Our Publication Process and Timelines." Updated June 10. https://upcolorado.com/publish-with-us/our-publication-process.

Valles, Sarah Banschbach, Rebecca Day Babcock, and Karen Keaton Jackson. 2017. "Writing Center Administrators and Diversity: A Survey." *Peer Review* 1 (1). https://thepeerreview-iwca.org/issues/issue-1/writing-center-administrators-and-diversity-a-survey/.

Webster, Travis. 2021. *Queerly Centered: LGBTQA Writing Center Directors Navigate the Workplace*. Logan: Utah State University Press.

Young, Vershawn Ashanti. 2010. "Should Writers Use They Own English." *Iowa Journal of Cultural Studies* 12/13: 110–117.

Young, Vershawn Ashanti, and Aja Martinez eds. 2011. *Code Meshing as World English: Policy, Pedagogy, and Performance*. Urbana, IL: National Council of Teachers of English (NCTE).

SECTION ONE

Structural Marginalization

1
Of Budgets and Institutional Bumbling

New Writing Center Directors Reflect on Their First Year

ENRIQUE PAZ AND ELISE DIXON

The great irony of being a writing center (WC) scholar is that our expertise is not often regarded as central at our universities. Though institutions may acknowledge the wonderful work of writing centers, the wonderful workers dedicated to the research, theory, and practice of tutoring writing are regularly positioned at the periphery of academic ranks and respect. Or so say all the stories. We, Enrique and Elise, are two recent graduates of PhD programs in rhetoric and composition, now turned into tenure-track WC directors; like so many others, we were raised on these narratives. They were cautionary tales, like folklore passed down through the ages to warn of how institutions would exploit us, our labor, and our centers if we did not earn and preserve our position of legitimacy. Such tales constitute one of our field's enduring grand narratives—the marginalized writing center. Our mentors and programs equipped us with experience that might be used to subvert this narrative and earn respect among our academic peers. Our research is thorough, empirical, and theoretically sound. We have participated in building innovative programs and strategies for multidisciplinary writing support. And we recognize the need to build centers that are inclusive and antiracist. These experiences—we were told—are what we would need to be taken seriously and to build transformative centers that can transcend the marginality of yore.

https://doi.org/10.7330/9781646426119.c001

Our lived experiences in our first year on the job have instead suggested that the skills we needed to transcend the margins were more managerial. We arrived at our posts during the COVID-19 pandemic, finding writing centers already on the margins of their institutions, having spent years with little oversight or support. We have had to rebuild—reforging relationships on campus, renewing training for staff, and remaking services and resources for students—and often found our research acumen or innovative program designs were not suited for the task, especially at such precarious times for our institutions. Instead, we spent our days learning to navigate our institutional structures—mucking around with mysterious budget lines, organizational charts, and managerial tasks that had no obvious direction. Before we could pursue dynamic writing services or establish our centers as sites of empirical research or push for inclusive writing practices and curricula, we had to pull our centers out of the margins. As we've learned, to see such work continue fruitfully in uncertain futures, emerging WC professionals must become familiar with the day-to-day, institutional entanglements of WC administration. Equal command of the empirical, the theoretical, and the managerial may be the best way to ensure that the intellectual rigors of WC work continue to be appreciated by our institutions and are, in turn, supported enough for our replicable, aggregable, and data-supported (RAD) research practices and radical equity work to gain momentum.

In this chapter, we suggest that the writing center community's commitment to subverting the grand narrative and counteracting marginality has led to an abundance of theoretical knowledge on how to create transformative learning spaces. However, for many WC contexts, these pursuits can only succeed when supported by practical knowledge of how to navigate the black box of academic institutions (budgetary concerns, programmatic structures and relationships, university chain of command, etc.). Creating centers that lead campus writing innovatively, inclusively, and professionally requires the practical understanding of administration and administrative formations. Accordingly, we call for equipping emerging scholars and professionals with a deeper understanding of daily institutional navigations that are crucial to WC work, with a specific emphasis on graduate programs.

We begin by providing a brief literature review of past disciplinary responses to marginality in the writing center. We then add to these reports our own stories of marginalized centers in 2021, building upon that scholarship and adding to the record of lived experiences of WC directors begun by Nikki Caswell, Jackie Grutsch McKinney, and Rebecca Jackson (2016). Our narratives are not of linear success but of stumbling, incremental learning, and progress as we become nimbler and more responsive to the contexts of our universities. We conclude by reflecting on the impact of our disciplinary response to marginality and with suggestions for administrative training in graduate school so that new WC professionals may become agile administrators pressing inward from the periphery.

Research and Theory as Disciplinary Response to Marginality

"No other word haunts writing center scholarship more than *marginal*," writes Grutsch McKinney (2013, 39; emphasis in original). These narratives of marginal writing centers, their humble(d) administrators, and the students they serve endure throughout all our professional history and scholarship. While McKinney lays out many different responses to marginality (including claims of subversive marginality and post-marginality), we focus here on two responses that have informed the identity of WC scholars and professionals today: (1) an emphasis on research to drive practice and afford WC scholars' academic credibility and (2) a development and integration of theory into our administration and practice. These two responses represent the purpose of much WC scholarship, developing the empirical and theoretical depth of our work. Turning toward RAD research and theoretical WC scholarship has been a key strategy among writing center scholars to show how writing centers are not sites of marginal, managerial labor. However, we argue these responses have also contributed to a lack of scholarly attention toward the daily administrative labor of WC work, which, while not glamorous, is central. By ignoring or avoiding discussing daily managerial tasks in scholarship, the writing center community may be only further facilitating its own marginality by keeping early career directors in the dark about how to navigate the ins and outs of a center.

Early in the history of our disciplinary publications, founding editors Muriel Harris of the *WLN* and Lil Brannon and Stephen North of the *Writing Center Journal* encouraged WC scholars to publish to prove the rigor of our intellectual work and proved our academic professionalization. In 1979, Harris called for "more publications on labs and the whole process of tutoring instruction in writing" after lamenting that labs "still exist at the periphery" (1). Lil Brannon and Stephen North's (1980) introduction to their first issue described the journal "as an outward sign of a growing professional legitimacy" that would pull writing centers and their professionals out of the periphery (1). The editors warned that writing centers would "surely, deservedly, wither away" if WC professionals did not press into academic legitimacy through research publications and the respect they reap (2). As that research became more complex, scholars have assessed the caliber of our scholarship and what standards are necessary to grow our intellectual capital and grow out of the margins. Dana Driscoll and Sherry Wynn Perdue's (2012) "Theory, Lore, and More" scrutinized our published scholarship and concluded that much of the WC scholarship to that point "does not meet the test of what other disciplines define as evidence-based research" (35). Driscoll and Perdue call for replicable, aggregable, data-supported (RAD) research to articulate and defend the legitimacy of our practice, knowledge, and intellectual work so that we can "move our field into the future" (36). A proliferation of publications teaching research methods in writing centers (e.g., Thonus and Babcock 2012; McKinney 2015; Mackiewicz and Babcock 2019) takes up this call to show how WC research can become a central—rather than peripheral—contributor to many academic discussions. If we don't, Anne Geller and Harry Denny (2013) warned, we "may become agents in our own intellectual/disciplinary marginalization" (120).

In addition to calls for empirical studies, many scholars have developed theoretical orientations toward WC work's deep connection to identity, social justice, and inclusion with the goal of situating our work at the center (and not the margins) of contemporary conversations about equitable writing instruction. Scholars have explored the linguistic implications of writing center work, especially questions of what the "better" in "better writers" means (Bawarshi and Pelkowski 1999, 41–58), of how to facilitate students' rights to their own language (Young 2010; Green 2016), of connections between writing and identity and its implication for writing centers (DiPardo 1992; Blitz and Hulbert 2000; Denny 2010), and of how to best serve multilingual writers (Severino 2004; Phillips 2014; Rafoth 2015), in addition to engaging with theory scholars like Martin Heidegger, Jean Lave, Etienne Wenger, Jacques Derrida, Jean Foucault, bell hooks, Geoffrey Sirc, Michel de Certeau, and Judith Butler (Boquet 2002; Denny 2010; McKinney 2013). As Emily Isaacs and Melinda Knight (2014) describe, "The theorizing . . . functions to demonstrate that writing center scholarship is bona fide intellectual work . . . [and] therefore an effort toward legitimizing the intellectual underpinnings of writing centers as a site of inquiry" (60). Engaging with theory in the same manner as our colleagues in English studies and rhetoric and composition has indeed complemented and demonstrated the intellectual depth and complexity of our practice.

Of course, administrative realities were never ignored either. Book collections such as *Writing Centers: Theory and Administration* (Olsen 1984),

Intersections: Theory-Practice in the Writing Center (Mullin and Wallace 1994), *Administrative Problem-Solving for Writing Programs and Writing Centers* (Myers-Breslin 1999), and the *Writing Center Director's Resource Book* (Murphy and Stay 2006) include discussions of administrative practicalities including funding, hiring, training, and physical location. These texts include instructive local stories and solutions as well as theorizing of generalizable practice based on those experiences. Recently, Caswell, Grutsch McKinney, and Jackson's (2016) *The Working Lives of New Writing Center Directors* has documented the lived material experiences of administrative labor common to our practice and created a nuanced understanding of the whole practice of WC administration.

But these critical inquiries into administrative labor have not had the same impact on our emerging sense of professional identity as imparted in graduate education. As research degrees, PhD programs train their students to be researchers and theorists, and WC training has been no exception, building on disciplinary conversations that place research and theory at the heart of our intellectual identity and practice. In essence, in our discipline's collective work to move out of the margins through a deeper focus on RAD and theoretical research, we create less space for conversations on the daily managerial tasks—and the institutional navigation necessary to do them—that are required to keep an individual writing center afloat. As Nicholas Mauriello, William J. Macauley Jr., and Robert T. Koch Jr. (2011) warn in *Before and after the Tutorial: Writing Centers and Institutional Relationships*, WCs enter "isolation" and "self-imposed marginalization" when they do not build relationships throughout their institutions (3). Without more conversations about these tasks, early career writing center administrators (WCAs) may relegate themselves and their centers to the margins of their own institutions through lack of knowledge or understanding. And while initiatives like the International Writing Centers Association (IWCA) Summer Institute provide some opportunities to develop in these ways, these opportunities are often limited and expensive and struggle to circulate administrative knowledge beyond their immediate participants. Thus, we add to the warning by Mauriello et al. (2011): navigating our institutions to find and build relationships comprises much of the administrative work that moves WCs out of the margins of their universities, and our field must find better ways of preparing aspiring directors for this labor.

We draw attention to precisely this kind of essential labor—namely, the institutional navigations that have the potential to develop young, underfunded, or undersupported centers. Like Botvin and Buck have done in chapter 2 in this collection, we share our stories as evidence of the complex institutional positions that WCs may inhabit and that systemically and structurally tend toward pushing WCs to the margins. To illustrate our day-to-day stumbling through those institutional structures, we offer our own stories—small glimpses of our working lives and labors in our first years as WC directors. We provide these tales not as lamentations extending the narrative of the poor WC professional. We take to heart Botkin and Buck's warning to resist the "advice narrative" common to these kinds of reflections. Instead, we hope that these narratives promote further visibility of the kinds of administrative and managerial tasks that directors must perform when they are at the periphery of their institutions. To build centers where innovative theoretical and research work can eventually take shape requires emerging WC professionals to develop the awareness of these institutional workings and the nimbleness to move among them.

Enrique's Story

Despite my nearly ten years' experience in writing centers prior to this post, the administrative luxuries of an established and well-funded center did not prepare me for work I would face when I began directing my own center at a regional research university. This center, embedded in the English department, had spent the last five years without a full-time director and showed signs of disrepair and neglect. Usage rates had been falling each year, and fewer faculty demonstrated understanding of how to work with the center appropriately. The physical space was filled with a mess of administrative documents without order or purpose. And a once-thriving team of many undergraduate tutors had dwindled to only four. I was eager to build the kind of innovative writing center I had worked in before. But at each step, I encountered hindrances: institutional and managerial problems that I had heard of but rarely faced myself. Untangling these messes proved tricky, and I present two of these problems here: learning the budget and developing a tutor-hiring and -training process.

ISSUE 1: DISCOVERING THE BUDGET

I'd heard many stories warn about the terrors of funding. The narratives advise that one must be aware of their budget and be judicious about their spending. Still, despite knowing such a trap may await me, I received little practical instruction to assist me in my first task as a new director: learning what my budget was and how to seek funding when needed. As I asked around, I received only vague answers from the department chair, the administrative assistant who handled purchasing and payroll, and the graduate student administrator. It was not until I started to arrange for hiring more consultants that I was given a specific number: $7,500. Annually. For all the center's operations.

After five years without a director to advocate for the center's needs, the budget had dwindled to almost nothing. I made clear that we would be closed before Thanksgiving with a $7,500 budget and received two points from the department chair in response. First, there was likely to be unclaimed or unused student employment money somewhere that the center could magically appropriate, although I was not given guidance for how. Second, I would need to write a memo to the provost asking for funding for the spring semester. I had little conception of the odd financial shuffling that was seemingly commonplace here and no experience in the genre of memo-for-the-provost.

A healthy budget—in my mind—would be essential to revitalizing this enfeebled center and pulling it out of the margins of the institution. While we made it through the year, all of my available funds, including the extra money from the provost's office, could only support paying tutors. No sustained solution was developed, and I am told my budget is unchanged for the next year. With no money to fund anything other than tutoring, I cannot imagine how to support additional services or tutoring experiences, such as paying for regular ongoing training, support for WC research led by tutors, tutor travel to WC conferences, or even front desk workers to greet students and answer phone calls. How am I going to move the center out of the periphery while answering the phones?

ISSUE 2: HIRING PROCESS

Knowing that a strong center that breaks free of marginality begins with diverse and capable consultants, I set my intentions on creating a robust tutoring staff. I asked the department chair and the graduate administrator about hiring practices—what were the current hiring practices, how did we recruit, and which campus policies should I be aware of? Again, no one had clear answers. I thought there had to be a codified list of policies somewhere, right? My graduate school mentors always seemed to know what the rules were—how did they know? In my new center, the standard hiring process had always been that the administrative assistant would print a generic list of students who had uploaded resumes to the university's job website. New hires would come from that list or from cold emails from interested students. Then the administrative assistant did the paperwork, and new tutors participated in a few crash-course training sessions with readings and observations before beginning tutoring and learning by doing.

Hoping to create a healthier recruitment and training structure, I was allowed to resurrect a defunct course as a training and recruiting ground for new tutors. I knew how to develop and teach such a course; what I did not know would be the difficulty in getting students interested in it. The campus visibility of the center had become limited, and very few students were actively interested in working there. Further, my limited budget did not allow me to make promises about employment after the course was completed. Why sign up for a WC training course that did not guarantee a WC job? So instead I had to retool the course to deliver material that would provide value for professional writing and English education students, while also providing a solid foundation for tutoring. My colleagues advised me to create a course flier and to personally speak to advisors in all the colleges, seeking their help to recruit students across campus. I ended up with twelve students, only three of whom ultimately sought to work at the center.

I called student employment directly to discuss these hires and nine months into the job, I received answers. I learned about the student employment site, about the student employment guidebook for supervisors, and orientations on hiring practices. These resources taught me about student pay levels, hiring international students, and how work-study interacted with my budget, as well as how to post a proper job ad and reach interested students beyond my classroom and my very limited connections on campus (in my first year and during a pandemic).

These excerpts reveal practical, everyday ways my WC had been kept on the margins and how unprepared I had been to work through those structures. These were tasks that I never had to face, audiences I never had to consider, institutional structures I never had to untangle. My experiences only illuminated my inexperience—a lack of knowledge that threatened to keep my center on the periphery. When I was a fledgling graduate student administrator, budget memos or campus hiring policies were issues that I had read about and discussed in coursework but were abstract possibilities, foreign to my lived experience. But those experiences were essential to establishing my center as a central force for writing at my institution—and to moving out of the margins. My training professionalized me as a WC researcher, theorist, and scholar, but rather than the empowered, innovative, and professional scholar-director I had imagined myself to be, I instead found myself cast in the likeness of many of my predecessors: struggling administrators managing their way through local problems and solutions while imagining the possibilities on the other side. Nonetheless, these navigations serve to provide stability, sustainability, and strength necessary for those future ventures. They pull my center from the periphery and provide actionable means to disrupt that grand narrative in my local center.

Elise's Story

My writing center at a regional master's-granting university is funded by the academic unit known as the University College and is housed within the University College Building, but my tenure home is in the English department. This placement means that my administrative work remains largely unsupervised: for example, my yearly self-evaluation I submit to the English department chair does not include an option to discuss my administrative duties, and the dean of the University College is not tasked to oversee my administrative work either. I quickly learned that this lack of connection between my tenure home and the WC's home meant no one quite knew how to help me settle in. Thus, in the weeks leading up to the first day of fall semester, I found myself navigating the institutional maze of a university in relative solitude and from the margins from the very beginning.

I set to work first on the physical logistics: keys, cleaning up my office, and getting my technology set up. On my first few days, I wandered the halls of my building, searching for friendly faces who might point me toward those to speak to. Then I set to work on the less physical issues: What was my budget? *Where* was my budget? Who managed it? Or how should *I* manage it? What were the log-ins for WCONLINE and who could grant me administrative status? What systems were in place for gathering tutors' work schedule preferences? How did I approve timesheets? What forms were needed to make sure the tutors could be paid? In many ways, my first few weeks mirrored Enrique's in the sense that each question was shrouded in mystery. Each day I began with questions and chipped slowly away at better understanding which individual to contact about what, and who could provide me with helpful information. I learned from my dean what my budget roughly was, and I began receiving vague, confusing emails about how much the center tended to spend per month. I was never told how I could manage it, or ask for increases, or even what funds I could use for what. (Could I buy food for meetings? Decor for the center? Order new computers or furniture?)

Over time, through floundering email conversations and phone calls, I gained enough basic information to begin my logistical work of running the center, and I used that basic information and what I learned daily to chug my way through the first semester.

It was not until the second semester that I learned *I* was in charge of my budget and that since the fall, I had been authorized to make transfers and requests. Before the spring, no one had explored how I might be able to have more autonomy or control. By the end of my first year, I had uncovered enough information to feel that I was, in fact, running a writing center. Further, I *finally* felt like I had a handle on the day-to-day logistics enough to begin dreaming and planning for the future. It took me a year to feel as if I had enough control of my center to begin pulling it out of its marginal state. Truthfully, with each passing day and semester, I continue to feel as if I am bumbling my way out of the margins.

The experiences we have shared about the necessary practicalities of WC work for new administrators were complicated by the timing of our jobs. We both started during the pandemic, when both the virus and the switch to remote learning were still a bit of a mystery. Both of our centers and most of our campuses were fully online, so the option to find people in-person to ask about issues was limited and often took days of planning ahead. We spent little time in the physical space of our centers and sometimes did not meet our consultants in-person for months. It was clear we had been hired just under the wire before a hiring freeze, and faculty, staff, and students were too preoccupied with their own literal survival to attend to our welcome. Most new directors have similar stories of being lost or unsure of how to begin; fewer now have the story of beginning under the most unique circumstances of our lifetimes. Still, what would have been true regardless was how our imagined roles as WC directors (as radical agents of overarching change and cutting-edge research) were set in stark contrast to our reality (as practitioners literally fumbling for keys). In many ways, we realize now that our theoretical and scholarly knowledge did not prepare us to be nimble in the reality of our work as new WC directors.

No amount of WC theory, or even the practical guidelines that we are calling for in this chapter, could have prepared anyone to begin administrative work in the middle of a pandemic. However, our experience illuminates how necessary it is for graduate students hoping to become WC administrators to develop a clear sense of the day-to-day, foundational practicalities of WC work, before or alongside the more theoretical, RAD, and social-justice-oriented scholarship many of us have grown passionate about. While individual institutions may vary so much and limit the generalizability of training done in graduate programs, we suggest this training can and *should* be done and provide examples of such training in the following section. Focused attention on navigating institutional structures and understanding our managerial tasks are needed in order for WC directors to keep their individual centers from being marginalized within their institutions. A lack of familiarity with these tasks only further contributes to our marginality. Pulling our centers out of the margins *cannot* be done without the practical day-to-day understanding of procuring control of one's budget, understanding the administrative chain of command, compiling the order forms for supplies, sending reminder emails, and making coffee dates with longtime university faculty and administrators, among other daily tasks.

Re-Assessing Our Disciplinary Responses

Our discipline's efforts to develop theoretical and empirical scholarship highlighting the intellectual rigors of WC work are critical to our disciplinary survival and revising the narrative of marginality. However, in WC work, the practical, logistical day-to-day work often must supersede the theoretical; for if we have no command of the logistical inner workings of our university systems, the rest of the work simply cannot be done. We cannot do radical or research-based work if we don't know the process of understanding our budgets, which relationships are most critical for maintaining institutional support, or even where to go to get new keys cut. Graduate students with WC specializations will benefit from both a large-scale understanding of the theoretical and practical power of WC work *and* a small-scale awareness of how to get those things done through institutional relationships and small daily tasks. It is especially imperative to attend to such training in the current precarious job market situation, wherein many new graduates may begin their careers in undersupported or underdeveloped—that is, marginalized—centers.

For the remainder of this section, we provide a list of suggestions for training graduate students who plan to be WC administrators. While we understand that many, if not most, WC administrators come to their careers from trajectories different than ours (e.g., as staff or non-tenure-track faculty), we focus on graduate training as this is the position about which we understand the most. This bullet-pointed list is certainly not exhaustive, and we recognize that not all graduate programs and institutions have the resources to implement all these suggestions. They are meant to be a starting point for further conversations about making visible the day-to-day practicalities to build thriving centers.

- PROVIDE COURSES ON WRITING PROGRAM ADMINISTRATION in your graduate program. This may be the first step to providing students with opportunities to not only consider just how to tutor, teach, or coordinate elements of a center or writing program but also have a realistic understanding of the basic tasks of WPA work. Graduate students are often encouraged to operate in the theoretical realm. Grounding that theory in practice can occur in a course on administration. For example, the course may focus on the organization of your university's writing program, including how the program assesses itself, those it reports to, and how it has been (re)organized over the years.
- PROVIDE ASSISTANTSHIPS IN THE WRITING CENTER that make transparent the day-to-day work of directors. These assistantships should include experiences such as reviewing budget expenses and researching hiring policies. As graduate students, we were afforded such administrative opportunities that provided direction when we encountered new and unfamiliar tasks. Assistantships that provide more attention to the managerial could better equip future directors than could a research or tutoring-based assistantship.
- OFFER GLIMPSES INTO THE BUDGET. In Elise's WC administration course, she was assigned a project to develop a proposed budget for a program within the center she worked at. This assignment was helpful, but because she was in a well-funded center, the more precarious scrimping and saving that marginalized WCs often need to do were less familiar. Similar projects that might have explored the concerns of an undersupported center may include the next three suggestions.
- PAIR THEORETICAL WRITING CENTER TEXTS WITH PRACTICE-ORIENTED TEXTS, and ask students to consider what each text both asks and answers of the other. For instance, pairing Greenfield's (2019) *Radical Writing Center Praxis* with Caswell, Grutsch McKinney, and Jackson's (2016) *The Working Lives of New Writing Center Directors* can allow graduate students to think through the emotional labor attached to asking for additional resources for marginalized students, and how to avoid burnout in the process.
- CONNECT GRADUATES WITH MENTORSHIP OPPORTUNITIES for their careers as directors. Often, mentorship for WC directors is sparse within our institutions, and we rely on our community for help. IWCA's

Mentor Matching program is one such opportunity; this program could also focus more on providing the kind of practical and logistical guidance as well. Providing funding for graduate students to attend IWCA's Summer Institute might also be a way to connect future directors with mentors as well as administrative knowledge. If possible, extend your own mentorship to your students beyond graduation. We both found much direction and solace from our graduate school mentors and colleagues as we navigated our first years as directors.

- PROMOTE TRANSPARENCY ABOUT THE DAILY LABOR AS A DIRECTOR, PARTICULARLY THROUGH PUBLICATIONS. The training of graduate students and early career WC administrators can extend beyond our local programs and immediate students through greater visibility of our daily labors in the articles and books we publish. This call is not only limited to graduate student mentors but also includes all WC scholars, journal editors, and peer reviewers. Graduate students and new WC directors should be able to turn to our publications and find discussion and direction regarding the negotiations of institutional infrastructures and daily tasks. Editors and WC scholars more broadly may consider what publishing spaces might be made available to highlight administrative work and how to write critically about administrative issues.

Preparing graduate students for WC administrative work is ultimately about best preparing the next generation of scholars and practitioners who will change the field for the better. While engaging with critical, theoretical, and RAD research is an important aspect of preparing for administrative labor, recognizing the importance of the daily rigors of that labor allows a more realistic and practical understanding of how to run a center. We hope this list of possible strategies can be the start of fruitful conversations for many in our discipline.

Conclusion

The history of writing centers provides a story that is often taken as a warning to WC administrators and scholars against the marginalization of our practice within our institutions and in the wider communities of rhetoric, composition, and English. As writing center professionals, we find an occupational hazard to be that our research, our expertise, and our service are often undersupported, misunderstood, and pushed to the periphery of academic recognition. In response, WC scholars have produced their own counternarratives: they are professionalized with discipline-specific knowledge and expertise, driven by empirical research, and leading change on campus through student writing support, Writing Across the Curriculum (WAC)/Writing in the Disciplines (WID) programs, and attention to inclusivity and social justice. These counternarratives are critical to our collective disciplinary identity and often to our writing centers' survival, but those counternarratives have also generally only been understood and received in our *own* community, often while pushing out the stories of the practical and logistical work required to run a center. Thus, graduate students and new administrators like us may find ourselves with an abundance of stories about writing center professionals' capacity to do incredible scholarship, and a lack of disciplinary best practices for how to navigate our own institutional networks in order to just find printer paper or budget money. Without attention to the daily (and far less exciting) practicalities of administrative labor, these counternarratives cannot be fully lived out.

Our graduate training and experiences in writing centers prepared us to do the scholarly work of creating writing centers that subvert the marginalizing narratives that surround writing centers' histories. But when faced with an already-marginalized writing center, we often felt underprepared to respond appropriately to the challenges we faced. The managerial work of finding funding, navigating campus politics, or learning student employment protocols were not as visible in much of our training.

We see now how much the managerial tasks of budgeting (which, we realize now, often starts with *finding* or *creating* a budget and learning who runs it), emailing, cutting keys, learning the chain of command, tidying, and organizing are all required *first* to develop and practice the counternarratives that actually get our own centers and our discipline out of the margins of our individual institutions and scholarly fields of study. Writing centers continue to be radical spaces of social justice and change *because* of their constant engagement with rigorous scholarship *and* vigorous daily practice. We call for WC professionals and scholars to remember the importance of the basics so that we can do the good work we are here to do.

References

Bawarshi, Anis, and Stephanie Pelkowski. 1999. "Postcolonialism and the Idea of a Writing Center," *Writing Center Journal* 19 (2): 41–58.

Blitz, Michael, and C. Mark Hulbert. 2000. "If You Have Ghosts." In *Stories from the Center: Connecting Narrative and Theory in the Writing Center*, edited by Lynn Craigue Briggs and Meg Woolbright, 84–93. Urbana, IL: NCTE.

Boquet, Elizabeth H. 2002. *Noise from the Writing Center.* Logan: Utah State University Press. https://wac.colostate.edu/docs/books/usu/noise/front.pdf.

Brannon, Lil, and Stephen North. 1980. "For the Editors." *The Writing Center Journal* 1 (1): 1–3.

Caswell, Nicole, Jackie Grutsch McKinney, and Rebecca Jackson. 2016. *The Working Lives of New Writing Center Directors.* Logan: Utah State University Press.

Denny, Harry. 2010. *Facing the Center: Toward an Identity Politics of One-to-One Mentoring.* Logan: Utah State University Press.

DiPardo, Anne. 1992. "'Whispers of Coming and Going': Lessons from Fannie." *Writing Center Journal* 12 (2): 125–144.

Driscoll, Dana, and Sherry Wynn Perdue. 2012. "Theory, Lore, and More: An Analysis of RAD Research in 'The Writing Center Journal,' 1980–2009." *Writing Center Journal* 32 (2): 11–39.

Geller, Anne E., and Harry Denny. 2013. "Of Ladybugs, Low Status, and Loving the Jobs: Writing Center Professionals Navigating Their Careers." *Writing Center Journal* 31 (1): 96–129.

Green, Neisha-Anne S. 2016. "The Re-education of Neisha-Anne S Green: A Close Look at the Damaging Effect of 'A Standard Approach,' the Benefits of Code Meshing, and the Role Allies Play in this Work." *Praxis: A Writing Center Journal* 14 (1). http://www.praxisuwc.com/green-141.

Greenfield, Laura. 2019. *Radical Writing Center Praxis: A Paradigm for Ethical Political Engagement.* Logan: Utah State University Press.

Grutsch McKinney, Jackie. 2013. *Peripheral Visions for Writing Centers.* Logan: Utah State University Press.

Grutsch McKinney, Jackie. 2015. *Strategies for Writing Center Research.* Parlor Press. https://www.perlego.com/book/953906/strategies-for-writing-center-research-pdf.

Harris, Muriel. 1979. "Editor's Note." *Writing Lab Newsletter* 3 (9): 1–2.

Isaacs, Emily, and Melinda Knight. 2014. "A Bird's Eye View of Writing Centers: Institutional Infrastructure, Scope and Programmatic Issues, Reported Practices." *WPA: Writing Program Administration* 37 (2): 36–67.

Mackiewicz, Jo, and Rebecca Day Babcock, eds. 2019. *Theories and Methods of Writing Center Studies: A Practical Guide.* New York: Routledge.

Mauriello, Nicholas, William J. McCauley Jr., and Robert T. Koch Jr., eds. 2011. *Before and after the Tutorial: Writing Centers and Institutional Relationships.* New York: Hampton Press.

Mullin, Joan, and Ray Wallace, eds. 1994. *Intersections: Theory-Practice in the Writing Center.* Urbana, IL: National Council of Teachers of English.

Murphy, Christina, and Byron L. Stay, eds. 2006. *The Writing Center Director's Resource Book.* New York: Routledge.

Myers-Breslin, Linda, ed. 1999. *Administrative Problem-Solving for Writing Programs and Writing Centers.* Urbana, IL: National Council of Teachers of English.

Olson, Gary A., ed. 1984. *Writing Centers: Theory and Administration.* Urbana, IL: National Council of Teachers of English.

Phillips, Talinn. 2014. "Developing Resources for Success: A Case Study of a Multilingual Graduate Writer." *WAC and Second Language Writers: Research Towards Linguistically and Culturally Inclusive Programs and Practices*, edited by Terry Myers Zawacki and Michelle Cox, 69–91. Anderson, SC: Parlor Press. https://wac.colostate.edu/docs/books/l2/front.pdf.

Rafoth, Ben. *Multilingual Writers and Writing Centers*. 2015. Logan: Utah State University Press.

Severino, Carol. 2004. "Avoiding Appropriation." *ESL Writers: A Guide for Writing Center Tutors*, edited by Shanti Bruce and Ben Rafoth, 48–59. Portsmouth, NH: Boynton/Cook.

Thonus, Terese, and Rebecca Day Babcock. 2012. *Research the Writing Center: Towards an Evidence-Based Practice*. New York: Peter Lang.

Young, Vershawn Ashanti. 2010. "Should Writers Use They Own English?" *Iowa Journal of Cultural Studies* 12 (1): 110–117.

2
A Tale of Two Writing Centers

Navigating Fraught Institutional Legacies

JOSHUA BOTVIN AND ELISABETH H. BUCK

Our critique here is of a system. It is a system that enabled two writing centers to exist on our campus in direct conflict and competition with each other. We say very deliberately that our critique is *systemic* in nature because, as will hopefully become clear, it is difficult to pinpoint one party or entity that is singularly responsible for the events that transpired. Our circumstance is also partially attributable to the fact that writing center labor tends to be parsed, (largely) unseen, and often ambiguously structured, opening the door to systemic marginalization. Nikki Caswell, Jackie Grutsch McKinney, and Rebecca Jackson in *The Working Lives of New Writing Center Directors* assert that "the work of directing a center is often rendered immaterial and invisible . . . job seekers have no way of judging whether a director position is fair or feasible, relying instead on writing center lore about the perils of this or that type of position" (2016, 4). Anyone newly hired into a writing center administrative role must, in consequence, immediately navigate an often-complicated web of institutional history, both pertaining to the writing center's relationship to its campus and vis-à-vis the origins and perceptions of their position.

Our narrative will illustrate something of a worse-case scenario related to the preceding description. Due to a particularly difficult context, Elisabeth—a newly hired writing center administrator at a midsized regional institution—

https://doi.org/10.7330/9781646426119.c002

ended up splitting from the established campus writing center, the Writing and Reading Center (WRC), to found another center, the Multiliteracy and Communication Center (MCC). The MCC differed from the WRC only in its commitment to be attentive to writing on and through new media but otherwise served an identical campus population. For two years (2018–2020), the university maintained both the MCC and the WRC, resulting in widespread confusion for the entire campus. Elisabeth was initially hired as the faculty director of the WRC, and Joshua first served as one of the WRC's writing assistants, a catchall term for a staff administrative support role. Our goal is to explain how this circumstance unfolded and also to describe how we responded given our mitigated authority and positionality on campus. As brand-new and/or contingent faculty, we found that much of the background or context we might have needed to be successful, or at least more aware of what we were walking into, was invisible. In chapter 1 of this collection, Paz and Dixon also explore this theme of writing center positions that were not as advertised. Our roles began on the margins, but they have evolved into something more sustainable, largely due to the support of individuals within our department. These shifts in our labor were not without emotional and material costs.

Many current or hopeful writing center administrators may find parallels here in their experiences as new hires, especially coming directly from a graduate program, where, as Paz and Dixon describe, the lived realities of a role may be far different than what was articulated on paper. We do not wish this to be an "advice narrative"—which Caswell, Grutsch McKinney, and Jackson caution against—as "when we propagate advice narratives, we forward a very narrow viewpoint, one that often comes with minimal evidence" (2016, 9). In describing how two "rival" writing centers were enabled by institutional conditions, we hope instead to provide meaningful commentary on structures of (new) WCA positions and the often-tacit or explicit expectation to be an agent of change. We conclude by recommending specific, important queries to initiate at the interview stage to ascertain how "fair" and "feasible" the institution's perceptions are of both the center and its admin(s), thus addressing the gap in the lore that Caswell, Grutsch McKinney, and Jackson (2016) refer to. Our experiences of marginalization largely occurred as a result of systemic conditions that we suspect are not unique to our institution.

Elisabeth's Narrative

One widely accepted tenet of the grand narrative of academe, which also certainly manifests with/in writing center labor, is the primacy of a tenure-track position. In a good year, there might be five tenure-track writing center director positions *in the entire world*. This competitive and difficult job market means that folks do not always have the luxury of turning down a position, even one with obvious red flags. I do not wish to come across as a tenure-track individual wholly unaware of their privilege. Greater job security, pay, and institutional ethos tend to accompany many tenure-track roles. What I do hope to complicate here is the idea that *all* tenure-track jobs are *inherently* good jobs. Their scarcity does not always equate to a position that is sustainable, healthy, or stable.

I was hired in August 2016 right out of graduate school in the inaugural tenure-track role of faculty director of the Writing and Reading Center and assistant professor of English. At this time, there was already someone on campus with the title of director of the Writing and Reading Center. When my coauthor and I refer to the director of the Writing and Reading Center, we do not refer to me or my position. If this sounds confusing, well, it was. But to reiterate: in 2016, there was one writing center on campus—the Writing and Reading Center—and two directors, the newly created faculty director position (me) and the director (not me). In describing how this odd administrative structure came to be and what ultimately transpired, it will hopefully become clear that both the director and I were subject to systemic marginalization. The institution set us up to fail.

(NOT) STRUCTURED FOR SUCCESS

During my campus visit, I did not spend much time in the Writing and Reading Center space or with tutoring staff, so I was perhaps put into a position to assume that the director was planning to imminently retire. It was only when the director facilitated contact in the summer to "discuss plans for the fall" that I realized that I'd been very wrong in this assumption. I think I allowed myself to believe this partially out of self-preservation. I could not fathom why the institution needed both a faculty director *and* a director position. *So, surely, the director must be planning to leave soon . . . ?* It seems in retrospect a major oversight on my part that I did not ask for specific clarification on the director's role prior to accepting the job. At the time, I was just so grateful to have *any* job offer, and the fact that it was tenure-track and in my emphasis of choice contributed to my willfully unseen spot.

I try often to think about how I would feel had I been in the director's shoes. The director did not have a PhD but had served as the Writing and Reading Center's sole administrator for nearly thirty years, so it is understandable that she might have felt threatened by the university's decision to create the faculty director role. She was also not a member of my position's search committee, and I do not know the extent to which she was consulted about hiring me in particular.

Structural ageism likely manifested for both me and the director. I was twenty-seven when I was hired, but I'm often told that I look younger. My perceived youth did not signal natural authority, especially when juxtaposed with the director's long-standing position at the university. Conversely, it is plausible that the administration sought to replace the director with someone more credentialed, who could bring a fresh perspective to the writing center, but they could not fire her outright due to our campus's strong collective-bargaining units. I would wager that the faculty director role was created out of the administration's desire to make changes without initiating conflict with the campus unions. The burden of how to make our jobs workable on a practical basis therefore fell squarely on me and the director. I believe we both made good efforts to attempt to lead the center collaboratively, but my position was too fraught in its origins and too ambiguous in its delineations from her own.

While the faculty director job ad seemed to align with other position descriptions I had read for tenure-track writing center director roles, requiring a PhD and writing center research and experience, my actual job description—which I received during my first week on campus from the English Department—specified that I only spend five hours per week as a physical presence in the center; that I design tutor training; that I perform outreach to departments, colleges, and the community; and that I develop online support. The day-to-day labor of the writing center would be supervised and overseen by the director. The administration was also clear that they expected me to help innovate the Writing and Reading Center by applying my disciplinary expertise.

I was stuck then in an unwinnable position, as to maintain things as they were at the center would risk my being perceived by administration as ineffective but to seek out change would mean asserting my ill-defined directorial license. In eventually choosing the latter path, I sought to be as deliberate as possible and spent most of my first semester assessing the center's tutor training program. My recommendation was to make a major shift by eliminating the previous training model, a task-based checklist approved by the College Reading and Learning Association, and move to a for-credit, semester-long training course that I would teach. I still stand by my recommendations, but, with the benefit of hindsight, I also see my objective to shift tutor training as my attempt to carve out for myself some defined and meaningful purpose in the WRC, where one did not structurally exist. Despite my tenure-track status, I felt very much on the margin in that space. I had no ability to hire or supervise tutors, delegate to or coordinate labor with the other Writing and Reading Center administrative staff (composed of two writing assistants and a graduate assistant), or have wide-ranging conversations with faculty about how our center could best support their students. This authority all fell to the director. I had no idea how to be a campus advocate for a place where I played basically no role in its everyday operations. *Why am I here when nobody really needs or wants me to be?*

Another structural obstacle was the Writing and Reading Center's reporting apparatus and source of funding. All campus tutoring centers at the time were housed under the umbrella of the Academic Resource Center and funded primarily by a federal TRIO grant ("Federal TRIO programs" 2022). The Academic Resource Center had its own nonfaculty director, an individual to whom the WRC director reported. Randall Monty provides language for why this structure might have evolved as a response to the academy's shift toward neoliberalism. He writes that "even seemingly smaller changes, such as moving centers out of academic departments and reclassifying them as service programs, transitioning administrator roles from faculty to staff positions, renaming tutors as 'consultants,' and redirecting resources away from original research and towards grant procurement, are likewise attempts to imbue writing center work with an air of authority that only registers as coherent within a context that already assumes neoliberalism as its essential logic" (Monty 2019). Although our campus does include a large population of students who fall under TRIO grant criteria, the tutoring support centers were entire-campus resources eligible to be utilized by anyone. Many suggestions I made were rejected by both the ARC and WRC directors with the justification that such a shift would render us in violation of the TRIO grant's funding conditions. I had clearly been embedded into a (neoliberal) structure that had no place for me, as I was a faculty member with labor evaluated not by the ARC director but primarily by an English department.

TRANSITIONS AND SNAPSHOTS

Early in the fall semester of 2017, about a year after I started my position, conflict between me and the director had escalated to the point that I informed my English Department chair that I could no longer perform the faculty director role. My department chair had been my consistent advocate and was very sympathetic to the structural difficulties I was navigating in the WRC. I explained that the WRC writing and graduate assistants and tutors were being most harmed by the ambiguous administrative structure. I was acutely aware how universally confusing it was to determine who was actually *in charge* of the space. My chair agreed, and I was empowered not to be physically present in the WRC until some alternative could be found. I planned to explore whether it was possible to keep my assistant professor role and resign my faculty director position. The alternative ended up emerging from a meeting with an upper administrator at the university. She had asked what my solution would be and I said, half-jokingly, to simply break away from the WRC and start a separate, new writing center.

This, however, is exactly what came to pass. At the upper administrator's request, I spent the remainder of the 2017–2018 academic year (AY) putting together the proposal for what became the Multiliteracy and Communication Center (MCC). The MCC would serve the entire campus population, emphasize writing inclusive of new media technologies, and be funded outside of the TRIO grant, which was an important move that would enable much more autonomy in how we could allocate our resources. I was asked to have minimal contact with everyone in the WRC, and the proposal for the MCC was prepared with a great deal of secrecy. Very few knew what I was doing or why I was absent from the WRC's physical space. I look back on the administration's ready acceptance of my proposal with two views. Optimistically, one could see this as their belief that my plan represented the best way forward and that spoke to their confidence in my ability to lead a new center with a more twenty-first-century approach to writing. More cynically, it could be seen as the easiest solution to a very complicated problem, one that did not actually take steps to address the structural, funding, and staffing issues that had existed for decades.

The university's intention for the Writing and Reading Center was that it would shift to become a resource only for use by TRIO grant-eligible students in accordance with its funding mandates. There was no plan in place as to how TRIO students would be specifically informed of the change, how they'd be directed to visit the WRC instead of the MCC, or if they would be required to self-disclose their TRIO status. The upper administrator informed me that the MCC would take over the prime campus real estate currently occupied by the Writing and Reading Center, and the WRC would move to a windowless room in the basement of the same building. If the spaces writing centers inhabit reflect institutional perceptions of their importance, this reallocation sent a clear message. Current tutors could opt to work at one or both centers. All staff at the WRC were informed of this via a terse email sent to them by university administration in mid-April 2018. The resentment and confusion that resulted from this sudden announcement and shift were both unsurprising and, frankly, understandable.

Although I did not know Joshua well at the time, as they had accepted the writing assistant role right before I had successfully advocated to no longer be physically present in the WRC, they had struck me as someone very invested in student success. After the MCC became public knowledge and I was allowed to speak more freely, we had a conversation, and that is when I learned that their concerns about the WRC's operations largely paralleled mine. I had been assigned funding for an assistant director in the MCC and so asked at this time if they would be interested in applying for this role.

I conclude my portion of this chapter with several chronological snapshots. These hopefully provide narrative insight into how people perceived me as a person, my role in the center, and the confusion that resulted due to the campus maintaining both the Writing and Reading Center and the Multiliteracy and Communication Center. I began the faculty director job in August 2016, for clarity.

Snapshot #1 (October 2016)

It is a rare day in the Writing and Reading Center when I am the only administrator present. The campus's marketing team arrives unannounced, cameraperson in tow. "Hey," they say to me, "can you sit at this desk, and we'll take some pictures?" A few months later, a student informs me that my picture is on a billboard over Route 24 advertising the university's online programs. A colleague also emails me a print version of the ad, where I sit smiling in front of a computer at one of WRC's tutoring stations. "Are you supposed to represent a student or a professor here?" she asks. "I have no idea," I reply.

Snapshot #2 (March 2017)

Although I've been at the WRC for over a semester, I know only a handful of tutors well, the five folks who had signed up to take my writing center research workshop. As I pass by the lounge space where the tutors hang out during their off-time, a tutor I'd had very limited prior interactions with comments to me, wholly unprompted, "You seem like you'd be a really fun person to get drunk with." Another tutor, to her very great credit, immediately responds, "Wow, that is such an unprofessional thing to say to her." I manage to make it back to my car before I burst into tears.

Snapshot #3 (September 2018)

I'm sitting in the common area outside of what is now the Multiliteracy and Communication Center and watching the facilities team remove the names painted on the concrete wall of the former WRC tutors' lounge. It was a tradition that graduating tutors at the WRC add their names to the wall at the end-of-the-year party. Watching the erasure of the painted names is a sharp reminder of the legacy of this space. I staged a coup d'état. I might have "won" but at what costs—to the tutors, the director, the writing/grad assistants, and myself? There was a community here, and it needn't have ended this way.

The newly appointed chancellor and his coterie suddenly round the corner, catching me by surprise. I quickly stand and barely manage to catch the laptop I'd been balancing on my lap. Someone from his team introduces me as the director of the "new" writing center. He shakes my hand, and a marketing photographer takes our picture. Somehow, I doubt this will end up on a billboard.

Snapshot #4 (October 2019)

I am at a meeting where several faculty members from different colleges across campus are present, giving an overview of how the Multiliteracy and Communication Center can help assist students. One faculty member raises their hand and asks, "But wait, what happened to the WRC? That's where I used to send my students for assistance with writing." I mention that the WRC is still a center on campus but that it moved to the basement of the liberal arts building and is currently meant as a resource only for TRIO students. She continues, "But how do *I* know which center to send my students to? Do *they* even know their TRIO status? Why didn't the university make an announcement about this? I am so confused!" Another faculty member mentions that she wasn't aware of the changes and sent her students to the WRC, where they were provided with assistance even though she suspects they are not TRIO-grant eligible. I shrug my shoulders. "Well, the MCC is *supposed* to be the center that serves the entire campus population, and the WRC is *supposed* to be a resource only for use by TRIO students." I do not know what else to say. I've had this conversation so many times.

Joshua's Narrative

This narrative seeks to elaborate on how the situation outlined by my coauthor impacted my first year as a writing center administrator. In sharing my experience from the perspective of a contingent laborer, I hope to speak to others on the writing center margins whose stories often go untold, so that they may recognize if they themselves are in similar positions and have the agency to self-advocate.

In addressing the inherent marginalization of our work, Caswell, Grutsch McKinney, and Jackson (2016) bring attention to the haves and have-nots of writing centers. The authors cite Neal Lerner to outline this intended marginalization: "The terrain of our field seems separated into two types of directors: an active, enfranchised group with faculty or secure status and a part-time, contingent—and largely silent—group doing the best they can do under very difficult conditions" (2016, 6). As a contingent faculty serving as writing center administrator, I found myself belonging to the silent, latter group.

A bridge in the gap between the perceptions of the contingent administrator and my own experiences is Dani Nier-Weber's (2017) "The Other Invisible Hand: Adjunct Labor and Economies of the Writing Center," which provides an account of their time spanning several university writing centers. The narrative focuses on two features of writing center labor: invisibility and relational dispositions. Similar to the circumstance outlined by Wendy Rider in their contribution, chapter 3, in this collection, Nier-Weber describes the overlooked contingent faculty within the writing center as "the unsung and invisible hand . . . of writing center work" (2017, 104). Calling to attention the lack of scholarship centered on contingent faculty, Nier-Weber states, "Little corresponding discussion exists about the particular challenges, ethics, and economics of labor conditions faced by composition adjuncts and other professionals for whom writing center work comprises part, most, or all of their job" (2017, 104). They continue to state that this work largely goes "unnoticed and un-narrated," leading to unchallenged, false perceptions of labor and unclear expectations for this work. Nier-Weber's second feature is marked by a relational disposition shared by the vast majority of their consultants. This attitude is marked by "a compelling desire to help others" and attracting those "who wanted to contribute, be of service, and make a difference" (Nier-Weber 2017, 112). Core to this relational disposition, however, is the systemic exploitation of these groups of laborers, who often consist of marginalized, underpaid, and undervalued members of society (Nier-Weber 2017, 113).

Writing centers, then, are comprised of relationally oriented individuals typically underrepresented in scholarship. Nier-Weber makes explicit the fact that writing center directors must be aware of this reality and "protect individual adjunct faculty" (2017, 115). Their narrative, however, appears to play out under the best of circumstances, one in which a difficult system is navigated by a director who protects their staff. However, under less-than-ideal circumstances, the tentative employment of contingent faculty may put them in inherently marginalized positions.

I found myself accepting an administrative role in a writing center under those less-than-ideal circumstances. Due to my marginalization in a contingent faculty pool, I heedlessly accepted a position that would thrust me directly in the center of the institutional conflict that my coauthor has outlined in this chapter.

TENTATIVE EMPLOYMENT

For the past decade, I've been associated with the same university, receiving both my bachelor's and master's degrees and then working postgraduation as an adjunct instructor and writing center administrator. As contingent faculty, I've found my time in the institution has been defined by the dual reality that I am both supported by my department heads and also insignificant to the grander institution. This is both motivating and terrifying. It inspires me to pursue scholarship and professional development, while recognizing that my efforts could be for naught if enrollment dips and course numbers diminish.

The fraught nature of my positionality took center stage in the fall of 2017, when the university issued a course reduction for adjunct workers, cutting my salary by a third. While I already waited tables on the weekends, this drastic shift in wages threatened to put me in an untenable financial position, and so I applied to an administrative role in the university's Writing and Reading Center (WRC).

As a young professional and recent college graduate, I focused on financial stability and professional development and so disregarded even the most basic gatekeeping practices for a job search, like asking my trusted colleagues about the reputation of the WRC (with whom I had no existing relationship, as either instructor or student). Had I asked, I might have learned about its contentious institutional reputation, or the ongoing situation described by my coauthor. This rush to fill a vacancy ultimately put me in a position where I felt bound to the job and thus unable to comfortably speak my mind in a position with an ill-defined role.

ILL-DEFINED ROLE

In October 2017, while, unbeknownst to me, my coauthor was in the process of removing themself from the WRC, I assumed one of the two "writing assistant" roles. From the job description, I was intended to act in an administrative capacity, with duties such as program development and facilitating tutor training workshops. Duties were also discussed during my initial interview with the director (not my coauthor) as adaptive to the skills of the individual, which we identified as developing our social media platforms. Unlike Elisabeth's role, which was assessed by the English Department, my position fell under the director's immediate jurisdiction, and so my first priority became appeasing the individual who would be directly responsible for my contract renewal.

Since the position began more than a month into the semester, there was little formal training. Instead, the director assigned tasks each shift during one-on-one meetings, such as modifying the formatting of training materials, revising questions on surveys that were never used, or drafting emails that were not sent. While these administrative tasks seemed par for the course given my limited experience in a writing center, they did little to provide me a sense of agency in my position and instead kept me dependent upon the director, who would highly scrutinize any content I produced. However, as the semester progressed, and for reasons of which I was not yet aware, their physical presence in the center gradually diminished. Though it was replaced with phone calls providing vague direction, it became apparent that my role had no clear parameters. On days when I received no or unclear instruction, I did not know what to do. Being new to the role and in recognizing the micromanagement style of my supervisor, I was caught in a paradox of not wanting to step out of line by completing work that was not assigned to me, while also not wanting to be accused of lazing about during work hours.

Fearing the latter I attempted to carve out work for myself, but everywhere I turned it seemed I hit an obstacle: improper login credentials, conflicting feedback from the two directors, or, the most common setback: violation of the TRIO grant. These obstacles only served to exacerbate my internal conflict; my role was ill-defined, contingent, and, I assumed, performance based. Because I never had a clear sense of my job, I never once felt I was doing my job and as a result would ultimately lose my position when up for renewal.

ON THE MARGINS OF INFORMATION

A recurring theme throughout the year was the marginalization I felt as a member of the writing center administration. As a new employee, I expected a learning curve to acclimate to the workspace; however, as described in the previous section, there was no tangible training process. In contrast, information seemed to be kept from me. I was often made to feel more like a graduate student than an administrator, which was highlighted in a number of ways: the inability to make changes to day-to-day programming; exclusion from meetings the director held with the other, more established writing assistant; and having my training workshops mandatorily held in the director's office while they were present. I felt constantly watched and without autonomy.

As the semester moved forward, I began noticing idiosyncrasies in the chain of command. On the rare days of the director's presence, I worked right beside and met frequently with them. I had briefly met my coauthor earlier in the semester, but by then they were physically absent from the space. I understood them both to be "higher-ups" in their administrative roles of director and faculty director, respectively, but could not accurately define what each of those roles were. I did my best to toe the line between the two, making sure to include each on any email correspondence and updates regarding my work and trying my best to find the middle ground between each of their, often conflicting, directions.

I came to define my role through my lack of agency. I could not institute new training methods in the WRC; I could not answer the questions of the tutoring staff; I could not even send an email without the director first proofreading the draft. I was in a meaningless, abused role on the margin of this institution.

CONTINGENCY COMING TO A HEAD

The lack of my defined role came to a head on an evening in April 2018. About thirty minutes after the director departed for the night, a tutor approached my desk and asked me to explain an email she had just received. The email, addressed to the entire WRC staff, was 150 words describing the opening of "a new student support center, the Multiliteracy and Communication Center." It addressed the broader mission of the MCC, detailed that my coauthor would head it, and clarified that the WRC would continue under the leadership of its current director. The new center would be housed in the current WRC space. The WRC would be relocated to the "ground floor" of the campus, a generous way to describe the windowless basement.

I was given no prior notice of this news and as a result could relay nothing to the staff. There are few moments in my professional life when I have felt more powerless. As a peripheral member of the writing center administration, I was not included in meetings on the institutional, departmental, or programmatic level to discuss these decisions. And yet, I was the only administrative staff present in the center at the scheduled time the email was sent. Being near the bottom of a top-down system with little to no transparency, I was just as clueless, shocked, and scared as the tutoring staff.

In their section of this narrative, Elisabeth discusses what was happening in the WRC at this time from their perspective, but as a contingent faculty on the periphery of our institution, this email was the first I learned of the situation in any meaningful detail. I faced these strange, ever tensing day-to-day conditions while there were complex, institutional changes happening under my very nose. Caswell, Grutsch McKinney, and Jackson talk about these invisible dynamics as if they exist merely in the past, setting the framework for a role before a director accepts a position. Institutional invisibility is a danger to those in the job market because it leads to obtuse expectations about a position you might eventually fill. But when you are so far on the margin, as is the case with many contingent faculty, your current job, your current knowledge of institutional decision making, your current day-to-day reality, are also invisible.

REFLECTIONS

I write the final section of my contribution with the audience of fellow contingent faculty in mind, the group furthest on the margins. In the years following the events I've listed, I accepted a full time lecturer position with my institution. While still contingent, the role offers significantly more job security and a higher wage. I received this position with the help of advocates like my coauthor. I am writing, then, with an awareness that my situation unfolded in a unique and privileged fashion that will be a rare exception and so am leery to provide specific steps of advice. Still, I believe several broader factors that helped my situation unfold in the way that it did could be applicable to most folks on the margins of academia:

- DOCUMENT: After my first few weeks in my role as writing assistant, I had a feeling something was off about the position. While I was uncertain of the specific details, and as a result terrified to speak to anyone at the university, I began documenting days that seemed important or off kilter. In addition to a personal outlet to vent stress, this provided me with a detailed account of each incident I experienced at the WRC that I viewed as troubling or unprofessional.
- SELF-ADVOCATE: With this documented evidence in hand, I felt more prepared to speak my mind. This is admittedly a fraught position in which to find yourself, but if you are able to find others who might advocate for you, like I found with my coauthor, connect with them immediately.
- RECOGNIZE ALLIES: As contingent labor, we are made to feel invisible, so much so that we may overlook the individuals within the system who are willing to advocate for those on the margins. While you may be working against a system, allies exist within that system. I met with my coauthor following the news of the writing center split. In that time I found an ally willing to build a more equitable writing center and to fight to protect their employees. We made it through an arduous second half of April, where the tension at the WRC had boiled over, and I was eventually offered the position of program coordinator, which evolved into my current role as assistant director.

However, with this said, I feel that to suggest to fellow contingent faculty to follow my path—to suffer through the stress, uncertainty, and marginalization I underwent in my time as an adjunct writing assistant with the WRC—would be unethical. I bluntly encourage anyone in a similarly fraught or abusive position to be prepared to walk away from their work. While this is drastic advice, no job is worth sustained damage to your mental health. Those furthest on the margins of academia are made to feel invisible, but it is increasingly our labor that enables the system of higher education. There is no better way to become visible than to withhold that labor from an abusive system.

Conclusion: Looking to the Future

The Multiliteracy and Communication Center and the Writing and Reading Center existed simultaneously for two years. While the WRC was again meant to serve the population of TRIO students in compliance with its funding directives, neither the institution nor the WRC ever enforced this distinction, nor did they have much incentive to. Students ultimately visited whichever center they happened upon or their particular professor advocated for. Confusion reigned.

We feel more comfortable sharing our perspectives now as many of the parties involved have since left the institution or retired, including the WRC director. We cannot confirm, though would certainly surmise, that the power dynamics and move to the basement might have expedited the director's decision to retire. They left the university in fall 2019, and the administration then made the decision to permanently close the WRC in August 2020, when we were in the height of the COVID-19 pandemic and all operations had moved fully online. The 2020–2021 academic year marked the first time the Multiliteracy and Communication Center existed as the only campus center for writing support, but a substantial funding cut at the beginning of that year also left much room for uncertainty.

We both would have benefited immensely if we had been given earlier access to the hidden structural contexts that situated our positions, perhaps by getting answers to the questions we pose below. A dual-administrator situation like the faculty director / director split described here should also be seen as an immediate red flag, especially when a new hire supplants someone who has been in charge of a center previously. That is a recipe for resentment that is hard to overcome unless both roles are very specifically delineated from each other and each finds meaning and purpose in their labor.

Looking back on the stress, frustrations, and confrontations of our first years of operation, it is difficult to assess if it was all worth it. These events were bleak and in the moment seemed endless and irresolvable, and the reality is they took an undue toll on our mental health. Although we are now several years removed, between the ensuing competition of the centers, budget cuts, and the COVID-19 pandemic, we have yet to have a fully "normal" year of operation. Though our day-to-day work has taken on more traditional duties of writing center administrators, we still struggle with the repercussions of this fallout and the institutional memory of the WRC.

We end this chapter with a few targeted questions we hope candidates could ask during the interview stage that might be pointed enough to help others avoid the circumstances we navigated, or at least more empowered to make an informed choice about a job's prospects. We also hope these questions might help direct folks toward making their labor and the expectations for that labor more visible.

For director roles:

- Can you provide a brief history of the writing center?
- How is the center funded?
    - Will my position be allocated in the center's budget?
    - What department(s) or unit(s) on campus funds my position?
- What relationship, if any, does the writing center have to academic departments (e.g., the English department?)
- Is this role a nine- or twelve-month contract?
    - What are the expectations for working during the summer and/or winter terms?
- Who directed the center previously, and under what circumstances are they leaving the position?
    - If they are remaining at the center, how specifically will their role shift?
- Who (admin staff, tutors, etc.) will be remaining in the center when I assume the directorship?
- Who will report to me and whom will I report to?
- Has there been a recent internal or external review of the writing center? If so, could you summarize the major recommendations?
- When will you have available a full description of my anticipated responsibilities as director?
    - What will be the protocol or timeline for revising or revisiting my responsibilities?

For nondirector administrative, assistant director, or contingent roles:

- Can you discuss the last individual who held this role?
    - Strengths and weaknesses, disposition and compatibility with existing staff, projects completed, day-to-day job duties.
- Does this position have an associated course release?
- What are your personal expectations for an individual filling this role?
- What is the length of the contract associated with this position, and is there opportunity for renewal?
- What administrative duties are expected of this position?
    - Will I be involved in hiring, termination, scheduling, training, or other professional development of tutors and staff?

- How does this writing center fit into the wider scope of the institution? Which populations are we expected to serve, and how do we meet the needs of those groups?
- How does this role function interdepartmentally? Are there expectations of outreach between different institutions on campus?
- Can you describe the relationships with the existing administrative staff of the department? What are their work styles, values, academic interests?

References

Caswell, Nikki, Jackie Grutsch McKinney, and Rebecca Jackson. 2016. *The Working Lives of New Writing Center Directors*. Logan: Utah State University Press.

"Federal TRIO Programs." 2022. *U.S. Department of Education*. Accessed April 4. https://www2.ed.gov/about/offices/list/ope/trio/index.html.

Monty, Randall. 2019. "Undergirding Writing Centers' Responses to the Neoliberal Academy." *Praxis: A Writing Center Journal*, 16 (3): n.p. Accessed April 4, 2022. http://www.praxisuwc.com/163-monty-et-al.

Nier-Weber, Dani. 2017. "The Other Invisible Hand: Adjunct Labor and Economies of the Writing Center." In *Contingency, Exploitation, and Solidarity: Labor and Action in English Composition*, edited by Seth Kahn, William B. Lalicker, and Amy Lynch-Biniek. Logan: Utah State University Press. https://wac.colostate.edu/docs/books/contingency/chapter7.pdf.

3
Belonging in the Center

WENDY RIDER

Like many writing center professionals, I fell into the field by happy accident. My family had just returned to the States after a year of living overseas, and I needed a job. Moving from a tropical island to the Southern California desert was disorienting, but I expected to find some solid ground, as I always had, in academia. With three young children at home, I hoped to teach English part time at the community college where my husband had just been hired as a full-time librarian. Then a job announcement for a "learning specialist" in the Antelope Valley College (AVC) Learning Center caught my eye. I had no idea when I was hired how transformative it would be. Over thirteen years later, I am deeply immersed in my work as a writing center professional (WCP),[1] although I remain on the margins, in some ways, as a part-time faculty member.

As a new WCP, I was partially prepared for writing center work; I had even been a tutor myself. My father was a junior high school teacher who ran a small tutoring business on the side to help make ends meet. As teenagers, my sister and I worked for him, tutoring younger children in various subjects. The money we earned helped pay for our car insurance. My experience teaching college composition courses also intersected with writing center work, but learning assistance diverges from traditional classroom instruction. My colleagues explained the principles of Socratic dialogue, process over product,

https://doi.org/10.7330/9781646426119.c003

and metacognitive reflection, but I had to explore and internalize the nuances on my own. Similar to the experiences Botvin and Buck describe in chapter 2 of this collection, I also struggled to navigate "invisible [institutional] dynamics" I had no way of understanding at that time.

Like many WCPs, I learned my job by doing it. I was fortunate to join a welcoming team in the AVC Learning Center, but I did not receive any formal training, nor did I really understand how to advocate for myself. Not coming from a recent graduate program in rhetoric and composition, I knew little about writing center narratives, including the "cautionary tales" of marginalization that Paz and Dixon allude to in chapter 1 in this collection. My naiveté probably made me more content with my job initially, but I could have done better work with more context to draw on. Even more than other writing center professionals, adjunct faculty tend to be left out of the "grand narrative" that Jackie Grutsch McKinney (2013) describes in *Peripheral Visions for Writing Centers*. If WCPs are "positioned as a substrata of writing program administration," part-time WCPs are even further down the ladder (Geller and Denny 2013, 98).

This tendency is true not only in the field of learning assistance but also in the academic community at large. Although adjunct faculty perform vital labor in higher education, particularly at community colleges, their voices tend to be peripheral within their departments and within the larger scholarly community.[2] This is not because adjunct faculty lack expertise, nor because they have nothing to say. Simply put, the structure of their positions leaves them with little time or funding to research, publish, or attend conferences. Some college administrators and full-time faculty members also marginalize adjunct faculty, whether consciously or not, because of their institutional status. My personal experience has been largely positive, but I recognize that tension. I have often wished for a stronger seat at the table as well as the greater opportunity to participate in scholarly pursuits that tenured faculty enjoy.

Early in my career, I chose adjunct work because I wanted to devote time to my family.[3] Finding mentors and friends at Antelope Valley College mitigated some of the drawbacks of my marginal position. My full-time counterpart invited me to collaborate with her on tutor training and professional development events in my formative years as an adjunct WCP. As I became surer of my footing in learning assistance, I gained the confidence to work with other faculty and organizations across campus and to pursue further professional development. All of these experiences helped me feel more connected and appreciated. When my job expanded to teaching English classes again, I also found an enriching synergy between my writing center work and classroom practices.

Another important piece of my growth as a writing center professional has been my involvement with the Southern California Writing Centers Association (SoCal WCA), our regional affiliate of the International Writing Centers Association (IWCA). At first, I was keenly aware of my part-time status. Everyone else seemed to be a writing center administrator or at least a full-time WCP. Instead of relegating me to the margin, however, the wonderful members of the SoCal WCA encouraged my contributions. Over time, I served on the Tutor Conference Proposal Committee (including as chair) and as the SoCal WCA secretary. At the 2017 IWCA Summer Institute, I met other adjunct WCPs who shared my passion for writing center work and wanted a greater voice in it. Participating in the writing center world beyond my institution gave me a broader perspective on my role and inspired me to reach higher.

Unfortunately, there were no full-time faculty positions available in the AVC Learning Center. As the ubiquitous image of the "freeway flyers" transporting themselves and their materials from college to college illustrates, tenure-track positions are limited, and competition is fierce. Meanwhile, educational institutions benefit financially from the hiring structure that simultaneously invites adjunct faculty to contribute and denies them the full privileges of the academy. Part-time faculty and staff always experience tension between the time and effort it takes to do their jobs well and the hours for which they are compensated. Like most educators, we invest ourselves intellectually, emotionally, and physically in our work because we care about our tutors, our students, our colleagues, and our centers. Simultaneously, many adjuncts struggle to obtain professional recognition, not to mention a living wage and adequate health insurance. In her incisive article "In the Name of Love," Miya Tokumitsu (2017) takes issue with the widely quoted saying "do what you love" (DWYL) and the corresponding myth that pursuing one's passion makes up for poor working conditions or insufficient pay. "Nowhere," she argues, "has the DWYL mantra been more devastating to its adherents than in academia." After describing the dilemma of adjunct professors, Tokumitsu suggests that the problem is ignored because "few other professions fuse the personal identity of their workers so intimately with the work output" (399–401).

Tokumitsu's perspective resonated with me more than I wanted to admit the first time I read her essay. I wrote "me" and "amen" in the margins of my book, but in my head I said, "Yes, but I still love what I do." Looking back, I find it interesting that I grappled with my professional marginalization on the physical periphery of a page. (I'm sure that fits a literary theory somewhere! Virginia Woolf, for one, would approve.) Like me, many part-time academics, including WCPs, do persist because they find emotional fulfillment in helping students succeed. That does not erase the inequitable aspects of their positions, however.[4] As Geller and Denny (2013) state, most writing center professionals "willingly make the best of the conditions we inherit" and demonstrate "tolerance for rising to the occasion" (124). Adjunct WCPs should consider the cost of exhibiting this attitude in a more precarious way from the margins.

Over the years, colleagues have asked me why I haven't applied for full-time English faculty positions at AVC. Part of the answer is because my heart is in the writing center. In her poem "To Be of Use," Marge Piercy (1982) describes people "who strain in the muck and the mud to move things forward, / who do what has to be done, again and again" (lines 10–11). Writing center work can feel like that at times. But as the poem also notes,

> . . . the thing worth doing well done
> has a shape that satisfies, clean and evident.
> . . . .
> The pitcher cries for water to carry
> and a person for work that is real. (lines 20–21, 25–26)

When WCPs connect with tutors and students one on one and see them grow academically and personally, we make a difference. Our work is satisfying and real.

My team is small, which has presented challenges but also given me the opportunity to participate in every aspect of our program. Through both my intellectual labor and my lived experience (Geller and Denny 2013, 104), I identify unequivocally as a writing center professional. Ironically, as this chapter is being revised, a new full-time, tenure-track Learning Center faculty position is finally on the horizon at AVC. Whether or not I am selected, I will continue to contribute to my field. I may work from the margins, but I belong in the (writing) center.

Notes

1. Writing center professional (WCP) is an inclusive term used to cover a variety of positions in the world of academic writing centers. See also Geller and Denny (2013).

2. At California community colleges, part-time faculty (commonly called adjuncts) teach approximately 70 percent of the courses, but they receive lower pay, fewer benefits, and less recognition than their full-time, tenured colleagues.
3. I was fortunate that my family situation allowed me that choice; many women cannot afford marginal employment.
4. Botvin and Buck (chapter 2 in this collection) support this point well with Nier-Weber's study of the systemic exploitation of contingent or adjunct faculty because of their "relational disposition" to serve and contribute despite their "inherently marginalized positions."

References

Geller, Anne Ellen, and Harry Denny. 2013. "Of Ladybugs, Low Status, and Loving the Job: Writing Center Professionals Navigating Their Careers." *Writing Center Journal* 33 (1): 96–129.

Grutsch McKinney, Jackie. 2013. *Peripheral Visions for Writing Centers*. Logan: Utah State University Press.

Piercy, Marge. 1982. "To Be of Use." Poetry Foundation. Accessed July 31, 2021. https://www.poetryfoundation.org/poems/57673/to-be-of-use.

Tokumitsu, Miya. 2017. "In the Name of Love." In *50 Essays: A Portable Anthology*. 5th ed., edited by Samuel Cohen, 396–402. Boston: Bedford / St. Martins.

4
Hidden in Plain Sight

Professional Tutors in the Writing Center

SHAREEN GROGAN, PAM BROMLEY, AND DENISE STEPHENSON

Not too long ago, at a regional writing center conference, I (Shareen) met colleagues who wanted to know, at my new institution, did I get to have peer tutors? When I replied no, that my new center had professional tutors as had my last one, I was greeted with expressions of sympathy along with hopeful assumptions that I would soon be able to change that.[1] My well-meaning colleagues clearly felt that I did not inhabit a "real" writing center. In writing center circles, my center and I remained somehow inferior due to a lack of undergraduate tutors.

This situation is far from unique. "Professional tutor," a complex term that we will reflect on and further define in this piece, can include faculty, professional staff, and/or graduate students who tutor in writing centers. In a recent WCenter post, a subscriber asked for a comparison of "peer versus faculty tutoring models" (Taylor 2020). The term "versus" already situates the different types of tutors in opposition, and the query assumes that writing centers have either peer tutors or faculty tutors, with peers given priority and with no mention of other types of tutors. One respondent in the scant discussion explained that her center was staffed by faculty tutors and gave a brief breakdown of the pros and cons of each, landing in favor of faculty tutors.

https://doi.org/10.7330/9781646426119.c004

She ended her post with the following apology: "I'm aware of being an outlier on this, but I do think each university has its own culture and needs" (Siemann 2020).

These exchanges reveal part of the "writing center grand narrative" (McKinney 2013), at least in the US,[2] that "ideal" writing centers are staffed by undergraduate peer tutors; indeed, as Jackie Grutsch McKinney notes, "It is not uncommon, in fact, for 'peer tutoring' to be used as shorthand for 'writing center tutoring'" (61). In the ideal writing center session, tutor and student collaborate as equals, where the student drives the agenda while the tutor asks open-ended questions. It is assumed that these students are (mostly) undergraduates,[3] and thus the tutoring session is a session between peers. In this ideal, peer tutoring is egalitarian and collaborative, nonhierarchical, and nonauthoritative. Because peer tutoring seeks to avoid domination, expertise is downplayed, as are any parallels to classroom teaching (e.g., Bruffee 1984; Trimbur 1987). However, as Grustch McKinney warns, a grand narrative can create "collective tunnel vision" (5). While recent scholarship is starting to acknowledge the work of nonstudent tutors, as discussed in this chapter, it is clear that peer (undergraduate) student tutors remain the standard and that the work of professional tutors is marginalized.

This chapter shows how idealized notions of peerness and collaboration have rendered professional tutors mostly invisible in the literature, their work undervalued. We explain first how undergraduate tutors are typically assumed in the literature before demonstrating that professional tutors comprise a meaningful proportion of staff working with students in US-based writing centers and provide significant benefits. We then establish that professional tutors are missing from the writing center grand narrative through a systematic evaluation of *Writing Center Journal* articles before reflecting on takeaways from our work and directions for future research.

The Presumption of Peer (Undergraduate) Tutors

The recent work on professional tutors underscores that undergraduate peer tutors have dominated writing center scholarship and practices to this point. For example, Beth Boquet (2021) notes that even as professional tutors make essential contributions to centers, training and scholarly conversations about undergraduate consultants have been "overrepresented" (xii). Here, we reflect on how undergraduate tutors and the peer approach came to be so central to the way writing centers understand themselves.

There is no doubt that working in a writing center provides enormous benefits to undergraduate students. The Peer Writing Tutor Alumni Research Project determined that peer tutors—who are quickly noted by the authors to be undergraduates—develop "a new relationship with writing," "analytical power," and "earned confidence" (Hughes, Gillespie, and Kail 2010, 14). And there is no doubt that directors take great joy in working with their undergraduate tutors. They study them (e.g., Bleakney and Pittock 2019), study with them (e.g., Fitzgerald 2014), mentor them (e.g., Ervin 2016), and promote their research and publication (e.g., Ianetta and Fitzgerald 2012).

The tenets of peer tutoring have their roots in the work of Kenneth Bruffee (1984), whose Brooklyn Project tapped into employing undergraduate tutors as a means of addressing the needs of increasing numbers of underprepared students who came to college in the era of open enrollment. While peer tutor feedback to student writers is typically "subjective," peer tutoring has generally been shown to be a cost-effective means to promote gains for tutors and tutees (Topping 1996, 337). Peer tutoring identified the position of the tutor as an undergraduate who works with undergraduate writers—very often in first-year writing classes—and simultaneously signified an approach to tutoring that is based in conversation and is collaborative, egalitarian, non-hierarchical, and set apart and in opposition to the hierarchies of classroom teaching (e.g., Bruffee 1984; Bishop 1990). Peer tutoring identifies both who the tutors are and what the tutors do.

Since Bruffee, writing center scholars have reflected further on what "peer" means. Often, the term "peer" is shorthand for "undergraduate."[4] In some writing centers, the term "peer" refers explicitly to undergraduate students (e.g., Sherwood 2007; Ianetta and Fitzgerald 2012; Ervin 2016), though these peers may be upper-level undergraduates (Scharold 2017) who tutor first- and second-year students (Bishop 1990). Peer denotes an equality of status: both tutor and tutee are students, and students at the same level. Irene L. Clark and Dave Healy (1996) seem to be outliers here; they were careful to identify tutors as being possibly undergraduates, graduate students, or composition teachers, cautioning, "Many are not peers in any sense of the word" and underscoring that no matter the status of the tutor, "writing center tutoring takes place in a hierarchical context" (39). Typically, though, writing center scholarship equates peer with undergraduate and considers peerness as a means to eliminate, or at least minimize, hierarchy between tutor and student. John Trimbur (1987) examined the notion of peerness in his discussion of how undergraduate peer tutors experience conflict in "social allegiances," between their classmates and the institution that employs them and between being a peer and being an expert (26). Peter Carino (2003) notes that Trimbur advocated nondirective tutoring strategies "to preserve the peer relationship as much as possible and to encourage collaborative learning rather than hierarchical teaching" while still defending the spirit of peer tutoring (96); in contrast to Trimbur, Carino argues that tutoring relationships are by nature hierarchical, but he also cautions that tutors might be trained "to recognize and use their power and authority without becoming authoritarian" (97).

However, an undercurrent in the literature suggests that teaching does occur in and by writing centers and that directiveness and tutor expertise can be useful. Linda Shamoon and Deborah Burns (1995) argue that an authoritative, directive stance has a place in learning how to write, and they show how faculty advisors are often quite authoritarian in their revisions and directives to their graduate students, which writers find beneficial. Isabelle Thompson et al. (2009), in a survey of undergraduate students who worked with a mix of graduate and undergraduate tutors, show that tutors' expertise is valued by students and that experienced tutors were more directive than inexperienced tutors, which students do not seem to mind (93–94). Clark's (2001) study of undergraduate students and (we believe) graduate student tutors, notes that students and tutors have different perceptions of what directive and nondirective mean in sessions, with students being equally satisfied regardless of their perspective of the tutor's approach. Clark (2001), Thompson et al. (2009), and Grant Eckstein (2019) acknowledge that tutors need to be skilled and make situational choices on the directive-nondirective continuum. Steven Corbett (2005) notes that his writing center is staffed by mostly peer undergraduate tutors and traces the history of noninterventionist tutoring and shows how it is positioned in opposition to classroom teaching; looking at the examples in the text, the reader can be clear that undergraduate tutors are the focus in this piece, as specified in the opening and closing anecdotes, and in the pieces Corbett examines. Reflecting on Carino's 2003 piece, Corbett says, "Writing center practitioners feel the need to promote a non-directive approach, which they view as sharply contrasting the directive, dominating, imposing nature of the classroom" (2005, 104). Corbett (2005) argues that classroom-based tutoring, whether one-off workshops where tutors facilitate peer review groups or writing fellows meeting regularly with students over the course of the term, requires that tutors position themselves differently in the classroom than they do in one-to-one sessions in the center. These classroom-based tutors are asked to be more comfortable with expertise and align themselves with the teacher and the course, not in opposition to them (Corbett 2005, 111). In these situations, Corbett argues that tutors must "(re)consider their roles as teachers" and that writing center directors must prepare them for this role (2005, 111).

In most instances, peer tutoring is as much about an approach as it is about defining tutor identity. As shown in the scholarship, peer tutoring is idealized as collaborative, egalitarian, and antiestablishment, and these notions can lead to the marginalization or absence of some practices in writing center conversations. An example of this pattern can be found in Mandy Suhr-Sytsma and Shan-Estelle Brown (2011), whose center, though staffed by graduate and undergraduate tutors, "encourages tutors to see themselves as peers to the writers they tutor" (20) while addressing the language used by tutors and writers that reflects on differences, such as race, class, or sexuality. Suhr-Sytsma and Brown (2011) come back to this notion in their conclusion, where they again suggest that tutors "see themselves as peer educators and learners" and suggest training strategies to "help keep [tutors] from slipping from peer to expert mode" when reflecting with students about the use of oppressive language, a topic about which these tutors have had substantial training (46). This center, it appears, minimizes the difference between undergraduate and graduate tutors to level any hierarchies that may exist by differences in student status.

In light of the centrality of the peer tutor approach, it is not a surprise that peer tutoring has moved to center stage as not just theory but as a rallying cry. In his keynote speech at IWCA 2015 in Pittsburgh, Ben Rafoth asserted all present at the conference espouse peer tutoring: "People like Ken Bruffee and Mickey Harris promoted peer tutoring and writing centers to advance this [student-centered] revolution, and today it is carried on by all of us here in this room, and now around the world" (2016, 18). Similarly, Neal Lerner's examination of thirty years of author and citation patterns in the *Writing Center Journal* (*WCJ*) identifies peer tutoring as a cornerstone of writing center ethos: "The values, attitudes, and strategies that writing centers and those who work in them have long stood for—collaboration, careful listening, student-centered learning, peer-to-peer interaction—would do well to be the values of our institutions themselves" (2014, 96). For Lerner, "peer-to-peer interaction" is on equal footing with "collaboration, careful listening, [and] student-centered learning" or may be a requisite for those acts to occur in writing tutoring.

Lerner's statement and Rafoth's keynote—as well as a consistent drumbeat of (undergraduate) peer tutors at the center of so many studies—place tutoring that is practiced by nonpeers firmly at the margins, outside the mainstream of writing center discourse. We find that little has changed since Connie Snyder Mick's 1999 *WCJ* article, in which she laments the lack of attention given to graduate student tutors:

> Some recent articles do not even identify the status of the tutors they are analyzing, suggesting by their oversight that graduate and undergraduate tutors are interchangeable, identical. But perhaps more disturbing is the pattern of self-abnegation which has emerged in writers who almost apologetically identify their writing centers as staffed by graduate student tutors, showing their reluctance to complicate the current discussion of peer collaboration theory. (34–35)

Given the centrality of peer tutors and the peer approach in writing center studies, it is not hard to see why writing center scholars would be hesitant to claim participating in anything so antithetical to collaboration as having professional tutors who share their expertise with student writers. It comes as little surprise, then, that tutoring by nonpeers is seldom discussed.

Professional Tutors in Writing Centers

Defining nonundergraduate tutors is complex. Taking cues from the NCW and WCRP—which both include professional, faculty, and graduate tutors as possible responses for who centers train and employ—we see professional tutors as encompassing three types of nonundergraduates who consult one-to-one with student writers in the writing center:

- faculty, who may also teach courses on campus and/or work primarily in the writing center
- professional staff, who often have master's or doctoral degrees and may also teach courses on campus or have other responsibilities not related to the writing center
- graduate students, who may also teach courses and are enrolled in a graduate program alongside their writing center work

Faculty, professional staff, and graduate students who are employed to tutor in the writing center are experts—in their academic disciplines, of course, but also in their practical, and often theoretical, knowledge of the most effective ways to work with student writers at specific stages of their writing processes and in different genres. We see these as broad and complex positions. For instance, faculty tutors at some institutions may offer writing center sessions

TABLE 4.1. Types of tutors working in US writing centers at four-year institutions

NCW	% (n = 482)	WCRP	% (n = 279)
Centers reporting tutors trained		Centers reporting who tutors are, by classification	
Undergraduate	78% (n = 375)	Undergraduate	37% (n = 104)
Graduate	37% (n = 179)	Graduate	27% (n = 74)
Professional	22% (n = 106)	Professional	15% (n = 41)
Faculty	15% (n = 72)	Faculty	7% (n = 19)
Volunteers	4% (n = 19)	Other (volunteers, etc.)	5% (n = 13)

Sources: National Census of Writing (n.d.a, n.d.b) and Writing Centers Research Project (n.d.).

only and have no classroom teaching, even as professional staff may teach courses as one of their primary responsibilities. Moreover, many writing center directors, whether they are classified as faculty or staff, tutor in their own centers. Graduate student tutors might well be "peers" when they are working with fellow graduate students, which is not true when they are working with undergraduates.

Despite the sense that centers with professional tutors are "outliers," the data reveal the contrary. As revealed in table 4.1, the National Census of Writing (NCW) and the Writing Centers Research Project (WCRP) both report that professional, graduate, and faculty tutors comprise around half of tutors working in writing centers; since these terms are not defined in these surveys, we assume there is some overlap in the categories in centers' reporting. Using data from the 2017 NCW, which shares responses from nearly 500 institutions to the writing center module of the survey, we found that of four-year institutions, over a third of centers reported that they trained graduate student tutors, more than a fifth trained professional tutors, and 15 percent trained faculty tutors (National Census of Writing n.d.a). At two-year institutions, where seventy-four institutions completed the writing center module of the survey, the numbers are considerably higher; more than 40 percent of institutions reported that they trained faculty tutors and more than half professional tutors (National Census of Writing n.d.b). For 2018–2019, WCRP reveals slightly lower numbers; of about 300 centers completing the portion of the survey that asked who tutors are, 27 percent employed graduate student tutors, 15 percent professional tutors, and 7 percent faculty tutors (Writing Centers Research Project n.d.). Professional tutor positions are regularly posted on WCenter, with most positions offering annual salaries and expecting graduate degrees and significant experience (e.g., Groundwater

2021; Paterson 2021). Many faculty positions also include one-to-one tutoring as a key aspect of the position (e.g., Lawrence and Myers Zawacki 2019). Clearly, nonundergraduates comprise an important part of who tutors in writing centers.

Recent scholarship has begun to focus on the lack of scholarship examining nonundergraduate writing center consultants. Megan Swihart Jewell and Joseph Cheatle's 2021 edited collection on professional tutors considers these tutors' work, with a specific focus on distinct perspectives for training, professional development, identities, and authority. It has chapters examining, for instance, professional and faculty tutors in community colleges (Miriam E. Laufer) and in science, technology, engineering, and mathematics (STEM) disciplines (Catherine Siemann). Reflecting on graduate student tutors, Susan Lawrence and Terry Myers Zawacki's 2019 edited volume on supporting graduate students in writing centers notes not only that there are growing numbers of graduate students using writing centers, something that has taken place since the 1980s (8), but also that "turning to graduate students complicates notions of peerness" (11). The authors also identify discipline, research methods, and degree level as ways that tutors may occupy peer or nonpeer positions. They suggest that student tutors, whether graduate or undergraduate, are the norm: "Definitional to writing centers is the identity as sites of individualized learning; that is, writers work one on one with a student peer or, in some writing centers, a professional tutor, to receive feedback specific to the writing they bring to their sessions" (14–15). Michael Pemberton argues graduate writing centers—"typically staffed by professional tutors and/or graduate students" (40)—serve graduate students more effectively than do centers staffed by undergraduate peer tutors. Pemberton ends on a note that admits pragmatism over pedagogy, noting that graduate writing centers can be expensive and may be beyond the budgetary commitment of some institutions. We find, however, that professional tutors remain in the margins of writing center scholarship and professional conversations.

Methods

To examine how tutors are presented in the field, we examined all articles (eliminating review articles, book reviews, and editors' introductions) published in the *Writing Center Journal* (*WCJ*) from 2005 to 2019. As the US flagship journal, *WCJ* is a good proxy for the US-based scholarly conversation. For the 182 articles published in that period, we coded each article by whether it defined "tutor." Then, if the author(s) defined what they meant by "tutor," we examined (or assumed via inference from surrounding text) what type of tutor(s) was included in the study: peer, undergraduate, graduate, professional, or faculty. An examination of the articles published in WCJ helps us triangulate how the field represents who tutors are and what tutors do when working with students, even as WCJ shapes (and is shaped by) the way the field understands itself.

Results and Discussion

In our analysis of pieces published in WCJ, we find that the term "peer tutor" assumes undergraduate tutor, and the peer tutoring ethos dominates the way all types of tutors are seen, in contrast to the broader range of tutors present in institutions, as highlighted in table 4.1. In a systematic examination of WCJ articles from 2005 to 2019, detailed in table 4.2, we found, of 182 articles, just a bit over half identified tutor type (dataset available from Author 1 on request).

Of the ninety-two studies that identified the types of tutors, almost two-thirds of articles mentioned peers or undergraduates as the only tutors. Just one-tenth of studies referred to graduate student tutors only, while 14 percent of studies mentioned a combination of tutor types, including undergraduates, graduates, and others (community members, lecturers). Only one article mentioned tutors who were not students: "All have master's degrees and teach" (Nakamaru 2010, 104). That neither the authors nor the editors of WCJ thought it was important to mention the tutor type in half of all articles published between 2005 and 2019 reveals an unseen spot in our collective vision. Just one in seven studies reported multiple types of tutors, and the percentage of studies in WCJ that engage with graduate and professional tutors is substantially lower than those who actually tutor in writing centers, with just 10 percent of studies considering graduate student tutors and 1 percent of studies looking at professional tutors. It is clear that graduate, professional, and faculty tutors are at, or even beyond, the margins of fifteen years of scholarly conversation taking place in WCJ.

Nearly half of the articles were not explicit about the tutor type being discussed, an omission that seems to confirm our assertion that a single type of tutor—peers—is assumed. For some articles, it can be inferred that the tutors are undergraduates because they attend a tutor-training course (e.g., Condon 2007; Davis 2006; Nordlof 2014). In Bonnie Devet (2015), it is clear she is referring to undergraduate tutors because she refers to their majors

TABLE 4.2. Types of tutors mentioned in *WCJ* articles, 2005–2019, by percentage

Tutor type as identified in WCJ articles (n = 182)	
Did not identify tutor type	49% (*n* = 90)
Did identify tutor type	51% (*n* = 92)
Of pieces that identified tutor type	
Undergraduate or peer only	64% (*n* = 59)
Graduate only	10% (*n* = 9)
Multiple types of tutors	14% (*n* = 23)
Professional only	1% (*n* = 1)

and to residence halls. In Harry Denny (2005), it can be inferred that these are undergraduates because they "narrat[e] their own *concurrent* experiences with joining academic discourse communities" (59; emphasis added). In some articles, the tutor type is mentioned sporadically (e.g., Ianetta 2006) or late (e.g., Malenczyk 2013, 81). The type of online tutor is not defined in Stephen Neaderhiser and Joanna Wolfe (2009) or Carol Severino and Shih-Ni Prim (2015). While some articles refer to "experienced tutors" (e.g., Thompson and Mackiewicz 2014, 40) or "knowledgeable tutors" (e.g., Conard-Salvo and Spartz 2012, 53), whether or not these tutors are undergraduates or otherwise is not made clear. The assumption of peer (undergraduate) tutors can clearly be seen in Denny, John Nordlof, and Lori Salem's (2018) study of working-class students accessing writing centers at three different institutions. Not until the very end of their award-winning article, when the authors suggest that professional or faculty tutors might better serve these students (87), can we deduce that all three centers must be staffed by undergraduates.

Only a handful of *WCJ* articles reconsider a key tenet of peer tutoring: nondirectiveness. For example, Kathryn Valentine (2017) complicates the assumption that teaching is directive and hierarchical while tutoring is nondirective and egalitarian. She asserts that casting peer tutoring as distinct from teaching "limits the kind of work tutors might do with students, particularly the kind of scaffolding that has become increasingly recognized as important in writing center practice" (106). Similarly, Phillip Gardner and William Ramsey (2005) note, "The cognitive impact of writing centers on students, at key stages in their development, is wholly congruent with the aims of the mainstream academy. Though writing centers do not focus primarily on field content, they focus intensively on how students dispose themselves to think in [the] field, and therefore are highly effective tools for academic maturation" (37). That is, Gardner and Ramsey, like Valentine, suggest that tutors, like teachers, provide directive feedback to help students in their academic journey. A tutor of any position who stands outside the classroom is not the person giving grades and so can sit beside the student to problem-solve how to best address the assignment and the audience. Peerness is not a prerequisite.

Along the lines of what Valentine (2017) and Gardner and Ramsey (2005) suggest, a handful of *WCJ* researchers note the benefits of tutor expertise, which assumes some tutor directiveness. Pam Bromley, Kara Northway, and Eliana Schonberg (2013) show that the writing centers that had more returning staff, and hence more experienced tutors, receive the most positive reviews. Nordlof's (2014) discussion of scaffolding suggests the importance of training and experience. Thompson et al. (2009) argue that "students are not likely to trust tutors who are not more expert than they are" (100). Nancy Grimm (2009) argues that hiding expertise (in the form of nondirective tutoring) denies students access to power. Susan Wolff Murphy (2006) argues that expertise is necessary for successful sessions and that showing expertise need not be an act of domination—and indeed recent writing center scholarship is leaning toward judicial use of directiveness (e.g., Dinitz and Harrington 2014; Driscoll 2015; Summers 2016) and advocates that all tutors own their expertise (Thompson and Mackiewicz 2014).

Expertise, of course, is something that all types of tutors can possess, but undergraduate tutors, while they grow in expertise (Hughes, Gillespie, and Kail 2010), will typically have considerably less expertise than graduate, professional, or faculty tutors who have substantial experience working with writers and in academic disciplines. Some *WCJ* articles suggest that professional tutors offer added benefits for student writers. Denny, Nordlof, and Salem (2018) suggest that professional tutors may be better poised to help working-class students, though they hedge that recommendation with an acknowledgment that many centers may not be able to add professional staff (87). It seems an admonition that student writers need more than many writing centers can afford to give. This admission, at least, pays attention to the practical needs of students rather than the ideal of peer tutoring.

The writing center grand narrative equates peerness with undergraduate tutors who collaborate in a nondirective and egalitarian way; in doing so, it fails to recognize the many who are neither peers nor undergraduates, who tutor in writing centers, and who bring their expertise to make choices about how and when to provide directive advice. The grand narrative marginalizes these individuals and their work in writing center discourse, even as these individuals do a great deal of writing center tutoring.

We argue that peerness is not a requisite for student-centered tutoring. We argue that expert tutors—be they faculty, graduate students, or professional staff—can tutor effectively without being authoritative or dominating. Professional tutors are capable of scaffolding as they navigate the directive-nondirective continuum; of assuming the role of the audience; and of helping students identify their purpose, clarify their ideas, and deliver a message without imposing their own ideas or voice. Undergraduate and graduate student tutors might perform these acts as well, but we ought to explore whether there is a benefit to students in the expertise and flexibility that professionals might offer in these realms (Thompson et al. 2009; Nordlof 2014; Salem 2016; Valentine 2017; Denny, Nordlof, and Salem 2018).

It can be argued that glorifying the employment of peer tutors in writing centers, and paying them a low hourly wage, perpetuates the notion that anyone can teach writing. Paying peer tutors low wages for writing center work aligns with the low wages universities across the country pay graduate students, adjunct instructors, and other contingent faculty to teach first-year writing (e.g., Colby and Schultz Colby 2017), something explored by Gorham in chapter 5 of this volume. It is worth noting that more than half of four-year institutions report that part-time faculty, graduate students, and postdocs teach first-year writing with one-year or shorter contracts (National Census on Writing n.d.a). As Mahala (2007) argues,

> The pressure to cut costs can be brutal, and teaching writing is labor-intensive. This does not bode well for improved working conditions in writing centers and can leave tutors in the position of picking up the slack for instructors teaching under conditions that may not encourage or even permit attention to individual students. Indeed, the major danger here is that writing centers could increasingly become a kind of fig leaf for universities wanting to claim the centrality of writing in their degree programs, but not actually willing to fund it. (8)

We suggest that clinging to notions of peers and peer tutoring may distract us from larger arguments about the need for highly skilled and trained teachers and tutors of writing.

Conclusions

In our review of *WCJ* articles from 2005 to 2019, the term "peer" typically refers implicitly or explicitly to undergraduate tutors and to a relationship between student and tutor that is nondirective and downplays expertise. We see the idealization of peerness in writing centers, and a disowning of expertise, as a fundamental reason that professional, faculty, and graduate tutors are so often at the margins of US writing center scholarship and organizations, even though these tutors are present in around half of centers.

If we dislodge the grand narrative a bit, we will see what is right in front of us—what is already there—that many centers have tutors who are not undergraduates and tutor students who are not undergraduates. The vast array of individuals who come to writing centers for writing support includes far more than just undergraduates in a first-year writing course. They include non-native speakers, first-generation and nontraditional students; they include graduate students writing master's theses and doctoral dissertations. Some writing centers serve the entire campus including faculty and staff, and the local community as well (Writing Centers Research Project n.d.).

We suggest that professional tutors might, for example, offer more stability, serve certain populations more effectively (e.g., first-generation, graduate, multilingual students), and provide additional depth in inclusive and antiracist pedagogies (e.g., Weaver 2006). We conclude not with how professional tutors are "better than" peer undergraduate tutors but with a reflection on the way that the ideal of peer collaboration masks the reality experienced in many writing centers and how that grand narrative can diminish and hide the roles of professional tutors and the complex work they do.

Instead of apologizing for being outliers, perhaps centers with professional tutors might serve as models for what is possible, so we, as a field, can argue for more institutional commitment and financial support. The fact that so many centers have professional tutors—and have deliberately chosen to do so, despite pervasive pressure and the assumption that peerness is better—flies directly in the face of "peerness" as the ideal. Continuing to perpetuate an ideal that does not seem to accommodate both the reality of how centers function and how best to support a diverse body of writers does not serve our profession well. Writing centers can be sites of inquiry into the complex relationships that tutors—both professional and peer—have with writers and the many ways they support their learning, thinking, and writing.

Notes

1. While we appreciate the complexity that goes into naming positions, and that the term "tutor" can be understood as "prescriptive" (McCall 1991, 163) or "remedial" (Runciman 1990, 30), we use the term "tutor" throughout this chapter, as it is the term most commonly used in the literature to refer to those individuals who work individually with student-writers.
2. Writing center professionals outside the US can understand the writing center grand narrative quite differently (see Scott 2017). This chapter, while acknowledging that writing centers are present globally, is generally situated in US scholarship.
3. In the introduction to a 2021 guide for professional, faculty, and graduate writing tutors, the editors note that writing center tutoring is "traditional[ly an] undergraduate peer-to-peer model," with most training literature focused on this group (Cheatle and Jewell 2021, 3).
4. When Shareen Grogan was on the IWCA Board, the board, in an effort to be more inclusive of its membership, created a peer tutor representative position; we were surprised to see that only graduate students applied. As there already existed a graduate student representative position, the board faced a conundrum: we had not noted explicitly that this was an undergraduate student position; "peer" for us had meant undergraduate student tutor—not just student, not just tutor.

References

Bishop, Wendy. 1990. "Bringing Writers to the Center: Some Survey Results, Surmises, and Suggestions." *Writing Center Journal* 10 (2): 31–44.

Bleakney, Julia, and Sarah Peterson Pittock. 2019. "Tutor Talk: Do Tutors Scaffold Students' Revisions?" *Writing Center Journal* 37 (2): 127–160.

Boquet, Elizabeth. 2021. "Foreword." In *Redefining Roles: The Professional, Faculty, and Graduate Consultant's Guide to Writing Centers*, edited by Megan Swihart Jewell and Joseph Cheatle, xi–xii. Logan: Utah State University Press, 2021.

Bromley, Pam, Kara Northway, and Eliana Schonberg. 2018. "L2 Student Satisfaction in the Writing Center: A Cross-Institutional Study of L1 and L2 Students." *Praxis: A Writing Center Journal* 16 (1): 20–27.

Bruffee, Kenneth. 1984. "Peer Tutoring and the 'Conversation of Mankind.'" *Writing Centers: Theory and Administration*, edited by Gary A. Olson, 3–15. Urbana, IL: NCTE.

Carino, Peter. 2003. "Power and Authority in Peer Tutoring." In *The Center Will Hold*, edited by Michael A. Pemberton and Joyce Kinkead, 96–113. Logan: Logan: Utah State University Press.

Clark, Irene. 2001. "Perspectives on the Directive/Non-directive Continuum in the Writing Center." *Writing Center Journal* 22 (1): 33–58.

Clark, Irene, and Dave Healy. 1996. "Are Writing Centers Ethical?" *WPA: Writing Program Administration* 20 (1/2): 32–48.

Colby, Richard, and Rebekah Schulz Colby. 2017. "Real Faculty but Not: The Full-time, Non-tenure-track Position as Contingent Labor." In *Contingency, Exploitation, and Solidarity: Labor and Action in English Composition*, edited by Seth Kahn, William B. Lalicker, and Amy Lynch-Biniek, 57–70. Fort Collins and Boulder: WAC Clearinghouse and University Press of Colorado.

Conard-Salvo, Tammy, and John M. Spartz. 2012. "Listening to Revise: What a Study about Text-to-Speech Software Taught Us about Students' Expectations for Technology Use in the Writing Center." *Writing Center Journal* 32 (2): 40–59.

Condon, Frankie. 2007. "Beyond the Known: Writing Centers and the Work of Anti-racism." *Writing Center Journal* 27 (2): 19–38.

Corbett, Steven J. 2005. "Bringing the Noise: Peer Power and Authority, On Location." In *On Location: Theory and Practice in Classroom-Based Writing Tutoring*, edited by Candace Spigelman and Laurie Grobman, 101–111. Logan: Utah State University Press.

Davis, Kevin. 2006. "The Writing Center as Last Best Place: Six Easy Pieces on Montana, Bears, Love, and Writing Centers." *Writing Center Journal* 26 (2): 22–30.

Denny, Harry. 2005. "Queering the Writing Center." *Writing Center Journal* 25 (2): 39–62.

Denny, Harry, John Nordlof, and Lori Salem. 2018. "'Tell Me Exactly What It Was That I Was Doing That Was So Bad': Understanding the Needs and Expectations of Working-Class Students in Writing Centers." *Writing Center Journal* 37 (1): 67–100.

Devet, Bonnie. 2015. "The Writing Center and Transfer of Learning: A Primer for Directors." *Writing Center Journal* 35 (1): 119–151.

Dinitz, Sue, and Susanmarie Harrington. 2014. "The Role of Disciplinary Expertise in Shaping Writing Tutorials." *Writing Center Journal* 33 (2): 73–98.

Driscoll, Dana Lynn. 2015. "Building Connections and Transferring Knowledge: The Benefits of a Peer Tutoring Course beyond the Writing Center." *Writing Center Journal* 35 (1): 153–181.

Eckstein, Grant. 2019 "Directiveness in the Center: L1, L2, and Generation 1.5 Expectations and Experiences." *Writing Center Journal* 37 (2): 61–92.

Ervin, Christopher. 2016. "What Tutor Researchers and Their Mentors Tell Us about Undergraduate Research in the Writing Center: An Exploratory Study." *Writing Center Journal* 35 (3): 39–75.

Fitzgerald, Lauren. 2014. "Undergraduate Writing Tutors as Researchers: Redrawing Boundaries." *Writing Center Journal* 33 (2): 17–35.

Gardner, Phillip J., and William M. Ramsey. 2005. "The Polyvalent Mission of Writing Centers." *Writing Center Journal* 25 (1): 25–42.

Grimm, Nancy M. 2009. "New Conceptual Frameworks for Writing Center Work." *Writing Center Journal* 29 (2): 11–27.

Groundwater, Ervin. 2021. "Position Announcement: Writing Specialist Position at UC Irvine." WCenter Electronic Mailing List, June 24. http://lyris.ttu.edu/read/messages?id=26657638.

Hughes, Bradley, Paula Gillespie, and Harvey Kail. 2010. "What They Take with Them: Findings from the Peer Writing Tutor Alumni Research Project." *Writing Center Journal* 30 (2): 12–46.

Ianetta, Melissa. 2006. "'Concerns Are Translated into Conversations of Sudden Community': Identification at the IWCA/NCPTW." *Writing Center Journal* 26 (1): 20–26.

Ianetta, Melissa, and Lauren Fitzgerald. 2012. "Peer Tutors and the Conversation of Writing Center Studies." *Writing Center Journal* 32 (1): 9–13.

Jewell, Megan Swihart, and Joseph Cheatle. 2021. "Introduction." In *Redefining Roles: The Professional, Faculty, and Graduate Consultant's Guide to Writing Centers*, edited by Megan Swihart Jewell and Joseph Cheatle, 3–14. Logan: Utah State University Press.

Lawrence, Susan, and Terry Myers Zawacki. 2019. "Introduction: Writing Center Pedagogies and Practices Reconsidered for Graduate Student Writers." In *Re/Writing the Center: Approaches to Supporting Graduate Students in the Writing Center*, edited by Susan Lawrence and Terry Myers Zawacki, 7–26. Logan: Utah State University Press.

Lerner, Neal. 2014. "The Unpromising Present of Writing Center Studies: Author and Citation Patterns in *The Writing Center Journal*, 1980 to 2009." *Writing Center Journal* 34 (1): 67–102.

Mahala, Daniel. 2007. "Writing Centers in the Managed University." *Writing Center Journal* 27 (2): 3–17.

Malenczyk, Rita. 2013. "'I Thought I'd Put That in to Amuse You': Tutor Reports as Organizational Narrative." *Writing Center Journal* 33 (1): 74–95.

McCall, William. 1994. "Writing Centers and the Idea of Consultancy." *Writing Center Journal* 14 (2): 163–171.

McKinney, Jackie Grutsch. 2013. *Peripheral Visions for Writing Centers*. Logan: Utah State University Press.

Mick, Connie Snyder. 1999. "'Little Teachers,' Big Students: Graduate Students as Tutors and the Future of Writing Center Theory." *Writing Center Journal* 20 (1): 33–50.

Murphy, Susan Wolff. 2006. "'Just Chuck It: I Mean, Don't Get Fixed on It': Self Presentation in Writing Center Discourse." *Writing Center Journal* 26 (1): 62–82.

Nakamaru, Sarah. 2010. "Theory In/To Practice: A Tale of Two Multilingual Writers: A Case-Study Approach to Tutor Education." *Writing Center Journal* 30 (2): 100–123.

National Census of Writing. n.d.a. "2017 Four-Year Institution Survey: Writing Centers—Consultants." Accessed July 5, 2021. https://writingcensus.ucsd.edu/survey/4/year/2017.

National Census of Writing. n.d.b. "2017 Two-Year Institution Survey: Writing Centers—Consultants." Accessed July 5, 2021. https://writingcensus.ucsd.edu/survey/2/year/2017.

Neaderhiser, Stephen, and Joanna Wolfe. 2009. "Between Technological Endorsement and Resistance: The State of Online Writing Centers." *Writing Center Journal* 29 (1): 49–77.

Nordlof, John. 2014. "Vygotsky, Scaffolding, and the Role of Theory in Writing Center Work." *Writing Center Journal* 34 (1): 45–64.

Paterson, Leslie. 2021. "Hiring: Academic Skills and Writing Specialist." WCenter Electronic Mailing List, April 23. http://lyris.ttu.edu/read/messages?id=26413638.

Pemberton, Michael A. 2018. "Rethinking the WAC / Writing Center / Graduate Student Connection." In *Re/Writing the Center: Approaches to Supporting Graduate Students in the Writing Center*, edited by Susan Lawrence and Terry Myers Zawacki, 29–48. Logan: Utah State University Press.

Rafoth, Ben. 2016. "Faces, Factories, and Warhols: A R(Evolutionary) Future for Writing Centers." *Writing Center Journal* 35 (2): 17–30.

Runciman, Lex. 1990. "Defining Ourselves: Do We Really Want to Use the Word 'Tutor?'" *Writing Center Journal* 11 (1): 27–34.

Salem, Lori. 2016. "Decisions . . . Decisions: Who Chooses to Use the Writing Center?" *Writing Center Journal* 35 (2): 147–171.

Scharold, Dagmar. 2017. "'Challenge Accepted': Cooperative Tutoring as an Alternative to One-to-One Tutoring," *Writing Center Journal* 36 (2), article 4. https://doi.org/10.7771/2832-9414.1825.

Scott, Andrea. 2017. "The Storying of Writing Centers outside the U.S.: Director Narratives and the Making of Disciplinary Identities in Germany and Austria." *WLN: A Journal of Writing Center Scholarship* 41 (5–6): 10–17.

Severino, Carol, and Shih-Ni Prim. 2015. "Word Choice Errors in Chinese Students' English Writing and How Online Writing Center Tutors Respond to Them." *Writing Center Journal* 34 (2): 115–143.

Shamoon, Linda K., and Deborah H. Burns. 1995. "A Critique of Pure Tutoring." *Writing Center Journal* 15 (2): 134–151.

Sherwood, Steve. 2007. "Portrait of the Tutor as an Artist: Lessons No One Can Teach." *Writing Center Journal* 27 (1): 52–66.

Siemann, Catherine. 2020. "Re: Peer versus Faculty Tutors." WCenter Electronic Mailing List, September 20. http://lyris.ttu.edu/read/archive?id=25837473.

Suhr-Sytsma, Mandy, and Shan-Estelle Brown. 2011. "Theory In/To Practice: Addressing the Everyday Language of Oppression in the Writing Center." *Writing Center Journal* 31 (2): 13–49.

Summers, Sarah. 2016. "Building Expertise: The Toolkit in UCLA's Graduate Writing Center." *Writing Center Journal* 35 (2): 117–145.

Taylor, Katherine. 2020. "Peer versus Faculty Tutors." WCenter Electronic Mailing List. September 20. http://lyris.ttu.edu/read/archive?id=25837472.

Thompson, Isabelle, and Jo Mackiewicz. 2014. "Questioning in Writing Center Conferences." *Writing Center Journal* 33 (2): 37–70.

Thompson, Isabelle, Alyson Whyte, David Shannon, Amanda Muse, Kristen Miller, Milla Chappell, and Abby Whigham. 2009. "Examining Our Lore: A Survey of Students' and Tutors' Satisfaction with Writing Center Conferences." *Writing Center Journal* 29, (1): 78–105.

Topping, Keith J. 1996. "The Effectiveness of Peer Tutoring in Further and Higher Education: A Typology and Review of the Literature." *Higher Education* 32 (3): 321–345.

Trimbur, John. 1987. "Peer Tutoring: A Contradiction in Terms?" *Writing Center Journal* 7 (2): 21–28.

Valentine, Kathryn. 2017. "The Undercurrents of Listening: A Qualitative Content Analysis of Listening in Writing Center Tutor Guidebooks." *Writing Center Journal* 36 (2): 89–115.

Writing Centers Research Project. n.d. "Writing Center Research Survey 2018–2019: Tutors–Tutor Classification." Accessed July 5, 2021. https://tableau.itap.purdue.edu/t/public/views/WCRP2018/Story.

5
From Pieces to Whole

Professional Tutors and Instability in the College Writing Center

AJA GORHAM

In quieter moments, I sew. The act of joining, easing, and uniting pieces of fabric reminds me of writing. The art of combining pieces to give birth to the new is the essence of writing and the foundation of sewing. Yet, when I sew, I prefer the ease of working with continuous yards of fabric as opposed to patchwork sewing. In patchwork sewing, smaller pieces are intricately joined to contribute to larger, unique designs. For me, the precision and effort needed for patchwork sewing add stress to an otherwise meditative craft. Putting forth hours of detail-intensive work in the hopes the final design will materialize reminds me of trying to craft a life from working as an adjunct composition instructor and a part-time professional tutor in a writing center. My three-year effort to piece together a financially stable life as an adjunct faculty member and professional tutor is increasingly more frequent and underdocumented. My and others' work to seam together a life from the remnants of academia inspired this research. To encourage discussion about degree-holding tutors, this qualitative study will spotlight the patchwork experience of four professional tutors at the Cortez Community College Writing Center. Spotlighting their working realities allows for speculation about contingency's influence on the writing tutorial.

Specifically, this qualitative research addresses these questions:

1. How do professional tutors experience contingency in relation to their work in a community college writing center?
2. How may tutors' working environments influence their work in tutorials?

Professional tutors working to piece together career stability in the writing center can be a varied group as noted in Grogan, Bromley, and Stephenson's discussion of hidden professional tutors (chapter 4 in this collection). For this discussion, professional tutors are understood to have the credentials to be faculty; however, they may not necessarily be teaching. The term *professional* is borrowed from Dani Nier-Weber (2017) in one of the few published accounts of professional tutors in the collegiate writing center. In telling the story of professional tutors at their own writing center, Nier-Weber (2017) documented the nebulous space of professional tutors who were both "employed yet not employed" and treated as transient workers despite some having worked at the writing center for nearly a decade.

Scholars seeking to explore the frayed position of professional tutors may find, as Nier-Weber's (2017) and Wendy Rider's narrative of fringe writing center work (chapter 3 in this collection) highlight, the fragility of a professional tutor's position comes with concerns. The study conducted by Dawn Fels et al. (2016) points to a potential concern in the uncertain nature of professional tutors' working environment. When surveyed, nontenured, off-tenure track, and contingent tutors felt their work in the writing center came with a compromise. Fels et al. (2016) note, "When questioned about the risks involved with a contingent position, another participant referred to the risks that her contingency held for her students. Certainly, a job loss would affect the participant's family's ability to make ends meet. . . . [However,] her contingent position put students at risk of not receiving the best possible educational experiences; consistency was key to providing the help students received. Despite feeling exploited, the participant felt that the primary risk of contingency was and is the quality of education provided by the institution" (A10). Even with worries about her financial instability, one tutor pointed to issues involving students—specifically how students' learning may be compromised because of contingency. The issue of contingency is one that has the potential to impact both tutor and tutee. Considering the profound impacts of contingency, it is necessary to explore the scope of influence instability has in practice.

The potential influence is especially pressing because of the consistent role of part-time professional labor in the writing center. In fact, when 127 two-year colleges replied to the National Census of Writing (2015) question "Are your writing center consultants faculty who teach in the writing program?" 55 percent (or 70 schools) answered "yes" (Gladstein and Fralix 2015). Nier-Weber (2017) also acknowledges this growth by showing that the Writing Center Research Project (WCRP) indicated an over 25 percent growth in professional tutors from 2001/2002 to 2007/2008. In the 2017/2018 WCRP, respondents at community colleges reported professional tutors accounted for 25.4 percent. Part-time professionals in the writing center follow a broader cost-conscious trend in higher education that has largely responded to reduced institutional and government funding by trying "to save monies and maximize work-force flexibility . . . [by] hiring of faculty off the tenure track, including adjunct, part-time, and full-time, non-tenure track positions" (Schell 2017, ix). The reliance on part-time labor is common practice in the writing discipline as most students are required to complete a composition course (Schell 2017). The same part-time writing teachers have increasingly become professional tutors in the writing center; yet the working environments of professional tutors remain an area of potential contradiction because the work is undermined by the employment structure.

Contingency values the flexibility of the temporal, while writing tutorials thrive from consistency. The writing tutorial depends, in part, on "build[ing] positive relationships, whether for the next thirty or fifty minutes, over the course of the semester, or even beyond" (Nier-Weber 2017, 112). However, because of contingency, these bonds are forged by professional tutors who exist in a liminal space where "little corresponding discussion exists about the particular challenges, ethics, and economics of labor conditions faced by composition adjuncts and other professionals for whom writing center work comprises part, most, or all of the job" (Nier-Weber 2017, 103–104). This research seeks to expand Nier-Weber's spotlight on professional tutors' underdiscussed labor conditions by examining instances of burnout and financial instability. While issues may not be universal to all writing centers or all structures of higher education, the stories of professional tutors are important to explore because their labor conditions prompt new questions of how the writing center accomplishes a student-driven mission in a cost-focused, insecure work environment.

Shortages that threaten livelihood may be a push toward the writing center for some; yet, using the writing center as a budget solution creates a new problem—burnout. Burnout is the result of stress individuals experience both from work and their working conditions. Burnout for this analysis is understood as a "gradual process whereby the stresses of working closely with individuals requiring support or guidance result in various symptoms detrimental to both professional and personal functioning" (Watts and Roberson 2011, 34). Burnout is typically examined based on workers' emotional exhaustion, approach toward others, and perceived job satisfaction. Similar metrics can be applied to professional writing center tutors who encounter similar demands but experience increased insecurity. The potential for exhausting challenges faced by some professional tutors combined with unstable employment complicates the writing center's dependence on relationships and relationship building in pursuit of student-centered learning.

Because of instability experienced by contingent, professional tutors, the writing center may become a site of stress for these employees. This study will explore some of the external factors involved in labor instability to speculate how such forces may impact tutorials. Moreover, this study will use interviews of four professional tutors at a metropolitan, community college writing center, referred to as Cortez College, and analyze their discussion of working conditions and student interactions.

Study Site and Participants

This study took place at Cortez Community College. At Cortez Community College the professional Writing Center and the corresponding English Department have a symbiotic relationship insofar as the writing center is considered a part of the English Department, and the two share some staff. In fiscal year 2018, the open enrollment institution had 13,671 students. The Cortez Community College Writing Center began in 2012 and was staffed with only adjunct instructors from the English Department. Tutors are paid a variable hourly rate. Students are limited to two scheduled appointments per week, which occur in sixty-minute intervals. Tutors are to use fifty minutes to work with the students and ten minutes to complete a tutoring report. Appointments are consecutively scheduled. A tutor is scheduled to have a thirty-minute, unpaid break after four consecutive hours of work.

This research initially secured Institutional Review Board (IRB) approval to interview tutors and record tutorials with students. However, because approval was granted in March 2020, the onset of the COVID-19 pandemic made students inaccessible. The study was then limited to professional tutors,

TABLE 5.1. Participant information anonymized

Pseudonymous	Pronouns	Description
Cameron	He/His	Cameron earned an advanced degree in English. Cameron joined the Cortez Writing Center in 2013 after several years of college-level teaching.
Edie	They/Them	After earning an advanced degree in English, Edie began working as an adjunct instructor teaching composition at Cortez College. They began working in the Cortez Writing Center in 2014.
Jerome	He/His	Jerome began working in the Cortez Writing Center in the 2012/2013 school year. He continues to work as an adjunct instructor teaching composition courses.
Rey	They/Them	After finishing an advanced degree in English, Rey began tutoring at the Cortez College Writing Center in 2013. In 2015, Rey stopped teaching after accepting a full-time position. They continued to work in the writing center at the time of the interview.

who were recruited through an email sent to the Writing Center coordinator. The email explained the study and asked for an attached document to be forwarded to thirty-two professional tutors on staff. The email outlined the purpose of the study and asked those interested to participate in one 60-minute interview. Participants shared their stories and experiences related to professional tutoring in the writing center in a recorded video call (see table 5.1). I conducted interviews between May and August 2020. The four interviews generated 361 minutes of data, which were transcribed and later coded. To create codes, I closely reread transcripts to identify repeated ideas, which were grouped into themes. These themes were a form of organization that became codes (Auerbach and Silverstein 2003). These codes allowed me to track major topics of conversations and quantify how often topics emerged.

The interviews were started with general questions, as listed in appendix 5A. These questions functioned as a basis for inquiry and were adapted over the course of the semi-structured qualitative interviews. Adjustments and additional questions were introduced to reflect the specific information shared by a given participant. I understood the interview to be a social process; thus, "The aim is not to coax preferred responses, but instead facilitate an interactive dialogue that more closely resembles everyday conversation than a formal interview" (Hathaway 2020, 109). Adjustments recognize respondents are not passive deliveries of information but are instead collaborating with the researcher in the construction of meaning. Information about the four participants is detailed in the following section, using their selected or assigned pseudonym with a corresponding pronoun.

Findings: How Do Professional Tutors Experience Contingency in Relation to Their Work in a Community College Writing Center?

The fact that the Cortez Community College Writing Center is housed within the English Department means there is an ebb and flow between the department and the writing center. In fact, when instructors at Cortez were unable to teach classes or their teaching offers were revoked, the Writing Center became a place they could supplement their lost income. This situation was noted by Cameron, one of the study participants, who said, "The English Department could supplement their budget by saying, well, instead of teaching three classes this semester, you're going to teach two. But we're going to give you 10 hours in the Writing Center and you're going [to be] okay. So, it tends to become more of a financial bargaining chip." In fact, three participants reported they both began and continued working in the Writing Center because classes could possibly be canceled or reassigned. Jerome, for example, began working in the Writing Center because one of his courses was canceled. Jerome recalled that the department chair recommended, "'You should apply at the Writing Center.' I think that I was talking about . . . getting classes and they were taking away one of my classes because of enrollment issues." In other words, a looming budget shortfall prompted Jerome to talk to the department chair, who, in turn, proposed he try to work in the writing center. For other professional tutors, the writing center functioned as a safeguard against future financial hardship. For example, when I asked Edie what prompted them to continue tutoring, even though they were teaching at a different campus, they reported, "If I lose my job I might need to work more hours at the Writing Center." A financial backup plan kept Edie working in the Cortez Writing Center in the same way that inconsistency of teaching as an adjunct instructor led Jerome to tutor. Because the Writing Center functioned as a safeguard against the economic hardship of canceled or reassigned classes, while also offering unstable hours and earnings, the Writing Center was an imperfect defense against loss of income.

Concern about loss of income was uncovered as a theme related to an underlying stress for participants. During interviews, conversations of contingency were inseparable from conversation of hours and tutors' earnings. For instance, Cameron revealed that reduced hours in the spring semester of

2020 created a financial hardship. He said, "So [beginning] from January . . . I'm working two hours in the Writing Center. Okay. My working hours, in terms of my overall pay hours from Cortez, were cut by 30 percent? I think 35 percent? As you could imagine, that's a massive hit to someone's budget." In Cameron's life, hours were conceptualized in terms of budgeting, and decreased tutoring hours had an immediate impact. Similarly, Rey also recalled a time when the Writing Center comprised a large portion of their budget. They shared that at one point they were working nearly twenty-seven hours per week, and the "Writing Center was more than half of my income." Both Cameron and Rey depended on time working in the Writing Center for a significant portion of their income, and a decrease in hours created financial stress.

The financial stress also had an emotional cost. For instance, Rey, who stopped teaching but remained a tutor in the writing center, discussed the financial pressure that felt overwhelming at the time of teaching and tutoring. They shared: "Not to be dramatic, but just generally . . . [I do] not feel . . . supported. It's a giving job, for sure. If you're not getting adequate income, where you need four jobs, and you're still on government support like I was, you don't feel valued. You don't feel supported, but you're expected to value and support your dozens and dozens of students. It creates a riff of insanity." Rey revealed that, despite several jobs, they were on government assistance. Overall, they felt the administration's poor pay and high expectations were irrational, and this idea was shared among participants. Edie pointed to the same consequence of unstable pay when they said, "It would be better if the adjunct staff . . . made more money. You would have much better workers, you would have much happier workers. And you'd have more people willing to invest in the longer-term health and wellbeing of the writing center. But I'm not holding my breath." Edie felt that low pay for adjuncts, who comprised the Writing Center tutoring staff, was a determinant to workers and the health of the overall Writing Center. Both Edie and Rey pointed to low pay as creating instability so profound it undermined relationships of tutors and Cortez College administration.

In addition to wages, reduced hours were another way participants felt administration being irrational. Cameron reflected: "The more you cut people's hours, you send a message, whether intentionally or unintentionally. [Like] yeah, how much do you really matter? Well, if you're struggling to pay bills, well that's not our [administration] problem. If you don't like it, get out. Maybe not as harshly as that, but that's the message there. [Administration is] asking you to do your best, show up every day and do your best. Be better for our students, but no one's going to be there for you." Much like Rey, Cameron felt the institution perpetuated a system of financial instability. Instead, the two felt the institution sent a message that tutors were expendable. This message was not overt, but, as Rey stated, "You don't have to be malicious or whatever. It was just completely demoralizing, too, 'cause I did not feel appreciated by the institution. My direct superior? Sure. But by the institution? I didn't. I didn't feel like they invested in me/us in general." Challenges surrounding inconsistent income caused participants to experience both financial and emotional shortfalls. In combination, reoccurring shortfalls created a fatigue that influenced how tutors perceived their work with students.

How May Tutors' Working Environment Influence Their Perspective on Tutorials?

Participants were aware that their attitude and working demeanor changed under the weight of fatigue. Contingency forced adjunct instructors, who comprised the study population, to seek additional work (McKenna 2014; Nier-Weber 2017; Supiano 2018). Yet, the high amount of student-facing work between teaching and tutoring created conditions for burnout (Lackritz 2014; García-Arroyo and Segovia 2019), as reflected in participants mentioning feeling stressed, drained, stretched, exhausted, or a combination thereof.

Cameron is an example of a tutor feeling stressed because of contingency. He shared, "[I] was working twice as hard to make sure that I did my best because I did not want to take out what was happening to me on my students, [but] not everybody felt that way." Though he reported giving additional effort with students to mask the stress of instability, he recognized that not all tutors' frustrations were hidden from students. Others recognized that feeling fatigued impacted their work with students and submitted to those feelings. Jerome, for example, was among the tutors who felt his work change over time. He reported that he went on autopilot each semester. He has begun, as he put it, to "gauge my level of energy by what week I turn autopilot on. And as I get more and more burned out, you know, it gets early. The autopilot goes on earlier and earlier." Feeling fatigued and burned out became a recurring theme of our conversation. When I asked him how burnout impacted his work with students, he replied, "I'm much more ready to give you an answer rather than letting you arrive at the answer. I am much less effective as a tutor because I'm gonna help you get a good grade instead of trying to teach you something." In addition to using automated responses, Jerome felt his manner in the tutorial change because he was too fatigued to facilitate silence or gaps in talking that allowed students time to process and respond. He shared that "when we're tired and burned out, I'm aware of those gaps, but like, I'm more likely to fill them in because I'm tired. And I'm like, I want to get out of here and I want to go home and have some soup and sleep then do this all over again. So, I'm much more ready to jump in and give you the answer and sort of get you out of there." Fatigue impacted how likely Jerome was to utilize tutoring as a teaching moment, and he was not alone. Similarly, Rey indicated, "[Students were] tired and hungry, and dehydrated, and emotionally fraught because a lot of my students in my classrooms were having issues, and the students I'm tutoring have more issues. I felt like I was an unlicensed counselor, which is very dangerous. I was, in all of the ways, exhausted constantly." Rey felt their tutoring changed as contingency stripped their physical and emotional energy. At the end of a long shift, the exhaustion would be inescapable. They shared, "There was one semester where I worked from, I think—I wanna say from four until we closed? Those last two appointments, I always felt bad, 'cause they were getting the moldy leftovers of me. It was just like, 'Oh my God, are we done?'" Rey, like Jerome, felt their work performance change as burnout set in. Rey acknowledged, "I don't know what it was like to be on the receiving end of my tutoring, but I can't imagine that that wasn't somehow conveyed to the student. That I'm hungry and have to pee and have no money, and I'm afraid of losing my job constantly." That both Rey and Jerome felt the fatigue brought on by the contingency's instability was evident in their tutorial, and though Cameron reported he tried to shield his fatigue from students, he was still aware of his exhaustion. Because students are absent from this study, it is unclear whether tutors' fatigue was noticeable. However, the fear and fatigue that participants thought were conveyed to students are pressing concerns when more closely considering tutors' ability to facilitate the writing center's mission.

Discussion

Participants' emotional exhaustion stemmed from contingency and influenced how some viewed their performance in the tutorial. Contingency's uncertainty demanded tutors work more; yet, working additional hours at the Writing Center and teaching multiple courses at various campuses meant participants were likely to experience burnout. When the Writing Center was used as a safety net in the ways Jerome, Cameron, Edie, and Rey engaged in the space, it intensified underlying stresses. Tutors become a part of a cyclical process of teaching under financial stress, seeking more financial stability in the writing center, and tutoring under unresolved financial stress. At no point was the financial stress alleviated; instead, the precariousness became a type of emotional exhaustion.

Participants found themselves in contingency's conundrum: they needed to work more to satisfy financial obligations but needed to work less to better engage students. Professional tutors' conundrum does not exist in a vacuum. Tutors serve students, and, as a result, a hindrance to tutors' work can become a detriment to students' experience. Students depend on tutors to facilitate a learning experience. Yet, when tutors are too hungry, fatigued, or stressed to build the relationships necessary to foster a student-centered learning experience, it is the student who may be alienated. The potential for student alienations is a threat to the writing center's overall mission because it may transform a tailored learning experience into a transactional situation in which the focus is on completing the tutorial and giving the customer what was required. The quest to save means "programs in many universities that offer remedial courses, affirmative action, and other crucial pedagogical resources are under massive assault, often by conservative trustees who want to eliminate from the university any attempt to address the deep inequities in society, while simultaneously denying a decent education to minorities of color and class" (Giroux 2002, 453). The writing center is a site that addresses inequities but because of cost safe measures also creates new equality issues. Current cost reduction principles have the dual power to disenfranchise the professional and the student. This dynamic of disenfranchisement is captured in participants' description of burnout, fatigue, and generally feeling unsupported. However, professional tutors do not exist in a vacuum. Students may also suffer as their learning becomes a peripheral concern as a result of the professional tutors' work to weave stability amid perpetual stress and fatigue.

The specific problem of financial instability points to a larger issue with contingency in the writing center and higher education more broadly. Pressure to reduce cost through unstable work shifts burdens onto workers, which has direct consequences on performance. As Jerome mentioned when he discussed going on autopilot, as instability grows so too does the "view of written work as a transaction between teacher and student [that] mechanizes the learning process, automates the role of faculty, and undermines the university as a place for democratic, critical thought" (Stone and Austin 2020, 1). In destabilizing tutors, schools are also undermining the services that facilitate the learning and development at the core of the education mission. The specific case of Cortez College Writing Center demonstrates that the pressure of contingency burdens tutors and has the potential to harm the student-centered experience at the crux of the Writing Center's mission.

Equitable and livable compensation for tutors has the power to safeguard the student-centered experience because it can be so transformative to tutors' working environment. This research recognizes the potential contradiction of discussing pay as a stabilizing force in a writing center. Because the writing center is already heavily focused on cost, it may seem reductive to consider money as a way to reduce ethical issues. This duality is explained by Randal Monty (2019): "Although there can be material benefits to positioning writing center work in the language and terms of the neoliberal academy (for instance, ensuring equitable and competitive tutor pay is a net positive), by focusing on monetary compensation, we reproduce the systemic biases we're hoping to critique. At the same time, holding these contradictory goals in mind is necessary for writing center workers to reconstitute their identities as promoting labor practices that are embedded in social justice, while also positioning other issues of social justice as inextricable from issues of labor and compensation" (44). Money is both a part of the problem and a part of the solution. Though controlling cost perpetuated the problem of burnout and potential alienation in the Writing Center, money is also a means of combating the problems created by insecurity. Financial stability reduces the exhaustive worry tutors experienced. Yet, it should not be used to justify more cost reduction in the writing center. Discussing compensation as a means of inclusion situates professional tutors in the sociopolitical reality that a focus on cost reduction has influenced higher education and the writing center to the extent that continued instability hurts both tutors in the form of burnout and students in the form of potential alienation. To rectify this damage, tutors must have adequate financial stability to ward off the emotional exhaustion.

Conclusion

This research seeks to situate the writing center in contemporary working conditions created by the cost-focused reality of higher education (Monty

2019). Showing that professional tutors have unique ethical concerns (Nier-Weber 2017), which may have consequences on students, pushes writing center discourse to be accountable to the needs of professional tutors both in future writing center pedagogy and theory as well as practice.

A system of creating financial strain can be looked at from a macro-, higher education level or a microlevel of a single writing center, as was the case in this study. In both instances, the adjunctification of higher education is evident. In the case of Cortez Community College Writing Center, the part cannot be separated from the whole—all the tutors are or were adjuncts in the English Department. The English Department hired part-time workers who were encouraged to seek financial stability in the Writing Center. Yet, the Writing Center did not alleviate instability. These professionals were invited into a perpetual system of low pay and increasing workload. Though this is the story of one writing center and a limited set of professional tutors, it is important to broaden the understanding of structures within various writing centers and acknowledge that the writing center, as a space, cannot be student centered when its leaders are emotionally exhausted, detached, and afraid.

This research was inspired by the change I saw in my own teaching and tutoring practices after finally gaining stability. I was drawn to these stories because I also spent my early teaching career as an emotionally fraught adjunct instructor and professional tutor. At the time, I erroneously blamed myself for bringing my constant stress into the tutorial. I did not understand that no amount of self-determination to do and be better for my students would create the working conditions necessary to foster such a learning environment. It was not until I gained full-time employment with benefits and promised support that I was able to be the best for my students. Just as in my sewing, I have seen the ease afforded by having enough. It is enough that I wish for all who enter the writing center. As a result, calling for increased support for contingent workers in the writing center is more than a way to improve the financial situation of employees; increased support for staff directly supports students and scholarship. It moves the collective from pieces to whole.

The mission of the writing center is not a scrap to be woven into the larger landscape of higher education. To address potential student disempowerment, professional tutors need to have a continuous voice, ongoing professional development, and constant security. Though remnants can be diligently worked into success, neither tutors' working realities nor students' learning experiences should be disconnected from the whole tapestry of education.

Limitations

My work history has allowed me to access resources that may be inaccessible to an outsider but also colors my opinion. While this study included other professional tutors in an effort to balance the interpretations, it cannot be denied that as the sole researcher and writer my previous experiences will color my data interpretation.

Additionally, there were a number of issues that limited the scope of data collection. This study was initially intended to involve students to help analyze the perspective of tutors. However, because of IRB delays, recording students in writing tutorials was not approved until March 2020. Student participation became unavailable as of March 16, 2020, due to the COVID-19 pandemic. Though the data set presented is limited, the voices amplified throughout this research do address a gap in current writing center theory and prompt future research.

Appendix 5.A: Tutor Interview Protocol

Topic	General Questions
Training	· Tell me about your education background · What is your degree background? · Tell me about your experience in writing centers · How many years of experience do you have in the writing center? · How many writing centers have you worked in? · Tell me about your training · When was it? · How did you get it? · What did you think about it compared to your responsibilities now? · Do you have formal training? · Did you get specific training about working with students with disabilities or ELL students? · Tell me about an experience you've had working with a student with disabilities/ELL · Can you tell a story about this experience? · How do you feel about working with students with disabilities?
Schedule	· How many places do you work? · How many hours a week do you work both in the writing center and among your other jobs? · What was your schedule like last semester? · What is your schedule like this semester? · What happens when you are unable to keep this schedule? For example, if you are sick or have a schedule conflict · Tell me about what your busiest day looks like: Commuting, busiest days, answering emails · What, if any, issues do you have with your schedule? · What would your ideal schedule be?

Contingent status	· Do you have any worries about your job or job status? · In your opinion, does your part-time status/schedule impact your effectiveness as a tutor? · With your current schedule and life demands, do you feel working in the writing center is sustainable? · Ideally, what would change in your day-to-day work life to make your job more sustainable / make you feel more effective in your position? · Do you want/feel you need more training about working with students with disabilities or ELL? · Are you aware of any resources the institution provides to help with additional training? · Why have you not utilized these supports?

References

Auerbach, Carl, and Louise B. Silverstein. 2003. *Qualitative Data An Introduction to Coding and Analysis*. New York: New York University Press.

Fels, Dawn, Clint Gardner, Maggie M. Herb, and Liliana M. Naydan. 2000. "Toward an Investigation into the Working Conditions of Non-Tenure Line, Contingent Writing Center Workers." *College Composition and Communication* 68: A10.

García-Arroyo, Jose A., and Amparo O. Segovia. 2019. "Work Overload and Emotional Exhaustion in University Teachers: Moderating Effects of Coping Styles." *Universitas Psychologica* 18 (2): 1–12. https://doi.org/10.11144/Javeriana.upsy18-2.woee.

Gladstein, Jill, and Brandon Fralix. 2015. National Census of Writing. Accessed January 2, 2024. http://writingcensus.swarthmore.edu/.

Giroux, Henry A. 2002. "Neoliberalism, Corporate Culture, and the Promise of Higher Education: The University as a Democratic Public Sphere." *Harvard Educational Review* 72 (4): 425–463.

Hathaway, Andrew D., Rory Sommers, and Amir Mostaghim. 2020. "Active Interview Tactics Revisited: A Multigenerational Perspective." *Qualitative Sociology Review* 16: 106–119. http://www.qualitativesociologyreview.org/ENG/Volume53/QSR_16_2_Hathaway_Sommers_Mostaghim.pdf.

Lackritz, James R. 2004. "Exploring Burnout among University Faculty: Incidence, Performance, and Demographic Issues." *Teaching and Teacher Education* 20 (7): 713–729. https://doi.org/10.1016/j.tate.2004.07.002.

McKenna, Laura. 2015. "The Cost of an Adjunct." https://www.theatlantic.com/education/archive/2015/05/the-cost-of-an-adjunct/394091/.

Monty, Randall W. 2019. "Undergirding Writing Centers' Responses to the Neoliberal Academy." *Praxis: A Writing Center Journal* 16 (3): 37–47.

Nier-Weber, Dani. 2017. "The Other Invisible Hand: Adjunct Labor and Economies of the Writing Center." *Contingency, Exploitation, and Solidarity: Labor and Action in English Composition*, edited by Seth Kahn, William Lalicker, and Amy Lynch-Biniek, 102–118. Logan: Utah State University Press.

Schell, Eileen. 2017. "The New Faculty Majority in Writing Programs: Organizing for Change." *Contingency, Exploitation, and Solidarity: Labor and Action in English Composition*, edited by Seth Kahn, William Lalicker, and Amy Lynch-Biniek, 102–118. Logan: Utah State University Press.

Stone, Erica M., and Sarah E. Austin. 2020. "Writing as Commodity: How Neoliberalism Renders the Postsecondary Online Writing Classroom Transactional and Ways Faculty Can Regain Agency." *Basic Writing Electronic (BWE) Journal* 16 (1): 1–23.

Supiano, Beckie. 2018. "It Matters a Lot Who Teaches Introductory Courses. Here's Why." https://www.chronicle.com/article/It-Matters-a-Lot-Who-Teaches/243125.

Watts, Jenny, and Noelle Robertson. 2011. "Burnout in University Teaching Staff: A Systematic Literature Review." *Educational Research* 53 (1): 33–50. https://doi.org/10.1080/00131881.2011.552235.

RESPONSE TO SECTION ONE
Structural Marginalization

KERRI RINALDI

Like the tutors in Gorham's piece, when I first started working professionally in writing centers, I made a living by weaving together multiple part-time, contingent jobs. And like Rider (chapter 3), I told myself I appreciated the flexibility that such an assemblage afforded me. I did not push for, and even sometimes resisted the idea of, full-time work as I clung to the notion of flexible freedom. Despite my contingent status, I still considered myself a scholar in the field (also much like Rider), writing for publication and presenting at conferences on my own time (and paid for out of my own pocket). When the university I worked for abruptly slashed my hours by half, and I suddenly couldn't afford necessities, I could no longer continue telling myself that the financial and job insecurity was worth the tradeoff of flexibility. I was given no warning, no recourse—and like the professional tutors Gorham describes in chapter 5, I felt the institution's actions communicated how little I was valued. So, I left for a full-time directorship, classified as a staff position with no teaching required.

When I first started that position, I told myself I preferred being staff rather than faculty line. I could choose when and how much I taught! I could publish only when I felt like it! I could research when and what I wanted to not because I needed to for tenure! Being staff gave me freedom to engage in nonadministrative activities like teaching and scholarship at my own discretion. But like Botvin and Buck warn of in chapter 2, as time went on, interview promises didn't quite match up to reality—limited funding for staff to attend conferences was available, but using it was frowned upon. Chronic staff turnover—a result of low pay—meant we were always understaffed, leaving me with little time to engage with current scholarship, let alone produce it. I had no input in or even warning about large decisions, like an institutional restructure of the center with new reporting lines. Ten years into my professional writing center career, I began to wonder if maybe the tenure-track (TT) writing center administrator position was what I should have been striving for this whole time.

When I read these chapters on structural marginalization, what I am confronted with is a sense of *powerlessness*. Powerlessness against the institution, against the purposefully obscure forces at play in decision making, against the systemic structures that devalue our work—while all the while benefiting from such devaluation. Professional writing center staff are not immune from the neoliberal academy's reliance on using full-time equivalent (FTE) and budget lines to make decisions. This neoliberal focus, coupled with a remarkable ability to prey upon our field's devotion to our practice and willingness to work for the love of writing, has levied unmistakable harm to the field of writing centers. As we saw in these chapters, structural marginalization plays out as job insecurity (Rider, chapter 3), rapid changes to job duties and hours (Gorham, chapter 5), devaluing specific staff (Grogan, Bromley, and Stephenson, chapter 4), difficult-to-navigate structures and managerial functions (Paz and Dixon, chapter 1), poorly defined roles (Botvin and Buck, chapter 2), and low pay and exploitation of our labor at the expense of our livelihoods and stability.

In chapter 4, Grogan, Bromley, and Stephenson uncover a lack of scholarship on professional tutoring, signaling these positions are devalued not only by their institutions but also by our own field. I would add that another likely reason for the lack of scholarship on professional tutors is that many directors who employ professional writing tutors are often staff or contingent workers themselves—with no time or resources provided to them to conduct research or publish about their writing centers. When primarily faculty-line directors who oversee "conventional" writing centers have disproportionate access to producing scholarship, the scholarship will not reflect the lived realities of those writing center workers who lack such access. An overreliance on nonfaculty labor means that many writing center professionals must financially sponsor their own participation in scholarship: funding their own conference participation or travel, conducting research with no institutional support, and writing for publication during unpaid time. Enshrouded in the marginalization of our positions and centers are looming implications for the writing center studies field at large—if fewer and fewer of us are granted access to the institutional resources, motivation, and recognition needed to engage with and produce new scholarship, what does that mean for writing center studies as a scholarly field? How can the field move forward—not even to grow but merely to exist?

In "A Triumph over Structures That Disempower," Yanar Hashlamon (2021) writes, "writing center scholarship often perpetuates an ethic of individual responsibility when it comes to caring for oneself and for clients" (249). I can see reflections of Hashlamon's argument in scholarship on labor conditions, as well: the "grand narrative" often locates the ethic of responsibility in the individual. This focus on the individual is often self-protective—in chapter 3, Rider notes that part-time and contingent writing center professionals, found at the bottom rungs of the academic hierarchy, have to advocate for their own needs. Within much of the writing center scholarship about improving labor conditions or making visible our intellectual and emotional work is the implicit assumption that the person responsible for doing so is the writing center professional, rather than the chair, dean, or executive administrator who oversees them. Intellectual invisibility is relentless and exhausting, which leads to burnout among writing center professionals (Nelson, Deges, and Weaver 2020). What would it mean to instead move that ethic of responsibility to the institution itself?

My own professional journey has led me to see the value in faculty-line writing center directorships. However, Botvin and Buck rightly argue in chapter 2 that in our current system, tenure-line directorships are extremely rare—and are not immune from marginality or fraught and complex circumstances. Beyond advocating for more TT directorships, these chapters demonstrate the need for ongoing scholarship on labor conditions in writing center work that not only observes and documents but also offers critical analysis of how to change the course of the field. Such critical analysis, as Randall Monty (2019) affirms, would do well to simultaneously critique the neoliberal shift of writing centers while also promoting socially just and equitable labor practices in our current system. Then again, how can folks in insecure or contingent positions risk challenging the very institutions that provide their livelihood? Much like scholars in composition and rhetoric have argued for, perhaps it is the tenured writing center professionals and those secure in their positions who should be the ones to loudly advocate for change to our field's trajectory as it inches toward exploitation, precariousness, and burnout.

References

Hashlamon, Yanar. 2021. "A Triumph over Structures That Disempower": Principles for Community Wellness in the Writing Center. In *Wellness and Care in Writing Center Work*, edited by Genie Nicole Giaimo, Kristi Murray Costello, Benjamin J. Villarreal, Lauren Brentnell, Elise Dixon, Rachel Robinson, Miranda Mattingly, Claire Helakoskim, Christina Lundberg, Kacy Walz, Sarah Brown, and Yanar Hashlamon, 229–260. United States: Press Books.

Monty, Randall. 2019. "Undergirding Writing Centers' Responses to the Neoliberal Academy." *Praxis: A Writing Center Journal* 16 (3): 37–47.

Nelson, Matthew T., Sam Deges, and Kathleen F. Weaver. 2020. "Making Visible the Emotional Labor of Writing Center Work." In *The Things We Carry: Strategies for Recognizing and Negotiating Emotional Labor in Writing Program Administration*, edited by L. Micciche, K. Navickas, K. M. Costello, J. Babb, and C. A. Wooten, 305–6. Logan: Utah State University Press.

SECTION TWO

Globalization and Marginalization

6
Becoming a Writing Center Administrator

A Transnational Counterstory

NANCY HENAKU

In *Peripheral Visions for Writing Centers*, Jackie Grutsch McKinney (2013) argues that "writing center work is complex, but the storying of writing center work is not" because underlying this storying is a "grand narrative," which, simply put, refers to discourses that follow "a relatively familiar pattern" (3). Grand narratives are techniques of power: they govern our storying by obscuring those narratives that do not fit the accepted pattern. We must therefore be attentive to the stories we tell (and do not tell) because how we tell writing center stories and who is represented in these stories have implications for why and how we envision the field and its future. Just as there is a grand narrative of writing center work, there is also a grand narrative about who works in the writing center that privileges North American experiences. The increasing significance of writing centers outside of the United States (see Santa 2002; Broekhoff 2014; Scott 2017; Hodges, Ronesi, and Zenger 2019; Richards, Lackay, and Delport 2019) challenges the field's American-centeredness, requiring more critical transnational theorization if we are to provide a broader vision of our work.

In this chapter, I present a "transnational counterstory" of how I came to work as a writing center administrator. I do so by reflecting on what my occupational trajectory, activities, engagements, discourses, and documents suggest about how my experiences are both similar and different from those of other administrators (e.g., Lerner 2000; Scott 2017). While interrogating a dominant American lens in writing center scholarship, "transnational," as used here, is not limited to stories outside of American contexts, because I tell stories about my experiences in both the US and Africa. "Transnational" emphasizes contact, relations, and flows of people, ideas, institutions, and so on that foreground cross-national dynamics and challenge homogenous narratives of being through, especially, their "implicitly other-oriented interactions" (Appadurai 1996; Doyle 2009).

I borrow "counterstory" from critical race theory (CRT) but extend it for transnational writing center theorization (Martinez 2020). I assume that stories by themselves are not necessarily disruptive: many sustain metanarratives. For me, it is in the telling (or framing)—how we make sense of narratives—that the disruption can happen. Transnational counterstories are disruptive of our grand narratives because they complicate the stories we tell about writing centers and the people who work within them by drawing attention beyond our professional center (the US), where, incidentally, CRT tends to restrict itself (Yao, Mwangi, and Brown 2019). Combining autoethnographic, transnational, and decolonial theories, my counterstory emphasizes the need to be attentive to the diverse individuated experiences of writing centers and their workers and the implications of these for providing a comprehensive narrative of the work we do globally. I begin by discussing transnational counterstorying as a critical method(ology). I then narrate my journey to becoming a writing center worker and the theoretical implications of this trajectory. My journey is presented in three sections: how I came to work in the writing center, how I acquired professional knowledge, and how I came to administer the writing center of a Ghanaian university.

Transnational Counter Storytelling as Critical Praxis

As a critical praxis, transnational counter storytelling (TCS) calls for a global recasting of writing center work in ways that transgress the field's dominant frames. Besides making visible cross-national/border experiences often obscured in our field, TCS is also about how this visibility points to tensions that challenge taken-for-granted approaches to writing center work. Transnational counter storytelling extends the interdisciplinary counterstory methodology of people of color researchers, including those in composition studies, for interrogating metanarratives and their intersectional racist underpinnings in academe and beyond (Martinez 2014, 2020). It examines how international dynamics complicate our disciplinary imaginings and their implications, especially for othered subjectivities in transit. This form of storytelling combines autoethnographic, transnational, and decolonial lenses.

Autoethnography—explained literally as "self + culture + writing"—is described "as both a method of inquiry and a genre of writing" (Jackson and McKinney 2021, 3) that examines culture by focusing on the personal (see Boylorn and Orbe 2014, 17; Jones, Adams, and Ellis 2016, 22). Through this lens, I see storytelling as a crucial rhetorical tool for understanding and conceptualizing writing centers as cultural sites. Their cultural dimensions are, for instance, evident in the labels, metanarratives, roles, relationships, paradigms, spaces/places, and so on constructed both locally (by individual centers and workers) and collectively (as a field). Because autoethnography examines what personal experiences suggest about larger culture, it allows us to study how individuated experiences complicate, align, and/or depart from the larger writing center landscape. It is also a "powerful method" for engaging diversity and identity as it "invite[s] readers into the lived experiences of a presumed 'Other'" (Boylorn and Orbe 2014, 15). As subsequent discussions indicate, not only are questions of identity, at several intersections, central to my trajectory as a writing center personnel, but the discussion also reveals at least two levels of *Otherness* connected to my geopolitical positioning at different times: one is related to my experience as an international (and senior graduate student) in a writing center in the United States; and the other is linked to my administrative work in a writing center in Ghana, an unrepresented space in the field. As a result, I also see autoethnography as a decolonial resource for making visible an (inter)subjective experience that would otherwise be invisible in our field.

Transnational counter storytelling challenges metanarratives by inviting diverse stories into the field. Though we tell an abundance of stories in writing center work, our storytelling—as McKinney (2013) observes—is still limited. For Marilee Brooks-Gillies (2018), this limitation implies the need to "theorize our stories and our storying" in ways that "get at the rich and complicated work we do" as well as our diverse experiences. For me, a transnational counter storytelling praxis allows for the kind of deep storying that is needed, but to do this we must also ask: What narratives are dominant in the field? And who has been telling them and in what manner? Postcolonial and antiracist scholars have underscored the colonizing aspects of writing center work. For Asao Inoue (2016), writing centers are dominated by "whiteness and whitely ways" that require intersectional social justice work. Eric Camarillo (2019) argues that writing centers are often constructed through a rhetoric of neutrality that seeks to present centers as "cozy" places inviting to everyone. This rhetoric—a key aspect of writing center grand narrative—is, however, problematic because it aims to flatten the varied experiences that people bring into this space to align them with academic institutional expectations. Romeo García's (2017) work is especially significant from a transnational perspective because it challenges the discipline's dominant postcolonial and antiracist thinking by identifying "reductive racial frames" that explain Mexican American experiences within a white/black racial binarism. These observations point to the essence of telling our stories with decolonial and transnational lenses.

A transnational counterstory complicates the storying of the discipline because narrativizing our diverse experiences through decolonial and global lenses opens the space to account for, in more complex ways, the epistemes of power in writing center work. The decolonial project recognizes that our discipline and its grand narratives are implicated in coloniality of power. For example, we cannot examine the historically close relationship between "Standard" English and writing center work without linking it to the colonial influences of modernity and its linguistic manifestations. This view explains how non-native and "non-Standard" English speakers have traditionally been interpellated in writing centers. Decoloniality also provides a language for interrogating master narratives while making it possible to acknowledge the "pluriversality"—as against universality—of experience (Mignolo 2011). Thus, TCS recognizes that there are many stories of writing centers to be told; however, to do this well, we must also be attentive to the growing transnational influences in writing program administration (Logan 2016).

Because movement is core to transnational engagement (Appadurai 1996; Park and Wee 2017), a counterstory with a transnational lens considers how flows of personnel, discourses, and resources of various kinds impact the workings of the discipline. Analysis of such flows must, for example, grapple with debates about the neocolonial dimensions of writing center expansion into the Global South (Villagrán Mora, chapter 7 in this volume), forcing us to ask: What happens when the idea of the writing center moves elsewhere? Besides the increasing admission of international students and faculty with varied linguistic backgrounds in the US, writing centers are steadily circulating outside the US, and US-trained personnel are often tasked to start, administer, or collaborate with centers elsewhere. The dispersions (and immersions) that characterize such mobilities complicate how metanarratives operate. Transnational counter storytelling accounts for convergences while recognizing the heterogeneity of operations in institutional and geopolitical contexts. Many international perspectives in the field point to differences (e.g., Santa 2002; Broekhoff 2014). What is less emphasized are linkages and how these sustain or unsettle dominant narratives in specific translocalities. The entanglement between difference and sameness in global writing center contexts, my analysis shows, presents intricacies for transformation work that transnational counterstories help us reflect on or navigate.

Becoming a Writing Center Worker

Here, I highlight the circumstances in which I came to work in the field as a starting point for linking my experience in the US and elsewhere. I first encountered the writing center, both as an idea and as a physical space, during my PhD at Michigan Technological University (also called Michigan Tech).[1] I started working at the Michigan Tech Multiliteracies Center (MTMC) mainly to maintain my status as an international student and not necessarily because of a personal interest in the work. At the time, I was in the sixth year of the rhetoric, theory and culture (RTC) doctoral program. My funding had ended, and anticipating that the dissertation would be completed by mid-January 2020, I applied for postcompletion optional practical training (OPT) to work for a year in the US after my program. Unfortunately, the corrections for the dissertation were not complete by this January deadline; because my OPT had begun, I had to work at least twenty hours a week to maintain my status. I was still revising my dissertation, so I preferred on-campus employment. That is how I came to work as a consultant at the MTMC from January to May 2020. Before this time, I was a graduate teaching instructor (GTI) from 2014 to 2019, teaching First-Year Composition, Public Speaking, and Research and Writing in Communication. Some graduate students in our program worked at the MTMC, especially in the summers, but throughout my role as a GTI, I had teaching assignments and did not work at the center.

As a composition instructor, I became aware of the writing center in two ways. First, the role of the writing center in the first-year writing program was emphasized, and we were often reminded to require/encourage students to attend sessions. Second, every semester, one of the writing center personnel visited my classes to introduce students to available services and to encourage them to book appointments. Thus, before working at the MTMC, I had only engaged with the writing center from a distance, as an instructor. Working in the writing center as a consultant, I saw a reversal in my role from that of an instructor to that of a tutor. Because I was nearing the end of my studies, I occupied a position that was not quite that of a student as is the case for "typical" writing center tutors. An introductory email sent (on February 3, 2020) by William De Herder (the assistant director of the MTMC at the time) to graduate students to "consider taking advantage of weekly appointments with a coach at the MTMC" described me as "a recent PhD graduate." This also meant that I often worked with graduate students, most of whom were internationals like me.

My peculiar situation highlighted dimensions of my "other" identity in writing center work. First, my transition from instructorship to tutorship placed me in a complex positionality, especially in situations requiring feedback for students on a course I had previously taught. This positional tension required a kind of pedagogical reflexivity on my part about the differences between feedback by an instructor and feedback by a tutor. Besides engaging in critical conversations about differences between teaching and tutoring with our assistant director, I also learned by observing the approaches of the mainly undergraduate tutors in my writing center who were more experienced. This situation points to a layered relational dynamic: I may have been the most educated tutor in the space at the time, but I was not the most experienced in terms of writing center tutoring. Second, as an international student from sub-Saharan Africa, a non-native speaker of English and a non-American Black person, I did not necessarily fit the "white racial habitus" that shaped much of writing center spaces (Inoue 2016; García 2017). Unfortunately, much of the antiracist scholarship did not address my specific concerns as an African in an American center.

However, it would be problematic to suggest that my racial and non-native background put me in a less-privileged position because my positionality was further complicated by my qualification as a "recent PhD graduate" and my formal designation as a "consultant." While my Ghanaian English accent did not fit our center's dominant American accent, it was within Braj Kachru's (1996) "Outer Circle" (Englishes in ex-British colonies), which, in the global positioning of Englishes, was privileged over Englishes from "the Expanding Circle" (more recent Englishes with no historical relations with the British Empire). This meant I have had significant exposure to English and because of this, my English was close to the "standard" variety. This complex positionality was brought to the fore when, in one instance, an international student (from a country in "the Expanding Circle") declared, "You're so lucky. Your English is very good." The truth is that I did not always feel that way; however, the student's comment emphasized for me other dimensions of linguistic power that are invisible in the field.

Working with international graduate students caused me to ask, Which international students are found in American writing centers? And why? I questioned why I never used the writing center as a graduate student. I did not perceive myself as the kind of international student who needed writing center support. I was from a country in the Outer Circle where English is the de facto official language. I had degrees in English and began communicating in English as a child. I saw the writing center as a place for people with deficit linguistic capabilities—despite my research on critical sociolinguistic issues; therefore, I considered a visit to this space as evidence of my limited English skills. To use the writing center was, in my mind, to suggest that my English was not proficient enough—a situation that I believed would impact my ethos as a graduate student. My stint at the MTMC challenged this idea. It caused me to reflect on why certain "international" students are present in the writing center while others are absent or invisible. Many North American writing centers have always been transnational spaces because they engage with international and multilingual students, but this relationship is informed by an ideology of deficitness, including remediation, that impacts both international tutors and tutees (Cirillo-McCarthy, Del Russo, and Leahy 2016). Though the language of deficitness has been critiqued, it has been argued that it continues to operate in writing centers (Tinoco et al. 2020). This ideology characterizes North American university culture and is often evident in proof of English proficiency requirements for international students.

Learning the Lore of Our Profession

Before working at the MTMC, I had little engagement with writing center lore besides passing references to the writing center in the composition scholarship I read. However, because of my teaching and research, I was knowledgeable in areas that influence conversations in the field: rhetoric and composition, applied linguistics, world Englishes, and critical discourse studies. At the MTMC, I had a two-pronged role as a researcher and tutor, with ten hours per week dedicated to each role. Both provided opportunities to engage with writing center scholarship. In the tutoring role, I interacted more with the assistant director, who introduced me to core readings and scholars in writing center work (e.g., North 1984, 1994; Grimm 1996; Bouquet and Lerner 2008). He also highlighted for me the importance of historicizing the writing center by drawing my attention to the history of our writing center (De Herder 2019). The research role required that I meet weekly with the director of our center (Abraham Romney) to discuss core ideas from readings related to a project on decolonial perspectives in writing center work. The post/decolonial scholarship (Bawarshi and Pelkowski 1999; Inoue 2016; García 2017) I read illuminated dimensions of power in writing center work and their resulting linguistic and material violence on people of color. Because this scholarship was American-centric, it became crucial to research writing centers in international (including African) contexts.

Besides these influences, our weekly staff meetings also highlighted for me the connection between theory (through readings) and practice (activities) and how the collaborative nature of writing center work deconstructed the traditional notions of academic engagement. I learned that writing center work moved beyond writing; it was also about relationships—and care. Care for students; care for colleagues. I learned that writing center work and how we construct it were not always benign and were riddled with multiple layers of power. It made me pay attention to center documents and resources for how they construct writing center relationships. While I had not taken a course in the theory and practice of writing center administration, I had, by the time I left the MTMC, acquired knowledge in the field, which prepared me, first, for my interview and, later, for work for an administrative position in Ghana. An awareness of the tension in writing center positionality was central to my vision for my new role in Ghana. In my mission statement for the job, I envisioned a critical writing center that would take the work of transformation seriously. Being aware that not all patrons feel welcome in writing center spaces, I intended to look beyond the "cozy" walls of the center and be attentive to the material conditions that shape its patrons' literacy practices. I was going to avoid the language of neutrality and directly interrogate the sociopolitics of literacy education in my work. But I learned eventually that context is everything and that what counts as transformation is impacted by time, space, and circumstances.

From America to Africa: Running a Center as Co-director

Transnational counterstories show how contradictions and connections can make metanarratives visible. My experience in Ghana underscored this point.

After six months at the MTMC, I began a new position as the co-director of the writing center at Ashesi University, a private university in Ghana, West Africa, with 1,253 students enrolled as of 2021. The university constructs itself as an institution focused on training a generation of ethical African leaders (Ashesi University 2017). Because communication is central to this mandate,[2] there is, unlike elsewhere, a general sense that the writing center plays an important role, especially in students' communication. For example, all final-year capstone theses and applied projects (which are all long essays) are required to go through the writing center before submission. The Ashesi Writing Center, compared to my previous workplace, was relatively new and was still crafting an identity in a (national) context with little writing center history. To my knowledge, the Ashesi Writing Center is one of two writing centers in a Ghanaian university (the other is at the University of Ghana) and is the only one that provides more traditional services (in the form of tutoring) for students. The university only recently (2021) introduced postgraduate programs; thus, the center's student population (both tutors and tutees) has been undergraduates. The university provides majors in the science, technology, engineering, and mathematics (STEM) and business disciplines. There are no majors in arts and social sciences, though students take courses in these areas (e.g., Leadership, African Popular Culture, Text and Meaning) as part of the university's multidisciplinary liberal arts approach. The background of our tutors, therefore, challenged notions that the writing center was a place for mostly English and humanities majors.

The students' linguistic backgrounds raise important issues related to doing writing center work in highly multilingual contexts. Most of the students are Ghanaians. Of the student population, 17 percent are international, with many coming from other African countries (e.g., Cameroun, Liberia, Nigeria, and Côte d'Ivoire). Ghana is an English as a second language (ESL) context; thus, English is the language of instruction in schools and the language of official government business. Because of Ghana's colonial history, British English is the variety of English taught and examined in Ghanaian schools. In reality, many Ghanaians use what has been designated as "Ghanaian English," which, despite its proximity to Standard English, has its unique linguistic features. (See Ahulu 1994; Huber 2008.) American English is also gradually influencing English usage in Ghana (Osei-Tutu 2021). Through teaching and tutorial sessions, I came to understand that some of our students identified as first-language speakers of English though they spoke non-native varieties of English, a situation that interrogated the simplistic distinction of native and non-native speakers in writing center contexts. Besides English, there are about fifty (or more) Indigenous Ghanaian languages. Students from other African countries (e.g., Côte d'Ivoire) may be English as a foreign language (EFL) speakers. These students, in addition to knowing English, may know some other ex-colonial languages (e.g., French) and one or more African languages. In this context, multilingualism is the norm, not a peripheral aspect of writing center work. Thus, multilingualism did not carry the same sense of otherness that it does in some American contexts. Yet, our students were not immune to the global, often problematic, reception of non-native English usage.

The structure of our center is similar to those in America, but its context, as evident in the preceding description, is distinct. This situation sometimes interrogated writing center grand narratives. For example, I noticed through tutoring sessions and comments from faculty that language and grammar were as important as higher-order concerns. Not only did we highlight language and grammar issues for capstone projects, but we also often received requests from faculty to provide feedback on (student) manuscripts before publication. In a draft of my first presentation to students about the center, I asserted that the center was not an editing shop, an idea that was informed by a grand narrative that writing centers are places for "conversations," not "answers," about writing (McKinney 2013, 58). My coworkers, in their feedback, indicated that this purpose might be misconstrued by students who may think that they cannot come to the center with their linguistic or editorial questions. This example highlighted the tension between my American influences and the practicalities of my new institutional context. Similar observations have been made about multilingual students in the US (e.g., Cirillo-McCarthy, Russo, and Leahy 2016) and non-American contexts (Turner 2006). For us, the issue was not whether or not we could tutor grammar. The issue was how to tutor grammar in ways that honor our students' multilingual background while preparing them to be attentive to the linguistic expectations of a global (neoliberal) context that already disadvantages them, often requiring them to prove their proficiency in English, because of their locatedness outside of the metropole. Our discourse grammar approach presented grammar as a crucial aspect of the production of interactional meaning in discourse. It interrogated the hierarchization underlying the higher-order/lower-order distinctions and, instead, highlighted the symbiosis between these elements. For us, concerns with grammar were not about surface-level error correction; we considered grammar as contributing significantly to information flow, foregrounding, stance taking, and style in communication.

The context impacting my administrative role at the Ashesi Writing Center was layered. When I was employed, the writing center was considered part of an emerging Writing Across the Curriculum (WAC) program. Its purpose was to enhance the communicative competencies of students especially, and the general university population. Besides introducing new courses (called lab courses), designed in conjunction with writing center co-directors, the writing center was envisioned as part of this multifaceted WAC program that would support student communication through tutoring and other services (e.g., workshops). My appointment as co-director was part of this effort to professionalize the center in ways that align with the vision for the WAC program. My position as co-director was mainly administrative, but it came with some teaching responsibilities. I was expected to administer the writing center, help develop the emerging WAC initiative, and teach courses like Written and Oral Communication. Faculty and university authorities in charge of the writing center explained that teaching writing courses would give co-directors a sense of what happens in the classroom, which would then provide important context for work at the center. I worked with another co-director (Gabriel Opoku) to provide the center's thought leadership. We reported directly to the provost of the university. The center also had a coordinator (Daniel Kwaku Bempah) and seventeen undergraduate tutors. The other co-director and coordinator had worked for some time with the center before I joined. From these colleagues and tutors (one was the longest-serving worker in the center), I learned the history and culture of the center I had come to meet. I did not have to perform my role out of context.

I came to this job not as a trained administrator (I had envisioned a more traditional academic trajectory), and what I knew about writing center administration was very much informed by what I had observed from the work of the directors at my previous institution in the US. I learned to perform as an administrator on the job with a significant appreciation of how context defines this role. Through my position (and other factors about our center's histories and relations), then, our writing center was linked to the US, but it was also shaped by forces in our specific context.

I joined the Ashesi Writing Center in September 2020 at the height of the COVID-19 pandemic. I was stuck in the US and administering the writing center (operating virtually because of the crisis) of a university physically located in Ghana. As administrators, we had as our immediate concern to ensure that the center continued to operate as smoothly as possible even as we instantly began the process of enhancing center professionalism. The period from September to December 2020 was characterized by intense planning and meetings in which we discussed extensively the WAC program and the role of the center in this initiative. We also identified the various components of a five-year strategic plan for the center and recast Ashesi University's learning goals through a writing center perspective. One of our goals was to intentionally build a departmental identity, culture, and ethos by, for example, formalizing tutor training and intentionally composing the center to increase visibility among students. Here too context determined what was possible or not. When I applied for the position, I proposed a twelve-week theory and practice of writing center course for tutors. However, I had to rethink this idea because there was no institutional arrangement, at the time, for such comprehensive training and because I came in when the semester had already begun, and in a crisis moment we had to improvise. We ended up having a crash training program, which was supplemented by our usual biweekly staff meetings.

For a four-day crash program, we discussed the following topics: "setting the goals for the training" (day 1), "the role of tutors in the writing center as workplace" (day 2), "providing feedback" (day 3), and "practicing tutoring sessions" (day 4). What seemed critical in the plan for the training was the readings I selected: Stephen North's (1984) "The Idea of the Writing Center" (for day 1), Muriel Harris's (1995) "Talking in the Middle" (for day 2), and Maureen McBride et al.'s (2018) "Responding to the Whole Person" (for day 4). I was aware that some administrators no longer use North's article, but I included it for two main reasons. First, because the text is often referenced and is considered a classic in the field, I wanted our tutors to know about it and engage with its ideas. Second, I thought that despite critiques, some of North's arguments are still relevant for understanding the challenges of writing centers in academe. I included the other articles to help clarify tutors' role in the writing center and emphasize the importance of listening in this work.

What is interesting is the absence of readings on African writing centers or non-native English contexts. For this specific training, the goal was to get tutors to start thinking professionally about their work. Thus, I chose these articles (and the activities) for more practical purposes—to introduce tutors to some foundational readings that can prepare them for the semester's work. The plan was to introduce African and second-language perspectives in our subsequent biweekly meetings. The postcolonial dimension, I felt, was a more direct political angle that should come after this initial practical training.

In hindsight, I realize we were moving from the global (larger Western-dominated writing center context) to the local (our specific context). I now see how beginning with an African perspective (the local) would have had a different impact. However, beginning from a global perspective also seemed useful because transnational influences were already present in the center. For example, because the Ashesi Writing Center is part of a network of Open Society University Network (OSUN) Writing Centers, there are opportunities for administrators and tutors from affiliated institutions to meet and collaborate globally. Besides creating cross-center connections, the network provides a comparative view of local practices across centers. My global approach was meant to help tutors see themselves as part of a transnational discipline; but in taking this approach, was I also (indirectly) reinforcing writing center metanarratives by divorcing the postcolonial from global writing center theory and practices?

Despite my approach, contextual differences and similarities always came up in our discussions, bumping up against ideas in the texts we read. The following entry from my director's journal, which I used to reflect on my actions and their impacts, highlights this point:

> We discussed the "Idea of the Writing Center," which generated intense discussion on some differences in context . . . there was also an indication that many of the issues North raises—the idea that writing centers deal with people with writing problems—are also prevalent and that this seems to shape the ways in which the role of the Ashesi writing center is constructed. This seems to suggest that nothing has really changed after several years of North's argument, but I also wonder whether this is also related to the circulation of the idea of the writing center to other places. Despite the ongoing conversations on rethinking writing centers—is there still a sense that the original ideologies shaping writing centers are still shaping how writing centers are viewed? (director's journal, September 15, 2020)

The excerpt above hints at the need to pay attention to the circulation of writing center ideas and how this can sustain metanarratives. My role and decisions also highlight the need to be attentive to how trained personnel from the US help circulate ideas—dominant or otherwise—in new spaces and their implications for how we envision writing center work globally as well as the possible tensions that arise. For example, when we discussed McBride et al.'s "Responding to the Whole Person," we agreed that empathic listening is important, but my co-director highlighted the significance of politeness in African communicative practice with its emphasis on respect and social harmony (Thompson and Anderson 2018), a sociopragmatic practice that characterized our center interactions.

Professionalizing a center during a pandemic came with challenges. For instance, we had to consider creative approaches for making the center visible and accessible. This issue of visibility dominated our conversation during an administrators' meeting on January 21, 2021 (see table 6.1). We, for instance, created what we came to call "FaceBook," a booklet that contained information about the center and its workers. The document provided the following description of the center.

> The Ashesi Writing Centre (AWC) exists to support the communication needs of all members of our community including students, alumni, faculty, staff, and the various departments . . . our work at the center moves beyond traditional writing. Our aim is to build and nurture a comprehensive communication culture characterized by an emphasis on multiliteracy, multimodality and multilingualism. We also highlight the important connections between reading, writing, and research.

While this mission statement may sound like any in a US context, context highlights dimensions of our work that seem invisible in this description. First of all, this description was part of an effort to intentionally reorient perceptions of the center. Though students are our main clients, we wanted to present the writing center as a democratic space open to everyone in "our community." By doing this, we indicated that communication was everyone's business, a perspective that we hoped would encourage students that they were not being targeted (for their "bad" writing). Additionally, since the writing center, based on conversations with some students, was still perceived as a space associated with "traditional writing," we needed to expand our idea of writing in a way that honors our students' multiliterate and multilingual backgrounds. This reorientation aligned with the WAC program's comprehensive approach to communication. For example, the newly designed first-year writing course emphasized multiliteracy, multimodality, and multilingualism. Among other things, students wrote essays, composed multimodal artifacts, and read resources on the politics of language in African contexts. We trained tutors in various components of this new syllabus so they have the background and knowledge to effectively engage our first-year patrons.

TABLE 6.1. Notes from administrator's meeting

Topic	Suggestions	Notes
How do we make the center visible this semester?	· Create short videos and share with lecturers to be played in various classes. · Tutors pop in on various classes. · Look at what's already working: move communication from email to WhatsApp (WhatsApp as an ideal communication channel). · Telegram—another option. · Use the FI channel on WhatsApp. · Package our information in more interesting ways. · Be consistent—e.g., send writing tips.	· Improve visibility. · Think up creative ways to reach students. · Students are not reading their emails... create a stronger line of communication with students. · Help students rethink the role of the center and student engagement with it. · Reinvent who we are.

Conclusion

Besides highlighting the need to pay attention to international experiences, this narrative indicates how a focus on individuated experiences can provide a basis for disrupting the dominant knowledge that shapes our collective understanding of writing center work and the people who make this possible. This is why counter storytelling is significant. It recognizes that there are many stories of writing centers to be told and that each can provide insight into how we understand the complex workings of the field. While aspects of my experiences are recognizable in the larger writing center narrative, this does not imply that my narrativizing of these experiences is not disruptive. Just by highlighting these experiences, I make visible dominant narratives and processes in our field. But the narrative also points to differences in experiences that challenge us to rethink our traditional theorizations such as the framing of multilingualism in our work. It means we must recognize the possibility that different metanarratives may exist and that what counts as best practice may not always be the same. For example, my experience differs from other experiences of writing center work even on the African continent (Broekhoff 2014), and issues related to the type of institution, nature of the center, organizational structure, geographical location, time of appointment, and so forth significantly impact the work we do globally. Because we are so focused on writing center culture in the US, we do not ask questions about who is sent elsewhere to do writing center work. A transnational view must ask: Where do administrators come from? What are their influences? Where do they go? And what do they do?

With the recent emphasis on decolonial approaches, how does the flow of personnel to other parts of the world complicate how we story writing center work? What does it mean to think about how certain structures and narratives are reproduced or interrogated in specific contexts? For McKinney, once a metanarrative is set "in motion, [it] excludes other ideas about writing centers that do not fit with the established writing center story" (11), but as my analysis indicates, contexts always have a way of rupturing metanarratives, calling forth a different story-theorizing. It also suggests that displaced metanarratives can sometimes operate invisibly, complicating the work of transformation. This is why we must be attentive to the dissemination of writing center theory and practice in other spaces and hear the stories that all writing center contexts are telling. If we built a writing center family tree that includes the complex stories of all of the people and places in our field, what would this look like? And what politics would this reveal? That is the challenge that a transnational counter storytelling praxis poses.

Notes

1. My former university (the University of Ghana) did not have a writing center when I was a student there but it now houses the University of Ghana-Carnegie Writing Centre.
2. Communication is one of the university's eight learning goals. See this link for more information: https://www.ashesi.edu.gh/academics/learning-goals.html.

References

Ahulu, Samuel. 1994. "How Ghanaian is Ghanaian English?" *English Today* 10 (2): 25–29.

Appadurai, Arjun. 1996. *Modernity at Large: Cultural Dimensions of Globalization*. Minneapolis: University of Minnesota Press.

Ashesi University. 2017. *Ashesi: Transforming a Continent*. YouTube video. 5:03. https://www.youtube.com/watch?v=V4ETDY-8j2E.

Bawarshi, Anis, and Stephanie Pelkowski. 1999. "Postcolonialism and the Idea of a Writing Center." *Writing Center Journal* 19 (2): 41–58.

Boquet, Elizabeth H., and Neal Lerner. 2008. "After 'The Idea of a Writing Center.'" *College English* 71 (2): 170–189.

Boylorn, Robin M., and Mark P. Orbe. 2014. "Introduction: Critical Autoethnography as Method of Choice." In *Critical Autoethnography: Intersecting Cultural Identities in Everyday Life*, edited by Robin M. Boylorn and Mark P. Orbe, 13–26. Walnut Creek, CA: Left Coast Press.

Broekhoff, Marna. 2014. "A Tale of Two Writing Centers in Namibia: Lessons for Us All." *Journal of Academic Writing* 4 (1): 66–78.

Brooks-Gillies, Marilee. 2018. "Constellations across Cultural Rhetorics and Writing Centers." *Peer Review* (2.1: special issue "Constellating Stories"). https://thepeerreview-iwca.org/issues/relationality-si/constellations-across-cultural-rhetorics-and-writing-centers/.

Camarillo, Eric C. 2019. "Dismantling Neutrality: Cultivating Antiracist Writing Center Ecologies." *Praxis: A Writing Center Journal* 16 (2): 1–6.

Cirillo-McCarthy, Erica, Celeste Del Russo, and Elizabeth Leahy. 2016. " 'We Don't Do That Here': Calling Out Deficit Discourse in the Writing Center to Reframe Multilingual Graduate Support." *Praxis: A Writing Center Journal* 14 (1): 62–71.

De Herder, William. 2018. "Composing the Center: History, Networks, Design, and Writing Center Work." *Praxis: A Writing Center Journal* 15 (3): 6–22.

Doyle, Laura. 2009. "Toward a Philosophy of Transnationalism." *Journal of Transnational American Studies* 1 (1). https://doi.org/10.5070/T811006941.

García, Romeo. 2017. "Unmaking Gringo-Centers." *Writing Center Journal* 36 (1): 29–60.

Grimm, Nancy. 1996. "The Regulatory Role of the Writing Center: Coming to Terms with a Loss of Innocence." *Writing Center Journal* 17 (1): 5–29.

Harris, Muriel. 1995. "Talking in the Middle: Why Writers Need Writing Tutors." *College English* 57 (1): 27–42. https://doi.org/10.2307/378348.

Hodges, Amy, Lynne Ronesi, and Amy Zenger. 2019. "Learning from/in Middle East and North Africa Writing Centers." *Writing Center Journal* 37 (2): 43–60.

Huber, Magnus. 2008. "Ghanaian English: Phonology." In *Varieties of English: Africa, South and Southeast Asia*, edited by Rajend Mesthrie, 67–92. Berlin: Mouton de Gruyter.

Inoue, Asao B. 2016. "Afterword: Narratives That Determine Writers and Social Justice Writing Center Work." *Praxis: A Writing Center Journal* 14 (1): 94–99.

Jackson, Rebecca L., and Jackie Grutsch McKinney, eds. 2021. *Self + Culture + Writing: Autoethnography for/as Writing Studies*. Logan: Utah State University Press.

Jones, Stacy Holman, Tony E. Adams, and Carolyn Ellis. 2016. "Introduction: Coming to Know Autoethnography as More Than a Method." In *Handbook of Autoethnography*, edited by Stacy Holman Jones, Tony E. Adams, and Carolyn Ellis, 17–48. London: Routledge.

Kachru, Braj B. 1996. "World Englishes: Agony and Ecstasy." *Journal of Aesthetic Education* 30 (2): 135–155.

Lerner, Neal. 2000. "Confessions of a First-Time Writing Center Director." *Writing Center Journal* 21 (1): 29–48.

Logan, Shirley Wilson. 2016. "Review: Where in the World Is the Writing Program? Administering Writing in Global Contexts." *College English* 78 (3): 290–297.

Martinez, Aja. Y. 2014. "A Plea for Critical Race Theory Counterstory: Stock Story versus Counterstory Dialogues concerning Alejandra's 'Fit' in the Academy." *Composition Studies* 42 (2): 33–55.

Martinez, Aja Y. 2020. *Counterstory: The Rhetoric and Writing of Critical Race Theory*. Champaign, IL: National Council of Teachers of English.

McBride, Maureen, Brady Edwards, Samantha Kutner, and Ash Thomas. 2018. "Responding to the Whole Person: Using Empathetic Listening and Responding in the Writing Center." *Peer Review* 2 (2). https://thepeerreview-iwca.org/issues/issue-2/responding-to-the-whole-person-using-empathic-listening-and-responding-in-the-writing-center/.

McKinney, Jackie Grutsch. 2013. *Peripheral Visions for Writing Centers*. Logan: Utah State University Press.

Mignolo, Walter D. 2011. *The Darker Side of Western Modernity: Global Futures, Decolonial Options*. Durham, NC: Duke University Press.

North, Stephen M. 1984. "The Idea of a Writing Center." *College English* 46 (5): 433–446.

North, Stephen M. 1994. "'Revisiting' the Idea of a Writing Center." *Writing Center Journal* 15 (1): 7–19.

Osei-Tutu, Kwaku. 2021. "The Influence of American English and British English on Ghanaian English." *Ghana Journal of Linguistics* 10 (2): 84–102.

Park, Joseph Sung-Yul, and Lionel Wee. 2017. "Nation-State, Transnationalism, and Language." In *The Routledge Handbook of Migration and Language*, edited by Suresh Canagarajah, 47–62. London: Routledge.

Richards, Rose, Anne-Mari Lackay, and Selene Delport. 2019. "Space, Place, and Power in South African Writing Centres: Special Issue in Honour of Sharifa Daniels." *Stellenbosch Papers in Linguistics Plus* 57: i–xiv.

Santa, Tracy. 2002. "Writing Center Orthodoxies as Damocles' Sword: An International Perspective." *Writing Center Journal* 22 (2): 29–38.

Scott, Andrea. 2017. "The Storying of Writing Centers outside the US: Director Narratives and the Making of Disciplinary Identities in Germany and Austria." *WLN: A Journal of Writing Center Scholarship* 41 (5–6): 10–17.

Thompson, Rachel Akusika, and Jemima Asabea Anderson. 2018. "Perception of Politeness: Some Perspectives from Ghana." *Journal of Politeness Research* 15 (1): 101–120.

Tinoco, Lizbett, Lou Herman, Shuv Raj Rana Bhat, and Alison Zepeda. 2020. "International Writing Tutors Leveraging Linguistic Diversity at a Hispanic-Serving Institution's Writing Center." *Peer Review* 4 (2): "Researching and Restoring Justice." https://thepeerreview-iwca.org/issues/issue-4-2/international-writing-tutors-leveraging-linguistic-diversity-at-a-hispanic-serving-institutions-writing-center/.

Turner, Adam. 2006. "Re-engineering the North American Writing Center Model in East Asia." *Praxis: A Writing Center Journal* 3 (2). http://www.praxisuwc.com/chang-102.

Yao, Christina W., Crystal A. George Mwangi, and Victoria K. Malaney Brown. 2019. "Exploring the Intersection of Transnationalism and Critical Race Theory: A Critical Race Analysis of International Student Experiences in the United States." *Race Ethnicity and Education* 22 (1): 38–58.

7
Harnessing the Periphery

A Community of Practice in México

ABIGAIL VILLAGRÁN MORA

When I established the writing center at the Universidad Popular Autónoma del Estado de Puebla (UPAEP), a private university in Puebla, México, over a decade ago, writing centers were just starting to emerge in my country. As many practitioners outside of the US, I did not have firsthand knowledge of writing centers, and I learned about them from scholarship. A simple online search led me to the *Writing Center Journal*, *Praxis*, and the *Writing Lab Newsletter*. I also participated in one of the International Writing Centers Association's Summer Institutes and presented in conferences. Eventually, I obtained a PhD in composition and applied linguistics, and I focused on the writing center field. From the start, I found this approach to writing support not just suitable but necessary for my context. I anticipated a need to adapt some of the principles in writing center pedagogy, but its core ideas were akin to our needs in terms of writing support; I was particularly drawn by the promises of the one-to-one peer approach. Because many Mexican students frequently see writing as a tortuous and impossible task, as exemplified in a common saying "la letra con sangre entra" (writing comes with blood), peer tutors represented the possibility of resignifying students' relationship with writing, making it at least more accessible. Thus, allowing enough one-to-one dialogue and providing a situated approach to our support were my primary concerns as I embarked in creating the writing center. To that aim, my first task was recruiting and educating peer tutors so they could bring to life these writing center principles.

Throughout the years, the writing center tutors have been negotiating with these principles as well as with the complex learning cultures of Mexican higher education, and the ever-changing reality of our particular context. These creative negotiations did not necessarily produce unique results that can outline the difference of writing center practice in our context; however, they do showcase a process by which writing tutors can use their own learning community to create the practice that they require. More specifically, a writing tutors' community of practice has a real potential for fostering a situated knowledge initiative that can inform and guide an endemic approach to tutor education. Situating tutoring practice is an essential first step in adapting writing center pedagogy beyond the Global North.

As more writing centers emerge throughout the world, it is important to critically approach dominant scholarship (Bawarshi and Pelkowski 1999). Some of the most cherished principles in writing center practice should be put to a test against what is needed by tutors and writers in particular contexts and cultures. Tutors' voices, knowledge, and experience are key against the sort of orthodoxy that would turn tutor education into a set of prescriptive rules (Santa 2002). Furthermore, in approaching only the "grand narrative" of Western writing centers (McKinney 2013) one risks reading a single story that can oversimplify and misrepresent different realities, as Chimamanda Ngozi Adichie (2009) masterfully explains in her famous TED Talk "The Dangers of a Single Story." Although the heterogeneity of practice and the diversity of practitioners throughout the world can seem an evident fact, the international expansion of the writing center movement can still fall into a self-serving form of neocolonialism (Bell and Holston 2021). These emerging writing centers not only need to acknowledge the particular constraints and affordances of their context and learning cultures but also harness them. To partake in the global conversation without risking assimilation or neocolonial marginalization, practitioners in the Global South could highlight each center's unique learning culture as a situated approach to writing center pedagogy.

It is crucial to acknowledge the progress in writing center research and practice and, at the same time, identify the affordances of context and culture through which tutors adapt and create their situated practice. With that purpose, I focused on the endemic practice that was evolving within the tutors' community and used this knowledge to create a situated approach for tutor education. It has been a challenge to track a practice in an ever-changing learning environment as well as creating and sustaining a knowledge initiative for the writing center; however, applying the community of practice approach to tutor education has been helpful. My research on the writing center I direct in Puebla, México, indicates that the community of peer tutors can sustain a knowledge initiative regardless of the ever-changing nature of their practice. A peer tutor education model that is built from the inherent learning culture within the tutors' community is an important step in harnessing the potentials of a peripheral position and authorizing tutors' voices globally (Santa 2002). What I observed in the writing tutors' knowledge strategies is indicative of a community of practice. I used this social learning framework to explore the knowledge initiative created for and by writing tutors so as to better steward their education and to explore ways for other writing centers in the Global South, and beyond, to harness complex learning ecologies.

In the Global South, a historically imbalanced position with respect to the Global North can result in reinforcing a situation of tutelage and subordination for writing centers. The Global South is a relatively new term used to describe, study, and transcend the negative impact that capitalist globalization has had on certain nations, states, spaces, and people. It is helpful to identify the "periphery and subaltern relational position" (Mahler 2017) with respect to the Global North, in order to resist and counter it. This denomination includes countries south of the US border, in the Caribbean, Africa, the Middle East, Asia, and in the Pacific region. For writing centers in the Global South, being in the periphery of the Global North can become a statement of differentiated identity, a response to counter Western misrepresentation, and a voluntary positioning away from the homogenizing "center."

This chapter presents my research on the knowledge initiative that came about as tutors collaborated, negotiated, and created the writing center from their own community of practice. It provides an insight into the tutors' inherent learning culture and their continuous knowledge construction strategies as they participated in creating their practice. Even though this study is deeply rooted in its particular context, it showcases the value of collaboration and community engagement, and it highlights the potential for the community of practice to flesh out endemic approaches to tutor education.

Literature Review

The Community of Practice (CoP) framework was introduced by Jean Lave and Étienne Wenger in a 1991 cornerstone study on the different learning practices of midwives, tailors, quartermasters, butchers, and nondrinking alcoholics. Communities of Practice are defined as groups of people who "share a concern, a set of problems or a passion about a topic, and who deepen their knowledge and expertise in this area by interacting on an ongoing basis" (Wenger, McDermott, and Snyder 2002, 4). From this perspective, learning is not considered an internalized activity but one that requires participation. The first work to theorize about writing centers as communities of practice introduced a shift in the way writing center studies were addressing collaboration (Geller et al. 2007); the focus was not so much on tutor-student interactions but on the learning community that was established by tutors. A few other studies have used the CoP framework to approach tutors' learning. Mark Hall (2011) studied reflective-dialogic tutor-to-tutor interactions in a blog to explore how these interactions foster learning and reflection; Hall (2017) also studied how tutors' CoP engaged in creating a shared repertoire of "20 valued practices for tutoring writing." Additionally, Thokozile Lewanika and Arlene Archer analyzed how academic identities of consultants have shifted through their experience within the writing center CoP (Lewanika and Archer 2011), and Marcelene Senese (2011) used the CoP framework to explore the daily practices of writing tutors and how they engaged in learning from each other.

This initial research on how tutors learn within their communities of practice shows that this learning framework can be a helpful tool to elicit the endemic learning culture within the tutors' community and gain more insight into how they construct their tutoring practice, like the strong cohesion among tutors found by Senese (2011). This particular study explores how tutors use their CoP to construct a knowledge initiative that can inform tutor education.

The CoP Framework

The CoP framework is a system of dynamic tensions that can yield a knowledge initiative (KI) that encompasses the collective processes of creating, preserving, and sharing knowledge. Broadly, a dynamic tension between the individual and the collective is a balanced approach to learning capable of (a) sustaining individual agency and (b) fostering a learning community. This dynamic system ensures that identities and meanings are negotiated by the community in its own terms: a crucial affordance for fostering endemic learning practices in writing centers to avoid a homogenizing approach to writing, learning, and tutoring.

The tension framing the system is between the tacit and the explicit knowledge dimensions, which are mainly discussed by Etienne Wenger, Richard McDermott, and William M. Snyder (2002) but are also mentioned in Etienne Wenger-Trayner et al. (2015) and in various studies from the management field that focus on knowledge management (KM). The tacit and explicit dimensions describe the opposing forces of the individual and the collective as well as internalized and externalized knowledge; these major tensions are crucial in most social learning theories. Resulting from the conceptual tension between the tacit and the explicit dimensions, a conflicting negotiation is described when the two major dimensions "collide," reflecting a negotiation at the core of the CoP.

This tension between tacit and explicit knowledge is negotiated within the CoP in building a knowledge initiative. Studying such a process requires the researcher to compartmentalize in three distinct moments—knowledge creation, preservation, and sharing (Wenger, McDermott, and Snyder 2002)—which potentially coalesce into a collective knowledge initiative. In a dynamic system, these three distinct moments can occur simultaneously and are not always as distinctly differentiated. Understanding this process is necessary in order to steward and foster learning and agency. As writing centers continue to develop throughout the world, and particularly in the Global South, focusing on the inherent writing tutor community could result in valuable contextualized knowledge. This case study shows how tutors created a practice and their own knowledge initiative from a continuous participation in their CoP.

Research Method

An exploratory case study approach is ideal for focusing on a contemporary phenomenon in its real-life context. It is also helpful for exploring cases in which the boundaries between the phenomenon (case) and the context are not evident, cases that cannot be isolated from their contexts (Yin 2018), such as with the writing tutors' community. There is a value in focusing on a single case, especially for emerging writing centers in the Global South, because one single case can provide evidence of the intricate relationship between a writing center and its community, an individual and its community, a learning culture and writing center pedagogy, and so on.

For Robert K. Yin (2018), case studies are "generalizable to theoretical propositions and not to populations or universes" (10); neither the case nor its populations should be thought of as samples. The researcher should aim at expanding a theory through analytic generalizations instead of looking to extrapolate probabilities through statistical generalizations. These analytic generalizations begin by understanding what findings reveal about the theory involved. Then, the researcher focuses on what implications this connection bears for similar or analogous cases. The case study of the writing tutors' community strived to reach analytic generalizations through the CoP theoretical framework to determine how the writing tutors develop a knowledge initiative. This approach could also support other writing centers in using their own learning culture for a more contextualized approach to tutor education.

Purpose of the Study and Context

This case study sought to explore how the writing tutors collaborate to construct knowledge from their particular practice. It was defined from the perspective of theory, specifically from the CoP framework through the concept of KI addressed in the description of the framework and briefly described as a community's move from tacit to explicit practice, which involves a dynamic tension between forms of bringing about knowledge creation, knowledge preservation, and knowledge sharing.

The setting for this case study was UPAEP, a private university at Puebla, México. A typical class at UPAEP comprises a diverse group of students. Approximately 40 percent of them are from the state of Puebla, the fourth-largest state in México, only eighty miles from México City. Another 30 percent of students come from the southeastern states of Chiapas and Tabasco; and the remaining 30 percent come mostly from Veracruz (on the Atlantic coast) and from Guerrero and Oaxaca (both on the Pacific coast). Universidad Popular Autónoma del Estado de Puebla is a private university, but it is affordable for a middle-class Mexican student and offers many types of scholarships and grants. This arrangement contributes to building a large group of students from various socioeconomic and cultural backgrounds. Our college offers over forty different bachelor's degrees to approximately 9,000 students. Each year, around 1,200 freshmen enroll. The writing center at UPAEP was created in 2010 as a support strategy for students in the writing program.

Since then, it has expanded its support beyond an academic approach, and the tutoring services are available online for anyone who requires them.

As the founding director of the writing center that is the focus of this study, I have had a professional relationship with every tutor who has ever worked in the center. My relationship with the tutors could have conditioned responses and led to tutors opting out of the study. To control for these concerns, I only included as participants former tutors who no longer had a professional relationship with the writing center. Although some former writing tutors were still students at the time of this study, they were selected as participants only if they were not currently providing tutoring services for the writing center and if they were not my students during their participation in this study.

A group of thirty-five former tutors were selected as participants. Their work in the writing center was either voluntary or part of the 480 hours of social service required by Mexican law for every college student. These former tutors were eighteen or older at the time this study was conducted, all Mexican citizens who identified as part of the mestizo population. To participate in the study, their work in the writing center had to be of at least one semester and no longer taking place.

Participants in this case study worked in the writing center between 2010 and 2019. At the time this study took place, some were still studying for their BA, others had graduated, and some were working and/or pursuing a graduate degree. Their first language is Spanish and, even though they are all bilingual or multilingual, their responses for this case study were provided in Spanish. All thirty-five participants gave consent for the study.

Research Questions

This study focused on the potential KI through the concepts of knowledge creation, knowledge preservation, and knowledge sharing (Wenger, McDermott, and Snyder 2002). The detailed research questions for this case study were as follows:

How do writing center tutors construct knowledge from their CoP?
a. How do writing tutors describe constructing knowledge from their CoP?
b. How do writing tutors perceive their CoP in terms of knowledge creation, knowledge preservation, and knowledge sharing?

Data Collection

From a qualitative approach and a constructivist perspective, this case study sought to collect data about the tutors' community from the perspective of each participant using an email questionnaire and a semi-structured interview. To gain insight into the tutors' account for bringing about knowledge from their CoP, an email questionnaire was sent as a first step.

To gain more insight into the specific narrative on the elements of the KI, an online, video-recorded interview was conducted with a selection of participants, as a second step. The questionnaire sought to elicit a possible central narrative or story (Galleta 2013) that was addressed in the interview, as the second stage of the study. For this second stage, ten participants were randomly selected to conduct a semi-structured, video-recorded, online interview. From a constructivist perspective, any grouping would be a relevant source to study the CoP's learning culture and knowledge construction processes.

In the semi-structured interview protocol, I followed Anne Galleta (2013) to guide the conversation around a narrative or central story through three major segments (see figure 7.1). These move from open-ended questions that convey an account of an experience within the CoP, toward more specific questions that explore nuances and, eventually, connect with the theory and the KI.

FIGURE 7.1. The three segments of a semi-structured interview. Adapted from Galleta (2013).

The online questionnaire was open-ended and exploratory in the form of writing prompts. Table 7.1 presents the data collection prompt used in the questionnaire to elicit themes pointing to a possible central narrative for research question A.

The semi-structured interview questions considered the themes found in the questionnaire and varied slightly according to the story that each participant created throughout the interview. To account for these variations, the protocol was designed to weave a conversation from general insights to specific topics and concepts. The sample questions for the interview as presented in table 7.2 are arranged in terms of the categories for coding; however,

TABLE 7.1. Data collection from the online questionnaire

Research question	Data collection
A: How do writing tutors describe constructing knowledge from their CoP?	· Describe one contribution accomplished by your group of tutors that affected the writing center or beyond. · How did this come to be?

TABLE 7.2. Data collection from the semi-structured interview

Semi-structured interview

Research question	Data collection	Coding categories
B: How do writing tutors perceive their CoP in terms of knowledge creation, preservation, and sharing?	· How do you think other tutors made sense of this situation? · How did you know what to do in that specific situation? · What changes came about after this experience? · Did this experience translate into valuable knowledge for you and for the tutors' community? · Was your learning formalized in any way? (written, discussed, set to action...) · How would you rate the value of the community of tutors in terms of their contributions to generating knowledge? (1 = not valuable, 5 = very valuable)	KI: KC, KP, KS

during the actual interview they followed the narrative order in the three segments of the protocol, as proposed by Galleta (2013).

Data Analysis

I coded question A ("How do writing tutors describe constructing knowledge from their CoP?") looking for claims of knowledgeability. According to Wenger-Trayner et al. (2015), knowledgeability is defined as "the complex relationships people establish with respect to a landscape of practice, which make them recognizable as reliable sources of information or legitimate providers of services" (23) and ultimately translates into the possibility for a KI. These claims were identified in the data through actions that were perceived as impactful or as having contributed to the writing center.

The specific elements of the KI in question 2B ("How do writing tutors perceive their CoP in terms of KC, KP, and KS?") were already categorized from the design of the interview (see figure 7.1) according to these definitions:

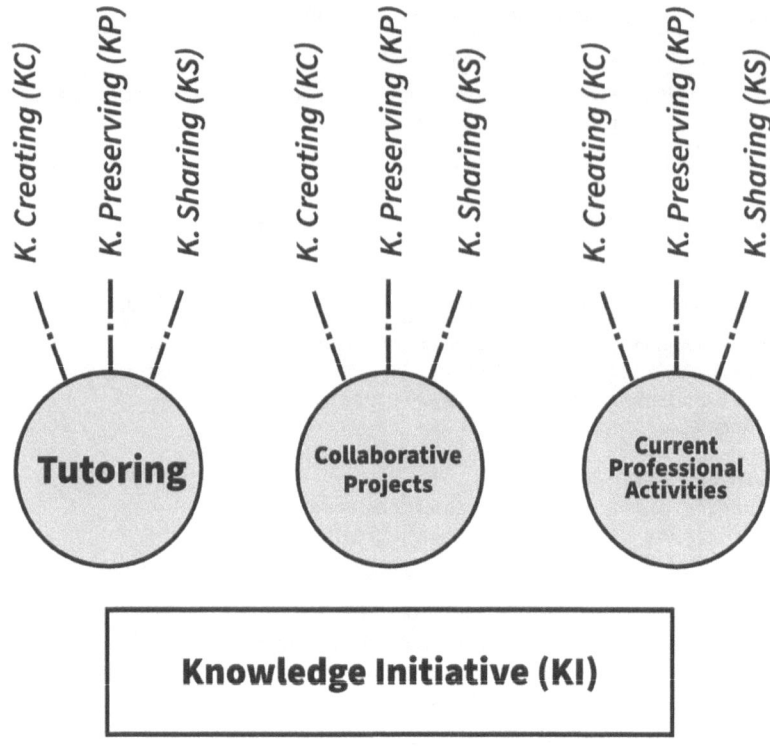

FIGURE 7.2. Coding for the specific elements of a KI within three types of practice: tutoring, collaborative projects, and current professional activities.

- Knowledge creation (KC): "the process of making available and amplifying knowledge created by individuals as well as crystallizing and connecting it to an organizations' knowledge system" (Nonaka, von Krogh, and Voelpel 2006, 1179).
- Knowledge preservation (KP): the selection, storage and actualization of explicit and tacit knowledge that prompts knowledge creation and allows for knowledge sharing (Davidavičienė and Raudeliūnienė 2010).
- Knowledge sharing (KS): involves the "intersection of personal meaning and strategic relevance" (Whalen and Bobrow 2002, n.p.) in negotiating what comes out of the community for the use of third parties.

Data from the interview were also coded for the elements of the KI. However, they were first classified according to the three main practices mentioned in responses (see figure 7.2):

- Tutoring: activities and skills related to the tutoring session
- Collaborative projects: activities and skills derived from teamwork undertakings among tutors inside and outside the university to engage with different groups of people
- Current professional activities: activities and skills mentioned by tutors who were already out of college and employed

Hence, a very important first finding is that each practice could potentially yield a KI on its own. Additionally, looking closely at their claims of knowledgeability, I was able to find interconnections between practices that were motivated by collaborative responses to challenging situations.

Results: How Do Tutors Construct Knowledge from Their CoP?

To develop a KI, the CoP focuses on knowledgeability, which places the attention on the "landscape of practice" (Wenger-Trayner et al. 2015, 23). In other words, knowledgeability establishes participants as reliable sources of their CoP knowledge also vis-à-vis external agents, while practice is generated and creates belonging within the CoP (Wenger 1998; Wenger-Trayner et al. 2015). By stating their perceived contribution, former tutors in this study considered aspects that identified them within the CoP and were valued outside of it.

How Do Writing Tutors Describe Constructing Knowledge from Their CoP?

To address the process of knowledge construction in general, the study looked at the tutors' perception of the CoP's knowledgeability. The main finding is that most former tutors perceived themselves to be knowledgeable in their capacity to collaborate in engaging external agents with writing or reading activities. Interestingly, in the questionnaire, only a minority of former tutors mentioned a contribution associated with the act of tutoring. The emphasis was on describing their knowledgeability as collaboration in getting others to engage. Responses focused mostly on the activities that former tutors did as a group, particularly in their social service projects. Former tutors refer to projects such as "Procrastination Night," reading and writing activities at Zaragoza Public Library, visits to various public elementary schools, and different reading and writing activities in public places.

The type of knowledge construction process that they described had more to do with creating opportunities for particular events than creating strategies for the tutoring session. Thus, a limitation about the questionnaire is that it did not help address the process by which former tutors constructed knowledgeability about tutoring itself. Nevertheless, it signaled the importance of collaboration in how and why the CoP constructed knowledge: to establish knowledgeability, former tutors refer to their collaboration.

How Do Writing Tutors Perceive Their CoP in Terms of KC, KP, and KS?

To explore the potential knowledge initiative in the CoP, it is necessary to trace the processes of knowledge creation, preservation, and sharing across the particular landscape of practice depicted by former tutors. In the interviews, former tutors' accounts signal three main areas where they experienced knowledgeability: tutoring sessions, social service projects, and their current professional activities. These areas are in line with the concept of landscapes of practice, where practice is extended to other communities, and participants are involved in different learning activities (Wenger-Trayner et al. 2015). Across these landscapes of practice, knowledgeability is a sort of currency that identifies members and is used to negotiate boundaries. I present results on how knowledge was created, preserved, or shared throughout the landscape of these three practices.

TUTORING

When interviewed about learning with and from the group of tutors and about significant lessons, most former tutors mentioned learning about tutoring from other tutors. This area in the landscape of practice describes all three processes composing a KI. Even if "tutoring" was not mentioned when discussing knowledgeability, findings show that knowledgeability translates to collaboration between tutors, which successfully produced a KI about tutoring. This means that tutors create, preserve, and share knowledge about tutoring. As newcomers, tutors first experienced the KI as observers who imitated and began to experiment with tutoring on their own. This represents a learning position described by Lave and Wenger (1991) as Legitimate Peripheral Participation (LPP), "an analytical viewpoint on learning" (40).

COLLABORATIVE PROJECTS

Collaborating with other tutors is a constant leitmotif throughout the questionnaire and the interviews. Most former tutors mention collaborating to engage others as the main descriptor of their knowledgeability, so it is understandable that the KI also revolves around collaboration. Most collaborative projects that were mentioned by former tutors were part of the social service requisites and involved activities outside of campus, such as workshops, reading activities in public spaces, writing love letters on Saint Valentine's Day, among others. These activities were created to promote reading and writing among different audiences: children, older adults, or general audiences in public spaces. No clear strategy of knowledge sharing emerged from the data about collaborative projects, even if they happen annually. This meant that tutors had to start from the beginning when planning each collaborative project. Nevertheless, relying on collaboration is at the center of their concerns when creating and preserving knowledge, even if a strategy to share knowledge is not observed.

Former tutors described their contributions in terms of knowledgeability (in the questionnaire responses), and most referred to their collaborative projects. So, how is it that they established knowledgeability in their collaborative projects but did not describe a complete KI for these projects? (Knowledge sharing was missing.) This omission points to the need of looking at the landscape of practice as a whole; instead of expecting a KI in all three areas, it would be expected that each area affects the rest while it is simultaneously nurtured by them. This means that the knowledge that is shared for tutoring could come from other areas, like collaborative projects, and can potentially be applied to these other areas as well. The concept of learning trajectory (Wenger-Trayner et al. 2015) can be useful to understand how "learners seek to translate learning from one part of the landscape to another" (43) as they move across their landscape of practice and progress in their learning trajectories.

CURRENT PROFESSIONAL ACTIVITIES

At the time this study took place, five former tutors were already employed and four had graduated from college. Findings show that former tutors in this study were also able to capitalize on their experience in the writing center for their current jobs. In this sense, some interview responses focused on the knowledge taken from the writing center and applied to these current activities. As with the area of collaborative projects, here the KI is also incomplete, as a knowledge sharing strategy was not observed. However, this is not due to an absence of knowledge sharing itself. Instead, findings point to a variety of positions that former tutors now hold where the multiple possibilities for sharing knowledge are out of the spectrum of their writing center experience.

Some of the knowledge creation (KC) that this group of employed former tutors connected with their experience in the writing center also involved collaboration and included people skills, emotional intelligence, responsibility, empathy, and teamwork. This translation of knowledge is expressed as finding similarities between the focus of the tutoring session and that of their current activity. In terms of knowledge preservation (KP), former tutors referred to two elements: owning a process and gaining confidence. Two different approaches to process came out from tutoring knowledge: a more personal approach to process was applied to education, and a flexible approach was used for social interactions.

Together, these accounts highlight how tutors have preserved the knowledge of applying one baseline process to different situations or people and made it their own. This knowledge is accessible for them whenever they face a new situation that requires adaptation or a consideration of different scenarios. The borders between different landscapes of practice are porous; this porosity points to a learning culture that acknowledges boundaries but is able to negotiate with them and even transcend them.

Conclusions and Lessons Learned

The unstable and ever-changing conditions in which the former tutors in this study performed were crucial, not just for creating a practice but for establishing the grounds for a knowledge initiative. So much so that these tutors' knowledgeability was developed through their community projects and not so much using their tutoring experiences. An initial application for this type of collaborative approach for writing centers involves thinking about the informal aspect of the tutors' knowledge construction process as well as its implications for decision making and for tutor education in the Global South.

INFORMAL LEARNING

A CoP approach can potentially be applied to educating writing tutors in a de-schooled, collaborative learning community, where they are encouraged to explore, create, and rely on the relationship with their peers (Illich 2013). This case study found that the CoP approach to tutor education can bolster such an informal learning environment with the added possibility of creating a knowledge initiative. By juggling the forms of knowledge that require direct management (explicit) and those that need a degree of informality and autonomy (tacit), CoPs combine intentional cultivation with active practitioners managing their own knowledge (Wenger, McDermott, and Snyder 2002, 12–19). Geller et al. (2007) also mention that supporting the tutors' learning culture would, in turn, empower them to support the learning culture of other writers. Much research still needs to be conducted to link the KI within the tutors' CoP to specific outcomes in the tutoring session. Nevertheless, building a tutor education approach supported in the CoP's endemic learning culture can empower a situated practice and potentially produce a contextualized knowledge initiative. In following this endemic and situated approach, practitioners in the Global South can benefit from writing center pedagogy, curate a particular learning strategy, and harness their unique tutoring practice. For example, when tackling writers who expect a very directive session, tutors often use various scaffolding techniques that they learn from writing center scholarship, but they also use strategies learned with other tutors in social projects, like connecting almost any conversation with the session's particular goals.

AN ECOLOGY OF LEADERSHIP

Acknowledging the tutors' agency requires relinquishing control in favor of a more student-driven agenda. To this aim, writing center leadership should be readdressed. The agency and empowerment expressed in the accounts of this study's participants proved decisive in their perceived capacity to create a practice and to claim knowledgeability. In order to thrive, CoPs should be able to have autonomy and control over their own knowledge management strategies (Wenger, McDermott, and Snyder 2002); therefore, too much supervision could be detrimental in this regard.

Nevertheless, a tutor's CoP still requires explicit actions to promote an environment of trust and empowerment and create opportunities for collaboration. Findings in this study also revealed that if a knowledge initiative is not intentionally created, any reification coming out of the CoP risks being lost. In other words, data show that even though former tutors created, used, and passed on valuable knowledge, because there was no intentional strategy to collect and analyze it, the knowledge was not preserved. Finally, an ecology of leadership would need to diagnose new training requirements that could translate into including other experts or leaders for specific learning purposes.

BEST PRACTICE IS INHERENT PRACTICE

Although this study is highly bound to its context, it is likely that other practitioners in the Global South experience similar circumstances when implementing their own writing centers. Different higher education cultures might result in challenging contexts for writing centers; there might not always be enough budget or even infrastructure to sustain a formal tutor education approach. Peripherality can also be represented as the constant juggling of contradictory expectations and an unclear institutional position, but this can be taken as an opportunity to take low stake risks for the benefit of learning. The need to adapt to constant change requires a strong community of tutors. This study also shows the need for more research on how to sustain informal learning environments and benefit from the affordances of peripherality for learning, even in more established writing centers.

Communities of practice can effectively create a learning culture to support writing centers, even in the most unstable of situations. As many writing centers adapted to keep their services going during COVID, it became evident that there was not much that could be taken for granted. Nevertheless, supporting a community of practice where tutors can act upon their own learning culture can prove to be a very firm foundation for the writing center as a whole. When writing tutors participate in a CoP, they learn about their own learning and the value of collaboration, which, in turn, can help them cope with continuous ambiguity throughout their professional careers. Fostering a CoP teaches writing center directors and tutors to negotiate boundaries and engage with tensions in learning and decision making. It is through these processes of negotiation that writing centers can cultivate agency and empower a learning culture.

References

Bawarshi, Anis, and Stephanie Pelkowski. 1999. "Postcolonialism and the Idea of a Writing Center." *Writing Center Journal* 19 (2): 41–58.

Bell, Stephanie, and Brian Hotson. 2022. *Writing Centers and Global Coloniality*. Accessed June 17. https://sites.google.com/view/writing-centres-coloniality/home.

Davidavičienė, Vida, and Jurgita Raudeliūnienė. 2010. "ICT in Tacit Knowledge Preservation." Paper presented at 6th International Scientific Conference, May 13–14, 2010, Vilnius, Lithuania.

Galleta, Anne. 2013. *Mastering the Semi-structured Interview and Beyond: From Research Design to Analysis and Publication*. New York: New York University Press.

Geller, Anne E., Michele Eodice, Frankie Condon, Meg Carroll, and Elizabeth H. Boquet. 2007. *The Everyday Writing Center: A Community of Practice*. Logan: Utah State University Press. https://doi.org/10.2307/j.ctt4cgmkj.

Hall, Mark R. 2011. "Theory in/to Practice: Using Dialogic Reflection to Develop a Writing Center Community of Practice." *Writing Center Journal* 31(1): 82–105.

Hall, Mark R. 2017. *Around the Texts of Writing Center Work: An Inquiry-Based Approach to Tutor Education*. Logan: Utah State University Press. https://doi.org/10.7330/9781607325826.

Illich, Iván. 2019. "¿Por qué debemos privar de apoyo oficial a la escuela?" In *Obras reunidas*, edited by Iván Illich, 191–213. México, DF: Fondo de Cultura Económica.

Lave, Jean, and Etienne Wenger. 1991. *Situated Learning: Legitimate Peripheral Participation*. https://doi.org/10.1017/CBO9780511815355.

Lewanika, Thokozile, and Arlene Archer. 2011. "Communities of Practice: Reflections on Writing, Research and Academic Practices in a Writing Centre." In *Changing Spaces: Writing Centres and Access to Higher Education*, edited by Arlene Archer and Rose Richards, 147–158. Stellenbosch, South Africa: Sun Press.

Mahler, Anne Garland. 2017. "Global South." In *Oxford Bibliographies in Literary and Critical Theory*, edited by Eugene O'Brien. Accessed June 17, 2022. https://www.oxfordbibliographies.com/display/document/obo-9780190221911/obo-9780190221911-0055.xml.

McKinney, Jackie G. 2013. *Peripheral Visions for Writing Centers*. Logan: Utah State University Press. https://doi.org/10.2307/j.ctt4cgk97.

Ngozi Adichie, Chimamanda. 2009. *The Dangers of a Single Story*. TED Global. TED video. 18:32. https://www.ted.com/talks/chimamanda_ngozi_adichie_the_danger_of_a_single_story.

Nonaka, Ikujiro, Georg von Krogh, and Sven Voelpel. 2006. "Organizational Knowledge Creation Theory: Evolutionary Paths and Future Advances." *Organization Studies* 27 (8): 1179–1208. https://doi.org/10.1177/0170840606066312.

Santa, Tracy. 2022. "Writing Center Orthodoxies as Damocles' Sword: An International Perspective." *Writing Center Journal* 22 (2): 29–38.

Senese, Marcelene M. n.d. *Peer Writing Tutors in Community Relational and Reflective Collaborations in the Writing Center*. PhD diss., Indiana University of Pennsylvania, Indiana, PA.

Wenger, Etienne. 1998. *Communities of Practice: Learning, Meaning, and Identity*. Cambridge: Cambridge University Press. https://doi.org/10.1017/CBO9780511803932.

Wenger, Etienne, Richard McDermott, and William M. Snyder. 2002. *Cultivating Communities of Practice: A Guide to Managing Knowledge*. Boston: Harvard Business School Press.

Wenger-Trayner, Etienne, Mark Fenton-O'Creevy, Steven Hutchinson, Chris Kubiak, and Beverly Wenger-Trayner. 2015. *Learning in a Landscape of Practice: Boundaries, Identity, and Knowledgeability in Practice-Based Learning*. New York: Routledge.

Whalen, Jack, and Daniel G. Bobrow. 2011. "Communal Knowledge Sharing: The Eureka Story." In *Making Works Visible: Ethnographically Grounded Case Studies of Work Practice*. Cambridge: Cambridge University Press.

Yin, Robert K. 2018. *Case Study Research and Applications: Design and Methods*. Thousand Oaks, CA: SAGE Publications.

RESPONSE TO SECTION TWO

Globalization and Marginalization—Nuancing Narratives of Marginalization in the Writing Center

Reflecting on Identity, Language, and Literacy

WEIJIA LI AND ESTHER R. NAMUBIRU

Prevalent understandings and scholarship about writing centers have come from a North American (i.e., US) "habitus" (Bourdieu 1991). For instance, the majority of writing center scholarship has been from the US (Kleinfeld, Lee, and Prebel 2021). Those understandings conjure "grand narratives," or Western-dominated stories about writing center work that either neglect (Henaku, chapter 6) or misrepresent (Villagrán Mora, chapter 7) the experiences of those on the margins of the writing center field. What most compels us about how Henaku and Villagrán Mora add nuance to the marginalization narrative is the way they reframe people who present as belonging to a marginalized group and show that they are not a monolith; rather, they have unique characteristics, experiences, and backgrounds that might not actually fit "the marginalized." We reflect on the tendency toward a single story when considering marginalization in the writing center. The narratives about the relationship between marginalization, on the one hand, and language and literacy in the center, on the other, need to be nuanced by considering personal identities and local contexts that impact writing center pedagogical spaces.

Like Henaku (chapter 6), our own identities also position us to dispute the narrative of marginalization. Yes, we are at the "margins" as two international scholars who have grappled with understanding the revealed and hidden

https://doi.org/10.7330/9781646426119.p002

(writing) curricular in American postgraduate programs and reconciling it with our non-Western academic expectations. We are also privileged to understand those curricular expectations through our writing center training and writing support programming. Further, as doctoral students, we have access to scholars and their research; we can ask questions directly and interact with the very people who study our international student population. And, being associate and assistant editors of *Connecting Writing Centers Across Borders*—a blog of *WLN: A Journal of Writing Center Scholarship*, we get to collaborate with scholars and practitioners and build our professional networks. Our linguistic identities are complex too: we both use English non-natively in our academic and professional lives, though one of us (Namubiru) grew up speaking English and is more fluent in it than her mother tongue. Thus, our stance toward writing center work sits at the intersection of our multifaceted experiences; our personal, academic, and professional identities are at once marginalized *and* centered.

The foundation of writing center work (i.e., one-on-one tutoring) essentially deals with writing as a literacy practice. Since literacy practices are inseparable from language, narratives around languages and multilingualism need to be reexamined. Writing centers are not attached to English alone as the language of input and production. At the Norman M. Eberly Multilingual Writing Center at Dickinson College, for instance, an international tutor who speaks English as an additional language might use a mix of their mother tongue and English to discuss a piece of writing in their mother tongue with an English-speaking learner of that language (Lape 2021). This approach is similar to what some international writing centers do: while facilitating English writing, many offer consultation in the local languages for writing in the local languages (see Kawamoto 2021; Lai 2021; Villagrán Mora, chapter 7 in this volume).

Another site where nuanced language is in the center could be relevant is opt-in programs, mechanisms through which some writing centers offer language support to non-native speakers of English. On the one hand, these programs bring visibility to the value of multilingualism and second-language writers in the center. Multilingualism is not on the periphery *in part because* these opt-in programs reorient and challenge the center's praxis to consider how the writing needs of these students are both similar and different from those of monolingual writers. On the other hand, we wonder whether these programs might perpetuate the narrative that non-native speakers of English mainly require language support and fail to show that native English speakers also need this kind of support (Eckstein 2016). There are other stories that we could offer here, but the gist is this: there is no one story concerning multilingualism and the writing center.

Let's offer one more look at language from the narratives surrounding Standard Edited American English (SEAE). Although many writing centers are embracing multilingualism and even encouraging all writers to use their varieties of English and/or their mother tongues during consultation (if possible), how might they remain creative and open to writers whose locally induced needs require SEAE usage? To wrestle with tensions between prescribed praxis and what is happening on the ground, in chapter 7 Villagrán Mora provides us a reflexive lens in constructing a knowledge initiative for tutor education based on an ongoing understanding of local needs and contexts. Villagrán Mora narrows down locality to her institution's geopolitical position (the Global South), the student body, and the daily activities in the writing center, as a way to resist the power of "grand narratives." Through their work, Villagrán Mora shows that languages (and literacy practices) are tied to locality, which affects the conception and operation of writing centers.

There is no one single story about writing centers. To emancipate us from grand narratives is to interrogate figurative ideation and lore of writing centers and rethink it as a pedagogical space for writing instruction, which is deeply rooted in language(s), literacy, and other contextual factors.

References

Bourdieu, Pierre. 1991. *Language and Symbolic Power*. Edited by John B. Thompson, translated by Gino Raymond and Matthew Adamson. Cambridge, MA: Harvard University Press.

Eckstein, Grant. 2016. "Grammar Correction in the Writing Centre: Expectations and Experiences of Monolingual and Multilingual Writers." *Canadian Modern Language Review* 72 (3): 360–382.

Kawamoto, Takeshi. 2021. "Hiroshima University Writing Center, Hiroshima, Japan." *Connecting Writing Centers Across Borders: A Blog of WLN: A Journal of Writing Center Scholarship*, February 12.

Kleinfeld, Elizabeth, Sohui Lee, and Julie Prebel. 2021. "Whose Voices Are Heard? Demographic Comparison of Authors Published in WLN 2005–2017 and Writers Interested in Publishing." *WLN: A Journal of Writing Center Scholarship* 45 (7–8): 11–17. https://wac.colostate.edu/docs/wln/v46/46.7-8.pdf.

Lai, Jose. 2021. "Intangible and Interactive Writing Center—Peer Tutoring Scheme @ The Chinese University of Hong Kong." *Connecting Writing Centers Across Borders: A Blog of WLN: A Journal of Writing Center Scholarship*, November 12.

Lape, Noreen Groover. 2021. *Internationalizing the Writing Center: A Guide for Developing a Multilingual Writing Center*. Anderson, SC: Parlor Press.

SECTION THREE

Embodied Marginalization

8
Tutors/Tutees Tango

Cross-Stepping [Dis]Abilities in Writing Centers

MYRA TATUM SALCEDO

I take a step forward to better hear the tutee.

Their space physically invaded, they step back.

Thus, we join in a dance to engage in the rhythm of writing. I risk revealing a hearing disability, and the student might later divulge a mental learning challenge in reading. We cross-step each other until meeting toe-to-toe, discovering that we both are visual learners, or discovering other commonalities. Our dance/communications halt when shushed by a nearby tutor for speaking too loudly. We feel pressure to whisper, despite Elizabeth Boquet's *Noise from the Writing Center*, which suggests that noise/volume can be both productive and transformative even while disturbing others. Therein lies the rub. Boquet states that their book asks readers "to consider the kinds of noise that we are allowed to make, that we are supposed to refrain from making, as we experience dislocations in our university communities and professional conversations" (2002, 6). Boquet even suggests that laughter be permitted. The grand narrative of a Texas public university's rules (in 2009)—which still holds today in 2023—states that whispering is essential in open cubicles and that, for the writing center, no hands of a tutor should touch a pencil to a paper during a writing session, even if the student requests such aid, because "non-directive engagement is encouraged." In other words, direct engagement is discouraged, no matter the tutee's needs or requests.

Born with a rare genetic bilateral hearing loss, I struggle to communicate in an environment that often requires near silence. Americans with Disabilities Act (ADA) protections do not address my decibel loss, due to a one-size-fits-all narrative. Rebecca Day Babcock, in her 2011 article "Interpreting Writing Center Tutorials with College-Level Deaf Students," did not consider decibel level or frequency levels of hearing loss in her study, as these are audist concepts (Lane 1992) in which hearing is the norm and deafness is described by the deviation from that norm. This is especially significant when approximately 15 percent of American adults (37.5 million) aged eighteen and older report hearing challenges, according to the National Institutes of Health (NIH) in 2023. While much of academic discourse focuses on accommodating the physical and mental challenges of students, little scholarship considers writing center tutors as the "text." In other words, now that you realize I have a disability, how do you "read" me?

Hearing impairment is part of my identity. I follow the lead of scholar Mark Mossman, who in his work states, "As a disabled person I plan to write this essay through the prism of personal experience and autobiographical information" (2002, 645). With the best global hearing technology in the twenty-first century—my custom-made hearing aids are produced in Sweden—I can achieve hearing and decipher 85 percent of sound. This means that I do not hear about 15 percent of the time, especially human speech (low tones, known as reverse hearing loss). The NIH statistics indicate that the realm of disabilities encompass a wide range. Accommodations should be fluid and addressed on a case-by-case basis.

Advocating largely for faculty and students with mental challenges, Margaret Price (2014) asserts that many mentally ill students and colleagues are "good at academic work, although the opportunity—or rather, the privilege—we have to engage in that work varies widely" (1). Price notes that individuals who make their disabilities explicitly known are not often on tenure tracks.

In his foreword to Price's book, Tobin Siebers (2014) states that educators not meeting the requirements of the status quo "exist at the margins of the schools as adjuncts, or as independent scholars, finding the entrance of education barred by the fact that they do not measure up to narrow and unspoken standards" (xiii). This description resonates with Simi Linton's description of someone with a disability as isolating the disabled person even more "like a guest invited to a party but never introduced" (2008, 88). I grasped—as a child in grade school—that a hierarchy of abilities existed. When the teacher asked: "Who cannot see the blackboard?" I learned to shoot up my hand in order to gain a seat near the teacher's desk in the front row when not hearing was considered woolgathering or not putting on my "listening ears." I had twenty-twenty vision. However, as a second grader, I already learned to feign squinting to be moved forward within hearing range of an instructor.

My disability is hidden, not unlike those with mental issues. I construct my ethos during the semester in much the same way that tutees build up their own reading and writing skills. I recently conducted a study on diversity at a Texas Hispanic-Serving Institution's tutoring center. It revealed that speaking a language other than English was accommodated; however, few tutors and tutees acknowledge how to assist students with physical or learning disabilities. One tutor stated: "We have a desk for a wheelchair."

More needs to be done to create awareness that abilities/challenges may not be visible. As a Texas university writing center tutor in 2009, I was asked not only to tone down my voice but also to not divulge my disability lest it diminish my authority and credibility with a tutee, as if this diminished my intelligence. This prohibition reflects a rhetoric of masculinity/authority rather than one of collaboration. I prefer to see tutors and tutees as partners in a tango. Garcia, in her chapter (chapter 10 in this collection), relates a yearning to "preserve the image of the academic I thought I would be and thought that admitting my limitations would be a sign of incompetence." Nonetheless, limitations and sites for growth should be addressed. Sarah A. Muceck's (2017) chapter, "Identity and the Disabled Tutor," in *Writing Centers and Disability* describes how a tutor who is deaf and wears hearing aids works to engage students in identifying her as a whole person, not just as someone hearing impaired (117).

It is often the average decibel of human speech where my hearing declines; the moment I need increased volume or repetition of a comment or question, I need to divulge what students often perceive as a loss. Brenda Jo Brueggemann and Debra A. Moddelmog (2002) state that when they tell students they are nearly deaf but adept at reading lips, it "risks that the academic may explode into the personal. Suddenly a precarious gap between facilitator/tutee opens up" (314). All at once, the facilitator has a body. Mossman (2002) conducted an experiment in which he waited until the final day of a semester to reveal a previously hidden prosthetic leg by wearing shorts for the first time. Mossman explained how his dynamic changed in the classroom with "its exterior physical constitution changed, became different, directly changed my interior self." He perceived that his students' new perception of him made his body "an event, a hot site of cultural activity . . . in a single moment were narratives of disability" (653). I have no such luxury to build up an ethos with students or to later reveal a disability with students at the end of the semester. Instead, the first time that I do not hear a student's question, often on the first day of class, I may respond to the question with an answer that does not correspond to the question. Laughter ensues, and I must step into the breach to explain that I did not clearly hear the question, and enunciation is significant. In that moment, I must come out as differently abled.

While there is some scholarship on tutoring deaf students, there is no middle ground for the hearing-impaired tutors or tutees who live in some gray area—a periphery of the hearing and nonhearing world. Hearing challenges exist on the margins of extreme definitions and thrive on a timeline of variations—too many not addressed in twenty-first-century writing centers. It is time to include tutor and instructor narratives of disability in tutor training.

One West Texas university offers enclosed glass-walled rooms for those who may need to raise the volume of their voices or others who need a modicum of quieter space in a bustling environment. For too long, nondirective approaches are reified through academic language designating what is appropriate engagement in a writing center. Graciously, at the behest of Babcock, the Literature and Languages Department at the same Texas public university, provided free face masks during the pandemic with clear panels revealing mouths for anyone who needed to read lips. There is no singular accommodation to assist everyone. One size does not fit many. Rigid rules (in some writing centers) address a standard of an ambiguous "norm." Garcia notes that even with the Americans with Disabilities Act in place, the protections aren't enough (chapter 10 in this collection). Mia Mingus states in an online reiteration of conference remarks (2017, n.p.): "It [accessibility] has looked like friendships that expect me to do all the work to educate them on disability and engage in conversations about disability and ableism. It has looked like a lifetime of supporting 'my communities' in 'their work' and them never showing up for anything related to disability."

My ethos as an educator merges with the development of my students as communicators. I agree with scholars who profess that teaching does not solve problems so much as articulate them and provide methods that can lead to solutions. Sometimes this may occur after a gap is created into which the problem falls. This gap, however, can serve as a juncture where inquiry and academic discourse can meet, where we acknowledge our own communication adaptations, successes, and fallibilities. How the teacher facilitates students in filling in this gap for themselves is the challenge; this is because there will be moments when no one dancer takes the lead in a tango. They cross-step together. Missteps can occur. However, the dancers can put one step forward, traversing intellectual and lived-in narratives to move beyond the periphery of the rigid rule-based and painted-on footprints of a floor model of the "correct" steps.

Sometimes I step forward and the tutee does not step back.

Yet, we may dance, side to side.

References

Babcock, Rebecca Day. 2011. "Interpreting Writing Center Tutorials with College-Level Deaf Students." *Linguistics and Education* 22, (2): 95–117.

Boquet, Elizabeth H. 2002. *Noise from the Writing Center*. Logan: Utah State University Press.

Brueggemann, Brenda Jo, and Debra A. Moddelmog. 2002. "Coming Out Pedagogy: Risking Identity and in Language Identity in Composition and Literature Classrooms." *Pedagogy*, 2 (3): 311–335.

Lane, Harlan. 1992. *The Mask of Benevolence: Disabling the Deaf Community*. San Diego: DawnSignPress.

Linton, Simi. 1998. *Claiming Disability: Knowledge and Identity*. New York: NYU Press.

Mingus, Mia. 2017. "Access Intimacy, Interdependence and Disability Justice." Conference remarks on the April 11, 2017, Paul K. Longmore Lecture on Disability Studies, Transformative Access Project (osu.edu), San Francisco, https://leavingevidence.wordpress.com/2017/04/12/access-intimacy-interdependence-and-disability-justice/.

Mossman, Mark. 2002. "Visible Disability in the College Classroom." *College English* 64 (6): 645–659. https://doi.org/10.2307/3250769.

Muceck, Sarah A. 2017. "Identity and the Disabled Tutor." In *Writing Centers and Disability*, edited by Rebecca Babcock and Sharifa Daniels, 105–125. Southlake, TX: Fountainhead Press.

NIH: National Institutes of Health. 2023. https://www.nia.nih.gov/health/hearing-loss-common-problem-older-adults.

Price, Margaret. 2014. *Mad at School: Rhetorics of Mental Disabilities and Academic Life*. Ann Arbor: University of Michigan Press.

Siebers, Tobin. 2014. "Foreword." In *Mad at School: Rhetorics of Mental Disabilities and Academic Life*, edited by Margaret Price, xi–xiv. Ann Arbor: University of Michigan Press.

9
Cripping Marginality

Disability and Directing a Writing Center

KAREN MOROSKI-RIGNEY

Okay, I say to myself, *Sit down and write this article. Tell them what it's like to live in your BodyMind. Tell them why it matters.* Then, I shock myself: *Does it matter? To anyone but me?* Then, I confuse myself: *You know this is a thing for you, Karen—not being able to understand innately what other people want from you. Are you psyching yourself out or are you reading the room?* Then, I steel myself: *Just begin at the beginning.*

How can I begin at the beginning? My brain doesn't do beginnings—it does webs, constellations, hurricanes, lotus flowers, mandalas, messes, miracles. And it doesn't pre-plan: the words come out, whether verbal or typed, without my being able to conceive them in my mind's eye beforehand. It's a very all-or-nothing brain, this brain of mine, and while I've learned to work with it over time, it certainly defies the normate structures of how to approach writing an article about . . . of all things . . . my brain. If you've read other things I've published, then you know I *can* "do things" the way you're used to seeing them done—linear progressions, smooth transitions, scaffolded arguments—but this time, I think I'd like to be a little more, well, me.

Lately, I've been doing quite a bit of this: by writing both through myself—as a disabled person—and about myself; by bringing together my

https://doi.org/10.7330/9781646426119.c009

own life with the theory and scholarship that help me to understand it, I hope to create something that will help us better understand the following questions (I am not arrogant enough to think we can fully answer them):

- How do disability and academia interface, creating a unique nexus of marginality?
- Why are disabled writing center practitioners underrepresented in our field?
- How does having an invisible disability make writing center work challenging?
- What can we do to foster disability justice in our work?

****

I am both autistic (autistic spectrum disorder, or ASD) and have attention deficit hyperactivity disorder (ADHD), which means my mind is regularly a hurricane of minutiae and stimuli, and I am forever sifting through it just to get to each singular moment in time where I am able to engage a world beyond my body. I am easily overstimulated, meaning that my BodyMind can't always assess which sensations, thoughts, sounds, and so on to notice most, and I don't think in linear ways. As a disabled writing center (associate) director, I am keenly aware of my *difference*. I am especially aware, in part, because my autism makes me aware. I live in a world of delineations and boundaries, a world where my need for clarity extends beyond a desire to check boxes and into a way for me to bring theory of mind into my work: *What—really—am I supposed to be doing?*

For a neurodivergent person (ASD and ADHD),[1] the open-ended world of writing center administration is both socially and professionally exhausting: the day-to-day minutiae of running a writing center is difficult for a person with executive dysfunction[2] and who struggles with both task-switching and much high-octane social interaction;[3] meanwhile, the open waters of imagination, developing programming, publishing, and so forth are just not structured enough to feel safe or reliable to me—though I still do them. My ADHD makes the minutiae of management an all-or-nothing focus jamboree; my ASD makes the flexibility and people-work of the writing center completely draining. And both conditions intensify the nebulous potentiality of writing center work, which is both liberating—*Flexibility! Self-determination!*—and terrifying: *Who am I? What am I? How will I know if I'm doing well?* This type of back and forth creates, for me, a lifestyle shaped entirely by cycles of extreme energy depletion and recovery.

While there are surely other directors like me, I don't know of any. The silence surrounding disabled writing center professionals may well stem from the fact that the general, ableist oeuvre of the Cheerful, Helpful Writing Center Person puts such pressure on the task of passing as neurotypical, as comfortable. It's too hard (and too professionally risky) to tell anybody about my neurodivergent brain, so for most of my career I've hidden it. My ability to mask ensures that I am congenial, calm, pleasant, even.[4] By default, I enact what Jay Dolmage (2017) has called "allegiance to a respectable form of ableist rhetoric—or ableist apologia" (45) in which I have so far spent my time and energy attempting to succeed by the standard markers of our field: I'm active in our field as a board member, a journal and book editor, a mentor, a writer, an invited speaker. I'm succeeding, right? Dolmage cautions: "If faculty and students can be seen to just try to accommodate some of the time, to play along with the game of accessibility and inclusion, they know that their own intelligence, ways of learning, and embodiment can be kept safe from stigmatization, can be unaltered and unexamined" (46). Masking keeps me safe.[5]

My writing this article is a first step toward rejecting that safety—it is a "coming out," of sorts, and a "coming toward" somewhere new.

But where? There is no room for disability within writing center work. Not for physical disability: no audiobooks, sprawling conferences, few virtual events, rare instances of translators or accommodations support. And not for invisible disability, either: as a field, writing centers' constant reaffirmation of power diffusion, face-to-face consultations, sociability, flexibility, and task-switching exiles those of us who wince at the pressure of so much interaction. Despite our best intentions to create an open-ended field, ripe for creation, I posit we have instead made a space where those who struggle to *know* in traditional ways cannot *be known* by our colleagues. Instead, we exist in the margins. I bet you don't even realize we're there, because we're trying so hard to act like we're just like you. In *Rhetorics of Overcoming: Rewriting Narratives of Disability and Accessibility in Writing Studies* (2021), Allison Hitt notes that "writing center discourses have reinforced rhetorics of overcoming by emphasizing diagnosis, particularly for learning-disabled students and autistic student writers" (97) and, I would posit, administrators. This marginalia is both dangerous and devastating, a rhetorical device intended to define, deplete, and deplace narratives that do not suit the warm, purportedly compassionate embrace of the writing center as an idea . . . unless the object of the device can find a way to overcome their own existence. Margaret Price (2011) aptly puts it thus: "Rhetoric is not simply the words we speak or write or sign, nor is it simply what we look like or sound like. It is who we are, and beyond that, it is *who we are allowed to be*" (27).

My experiences—including my difficulties—underscore the ways in which *my* grand narrative is different from that of the traditional "successful" writing center practitioner. I am writing this article as a longform demand: Please, let me be who I am.

Of important note: The symptoms and experiences of neurodiverse people are not unlike a buffet—not everyone has the same traits or experiences or to the same degrees. Throughout this article, I am speaking from my own experience and I am not claiming to speak on behalf of other people whose diagnoses are similar to my own.

Invisible Disability, the Academy, and Marginality

"Do I submit it?" I ask my wife, who is painting her toenails on the edge of the guest bedroom where my home office is housed. The cats are attempting to help. They are not helping.

"The proposal? Yes. It's good. Why shouldn't you?"

I sit and stare at the screen. I flex my fingers. I rub my heel on the seam of a carpet. I blink, hard, about thirteen times. I breathe a little irregularly. I stretch my shoulder blades.

I exhale: "Because then everyone will know. I can't take it back."

In "On the Rhetorics of Mental Disability," Catherine Prendergast (2001) makes a chilling claim: being diagnosed with mental illness or mental disability "necessarily supplants one's position as a rhetor" (202) and that to disclose diagnosis is to "be disabled rhetorically" (204). Hitt (2021) invokes this concept too, noting that "this turn toward diagnostic criteria as definitive guidelines for working with disabled [people] does more harm than good, as the resulting practices reinforce the pattern of diagnosis, accommodation, and cure" (97). I'm thinking about this as I write, wondering whether what I write will change what you think of me. Or if you'd prefer to cure me. I'm not the first person to worry about disclosing a disability to the academy or to their colleagues: "While the attitudes of coworkers and supervisors often create barriers for people with disabilities, their own attitudes sometimes compound the situation. People with disabilities are not immune from societal attitudes about disability and may internalize the same stereotypes and stigma as their nondisabled colleagues" (Evans and Brown 2017, 204). I wish it weren't true;

I feel ashamed that it is; I am trying to move through that shame and into claiming space for myself and others like me. But that work is hard. And in the world of writing centers, it feels uncharted.

I would guess that the reason we don't have a substantial body of writing center scholarship written by (*by* is the important part, here, not just *about*, though that is in short supply too) disabled writing center scholars—particularly those with invisible or mental disabilities—is threefold:

1. There is shame and stigma in disclosing a mental disability, especially if you "pass" as neurotypical most of the time.
2. The high-octane work of directing a writing center or working within one requires so much executive function, so much task switching, and so much social and relational activity that many folks with mental disabilities are precluded, from the get-go, from being able to carry out daily operations without extreme cost.
3. If a neurodiverse person does work within a writing center, they likely find many parts of the work difficult or extra fatiguing; they may not have the energy (or funding, or time in the day, or support) to sit down and write about it so that you or anyone else will begin to believe they exist.

And believe me, friends, the writing center is not special in this way. The academy at large has historically been an unsafe place for neurodiverse persons to make careers while maintaining their personal health—what Hitt (2021) has described as the "rhetorics of overcoming" (100). Dolmage (2017) wryly describes how "in no other profession is this stress better camouflaged behind other, supposedly inviolable, and more important, 'values' like autonomy, flexibility, and creativity" (56)—creating what he goes on to describe as "boutique stress" (56) wherein academics (including writing center directors) forego health or balance to claim some other method of self-determination, usually on the academy's terms and not their own. And so we wear ourselves down, proud of each new initiative generated by our writing centers, proud of each new campus collaboration or each new article proposal accepted. Only by burning the candle at both ends, with two other flames tickling our sides for good measure, all while loudly extolling how only as we embody the flexibility of melted candle wax can we truly respond with responsive, organic positionality to the prismatic and ever-changing demands of the academy.

Right. Okay. Well.

In my case, with each success comes the inevitable Autistic Burnout that concludes every herculean effort:[6] the home-run presentation requires a night of sitting in silence at home; the submitted journal article requires constant movement (stimming) for days; the completion of a major project takes my appetite and ability to sleep. Even still, I recognize the incredible (and ableist) privilege I have in that I *can* mask and thus complete my job responsibilities as they are originally designed, even though it comes at significant cost to my health—a cost that is invisible to the academy (and to colleagues in the office) but not to me or my family.

Even my willing engagement with this cost must be qualified, lest it be misinterpreted as complacency. In M. Melissa Elston's "Psychological Disability and the Director's Chair: Interrogating the Relationship between Positionality and Pedagogy" (2015), the author shares an anecdote about wrangling—successfully—with her own mental disability, but is then quick to add: "I do not include this story in order to contribute to 'super-crip' mythology, which builds upon anecdotal tales of disabled individuals rising 'above' their disability and overcoming it in order to pass as normative, thus contributing to and reinforcing ableism in the dominant culture's imaginary." I feel the same way as I'm writing today: I want to own the privilege I have in being able to mask and manage my task-switching and executive functioning well enough that my disabilities can go unnoticed. Not every disabled person will have that privilege. And the academy capitalizes on my having it: my disability—and the guilt, shame, and urgency I feel to professionally conceal its manifestation even as I disclose it to you in writing—will, in my case, rarely cost the institution anything precisely because I pay the toll myself. Price (2011) posits that academics with psychological disabilities do often "pass" as neurotypical much of the time—"Sadly, the necessity of passing for survival perpetuates the conventional view of the academe as an 'ivory tower,' an immaculate location humming with mental agility and energy, only occasionally threatened" (7) by the pushback of, say, someone like me. Usually, it's the other way around: the academy pushes; I move. The ticking is the bomb, in that I have no other choice if I want to stay here. And I do want to stay here—even if "here" often hurts.

Yes, the ticking is the bomb: despite the fact that all projects must, you know, begin at their beginning, writing centers engaging the project of ableism from "the beginning" will (and already does) mean retrofits, think pieces, and the oohs and aahs of many able-bodied scholars' misguided attempts to provide support that instead only further colonize bodies and accommodations. It's just: my body, brain, and BodyMind are my home. They are not new. They are not yours. They aren't publishing opportunities. They aren't checkboxes. I am not a CV line.

To be clear, the process of **beginning** is necessary, is meaningful, but also usually situates disability as *a problem to be solved, a pitiable deficit to be countered* instead of *considering disability itself as a creation of the parameters of writing center culture* that the field has designed for itself,[7] through "claim of not knowing, [which] is also, in a way, a claim that the ableism happening isn't really the case" (Dolmage 2017, 35). To exist (at present) in the eyes of the academy, disabled scholars and students must either become solvable or become invisible.

Why are there so few disabled writing center practitioners?

The first gesture toward a statistical understanding of this question might be, in fact, *measuring*—assessing, researching, trying to understand. But research on disability in faculty and staff at the university level remains very, very thin. In *Disability in Higher Education*, Broido Evans and Wilke Brown attempt to uncover what does exist, finding that "information as basic as the numbers of staff and faculty with disabilities working in higher education is unknown . . . and estimates are, most often, just extrapolations from larger population data about employment rates of people with disabilities, which indicate vast underemployment" (2017, 198). No doubt, there are at least two very clear reasons this dataset doesn't really exist: the shame and vulnerability of disclosure—which not everyone will formally endure despite a diagnosis, and the simple fact that the academy is staunchly uncurious about whether or not someone like me is *here*. This is, in part, due to a pernicious belief that disability is located in a person, not in the strictures of ableist workplace cultures. The (rotten) idea is that if a person can meet the measure—for example, get the PhD, secure the job, publish the article—that said person also (metaphorically) meets the price of *what the market will bear*—and that somehow, the cost of that experience is evenly distributed among abled and disabled people.

It's true that the needs of disabled writing center directors and consultants alike posit challenges to traditional notions of efficiency, productivity, organization, and engagement. Meanwhile, I'm left to ponder this irony: Why do the lives and experiences of real people matter less than a capitalist take on how we ought to carry out the work of helping writers take ownership of their own narratives?[8]

I'm here too, trying to own my narrative, just like a writing client.

Disabled writing center practitioners want and deserve to own their narratives.

To the institution, ignorance is bliss. Again, if disabled people are accepted or succeeding (by whatever metric) in the academy, then a general belief grows that disabilities are not incompatible with success within the academy. We stop wondering whether or not the expectations placed upon disabled scholars, teachers, or administrators are fair. It's easier, collectively, to *not know*: "This claim of not-knowing is also a claim to being a good person: separating the action or the implication from the individual. Because ableist apologia . . . are rarely ever personal apologies—they are apologies for a state of affairs, not claims of individual responsibility" (Dolmage 2017, 35). I don't think the academy is ready to apologize to disabled people; I don't think writing centers are either.

And so: there is little research on disabled academics, including writing center professionals, and there is no one person to blame but rather perhaps a structure that emboldens ignorance. It doesn't have to be this way; in this article's final section, I will describe the ways in which access intimacy provides more ways for the disabled community to be recognized.

This section is short, because it truly boils down to a very simple point: if disability can only be tracked when it has been disclosed, then the shame and stigma (and also genuine ignorance about what types of neurological experiences are actually attributed to disability) that prevent disclosure also prevent assessment of disabled people's needs, stories, or lived experiences. Evans and Brown go on to note that disabled faculty and staff "have the ability to provide counternarratives about the place of people with disabilities in the world" (2017, 199), and I am inclined to agree; however, only by identifying ourselves and then being assessed and identified in scholarly inquiry can those narratives be brought to light. Of course, I am not putting blame or responsibility on disabled faculty, staff, and writing center directors. I am simply saying that at present, the academy cares very little about if we are here or what we need—only whether or not we can do the job and do the job the way the university imagines it.

And for neurodiverse writing center practitioners, the job is a tough one.

Why Is Writing Center Work Difficult for the Neurodivergent?

Here, I will frame some of the reasons why neurodiverse writing center practitioners are either in short supply, never enter our field at all, or are already here silently in the margins, hoping you won't notice the ways we don't fit in.

Neurodivergent writing center practitioners who *are* here have to play the game—have to mask—and if we're doing so well enough, you might not even notice how hard we're trying. It is true that parts of writing center administration—specifically the executive function and task-switching tasks we each do all day long—can be taxing on anyone, including neurotypical folks. However, most neurotypical writing center practitioners I know find tremendous solace in the broader writing center community—a friendly, effusive, collaborative space full of networking and mutual support. And for writing center practitioners who are autistic or otherwise neurodiverse, what many see as the warmth and generosity of spirit that underscore nearly all writing center ethos represents a socially complex minefield. These social difficulties are where I'll focus my energies in the next section of the chapter, as I feel they are the least understood part of neurodivergence (especially autism) in writing center work.

On Autism and Professional Socializing

In Jackie Grutsch McKinney's oft-cited article "Leaving Home: Towards Critical Readings of Writing Center Spaces" (2005), the author notes that if writing centers are intended to be cozy, welcoming, home-y spaces, we encounter a significant problem. If we mark spaces with physical items we deem comfortable, "an unintended result . . . might be that these objects become prescriptions for these spaces . . . [but] 'home' is read differently by different people" (113). I'd like to extend this thinking to the socioemotional space of writing centers. The social environment of a writing center—face-to-face conversations, collaboration, reading out loud, eye contact, rapport building—are difficult for neurodiverse writing center practitioners of all levels (whether consultants or directors or anything in between).

Further, to cultivate job stability and career success (payment, promotions, respect, etc.) requires conference and campus networking, participating in social media and email lists designed to foster community, and creating a sort of "persona" that other writing center practitioners might gravitate toward in solidarity. And to the neurotypical person, perhaps these many points of entry into the community feel comforting. To me, as a neurodiverse (and specifically autistic) person, there are many times the warmth and sociality of our field feel prescriptive—as though you mustn't be a Real Writing Center Person if you don't fill your soul's stores of energy with memories of the latest unstructured networking event at which you talked to six strangers about their tutor training courses. Price (2011) writes, "A faculty member's performance of the required proportions of teaching, research, and service are often referred to as her 'productivity.' However, productivity is inflected by another factor, which may or may not be made explicit: collegiality" (113). She goes on to note that the American Association of University Professors' (AAUP's) policy statement's definition (American Association of University Professors 1999) of collegiality pushes against equating the term "enthusiasm" with "excessive deference," and notes that the AAUP emphasizes that collegiality should not be valued in ways that mask discrimination on the basis of race, gender, or class. The AAUP stops short of disability, however, leaving Price to do that work herself (2011, 114), recalling Lynn Z. Bloom's (2005) essay "Collegiality, the Game," which satirizes the academic culture surrounding forced socialization. Bloom suggests that mental disability will "hamper one's collegial efforts," and while Bloom is being facetious and Price knows it, the fact remains that Bloom is not wrong.

- If you struggle to make small talk at faculty meetings due to social anxiety or a generally autistic avoidance of unstructured social time, how will you build relationships on your campus? How will you get your dean to like you?
- If you attend conferences but spend each night in your room eating takeout because your autistic burnout is raging after seventy-two hours away from home, how will you find article collaborators or other ways to network across the field?
- If you never join the LISTSERVS, social media groups, or service organizations, how will you ever leave a mark upon your field?
- If you are not socially and emotionally accessible to your colleagues and your tutors alike, how will you generate the buy-in necessary to create a thriving writing center?

Most neurodiverse folks would likely find several or all of the those tasks very challenging for one reason or another. And if you were a neurodiverse person pursuing work in the academy, would you really seek to join a field wherein most of the measures of success or momentum require you to risk your physiological health? It's not for nothing that the academy—which, a little humorously in my opinion, provides a career-long haven to those of us who have intense interests and would like to spend our entire lives researching those interests (a spectrum-y trait, to be sure)—usually lets scholars work in relative isolation rather than in a traditional office setting. Writing centers depart from that more hermetic take on academic life in their pursuit of a research/community hybrid. I can see why the executive function, task-switching, and affect load of writing center work appeal far less than, say, a research position—even for someone who loves and values writing, writers, and the world-making done in a writing center.

I can tell you that in my own experience—I find these neurotypical moors of writing center work excruciating, and it makes me feel like a Bad Writing Center Person. I am most insecure about how stressful I find personal interactions or mentoring. Not because I don't care about my students; I care so much. But good, ethical, emotionally engaged mentorship requires so much "affect management" that it drains me more than I can express.[9] I am so hyperaware of my students' emotional states and growth needs that a day of providing engaged feedback can feel invigorating at the time but lead to hours of silence and stimming when I get home. I do not feel burned out by supporting emerging scholars; instead, I feel autistic burnout because I care so much about trying to socially, emotionally, and intellectually *get it right* and *perform it right*. And there's a real risk that sometimes I might not:

> Isn't it the case that a person with Asperger's, or anxiety, or schizophrenia, may unintentionally come across as dismissive, or even insulting? Isn't it possible that short term memory impairments might impede a candidate's ability to extend thanks, display knowledge of [the] unfamiliar . . . , and pay attention in approved ways? Are we comfortable treating these difficulties as dealbreakers in candidates? What sort of academic culture are we creating if the job candidates we accept are *only* those who can avoid outbursts, memory lapses, or outlandish coifs? (Price 2011, 120)

Even as I type that quote into this document where I'm composing, I sit with it and feel its sting. I know there are times my affect doesn't match expectations; I know I am seen as reclusive when I avoid work social events, or have hard boundaries about my time, or burn out by the end of a day. I know my need for breaks or to work from home seem indulgent to people who don't understand me. I know. I do know. I can't not know. It's the only world I get to know. Now, *you* sit with *that*.

I perpetually run the risk of being misunderstood, and the stakes are high—my fear of making social or professional mistakes guides my every move like caution tape wrapped around my heart. I'm willing to keep trying, but not all writing center disabled practitioners are, or can be, or should be. And what's more, very few neurodivergent people will be willing to tell you that they find all the things that bring others joy about our field *incredibly difficult*. To find community, socialization, and friendship difficult is, for me, the deepest shame wrapped within my diagnoses. Especially when I find these connections and relationships—which come at such cost for me—to be the most meaningful part of my work.

Which means, in short, that for me, trying to have a meaningful life often hurts very much. But to give up the hurt would be to give up the meaning. I wish there were another way.

There could be.

On Executive Function, Task-Switching, and Burnout

I won't belabor this section, as much has been written about the pressures writing center practitioners face to keep juggling about a thousand plates in the air at a time. I will note that as an autistic person, a lifetime's practice of masking has equipped me to manage the daily labor of my job, and the autistic burnout that comes with it. Meanwhile, an adulthood spent in recursive discovery of the self has also equipped me to realize that, as ever, disability is not defined by *how effectively you cope*. Disability is defined by what is hard. While it's tempting to believe that a neurodivergent writing center director's academic, social, and/or professional success means we've built a field that welcomes and integrates neurodivergence, don't be fooled. As I noted earlier, it's tempting to see the Successful Disabled Writing Center Person as proof that current writing center culture is *the price the market will bear*. Remember: our metaphorical debts are not the same. Remember the emotional, physiological, mental, and even, yes, financial price disabled colleagues pay to be here—and never forget that the structures and culture of writing center work enforce this cost.

Given the positionality of writing centers on college campuses, most offices are underfunded and understaffed—many writing centers might only have one professional staff member (it may be you!), and that staff member may be responsible for any and all of the following: developing a tutor training course, teaching that course, observing students while they are in practicum to become tutors, scheduling hours and tutors for the writing center, overseeing all office operations from ordering ink for the printer to watering the plants on the windowsill, to asking the dean for more money, to serving on university service committees, to handling momentary crises as they arise, to visiting the center on weekends to check on staff, etc. etc. etc.

Managing all these tasks is extremely taxing on a person's executive functioning. For a person with executive dysfunction, trying to assemble tasks into a priority order and then begin completing them feels like building a puzzle with all the pieces turned upside down (and only a hazy sense of whether or not all the pieces even belong to the same puzzle). For those who find this type of managing both the macro and the minutiae difficult, a writing center administrative role may not be a comfortable fit. With better institutional support (and more staffing), it could be.

It could be.

There is much that a writing center needs from its practitioners, and the work is complex. I have spent so much of my career thinking about what the writing center needs from me; I have only recently begun to ask: What do I need from the writing center?

Disability Justice in Writing Center Work

You know, you'd think this final section—this one where I talk about what I wish we'd do differently as a field—would be the easiest one to write. It isn't. I am heeding Jackie Grutsch McKinney's warning: Whose home? In this context: Whose hopes? Whose needs? I don't want to be prescriptive; I don't have answers, and I am not every disabled person nor am I our elected representative to this discourse. I do have suggestions, but I will keep them fairly short—while noting that there's much more left to say on restructuring writing centers to embrace disability justice and that you and I need to keep researching and writing. For now, what follows are some of my hopes for our field, and some ideas on how to get there.

ACCESS INTIMACY

In nearly everything I write about disability justice, I am drawn back to the concept of access intimacy. It feels like the way forward; it feels hopeful; it feels possible. In her blog *Leaving Evidence*, Mia Mingus (2011) describes access intimacy as "when someone else 'gets' your access needs." She continues, framing "a kind of access intimacy that is ground-level, with no need for explanations. Instantly, we can hold the weight, emotion, logistics, isolation, trauma, fear, anxiety and pain of access. I don't have to justify and we are able to start from a place of steel vulnerability. It doesn't mean that our access looks the same, or that we even know what each other's access needs are."

Access intimacy boils down to something very simple: believing one another and supporting one another. But access intimacy can only be made possible if we both create cultures in our own writing centers and in our field for neurodiverse people to disclose their identities/needs and then also respond to accommodating those needs from a place of dignity. I wish to voice my agreement, here, with Hitt, who writes, "Disclosure is not easy, whether you are a tutor, administrator, or student, and requiring disclosures in the writing center is both unethical and unnecessary" (2021, 120). Disclosure should never be forced; instead, a truly accessible space borne of trust and reciprocity should organically provide space for disabled people to simply express their needs and have them met.

I didn't write about accommodations in this piece—that's a story for another article. (Accommodations are the formalized ways in which disabled people are supported in engaging access on campuses.) But access intimacy suggests something deeper than a formalized plan signed off on in a sterile office: it suggests that we can have tenderness with one another. Real tenderness that moves beyond what seems traditional in our field and into genuinely asking what a person needs from us and then trying to provide it, without judgment. Here are some things that feel like access intimacy for me:

- If I don't want to attend something in-person, let me attend remotely.
- If I am uncomfortable in a social environment, allow me to sit it out.
- If I say I am overwhelmed, help me make a plan.
- If you communicate with me, be clear and direct.
- If you can't read my affect, ask me questions about how I feel.
- If I seem like I need space or quiet, let me have it.
- If I want to control my spatial environment—lights, temperature, noise—help me.
- If you plan to visit my office or space unannounced, give me a well-ahead heads-up.
- If I don't reply to your messages on nights or weekends, respect my access boundaries.
- If I seem standoffish or like I'm not playing ball, assume I'm setting a sensory boundary.
- If I tell you something in the environment is overstimulating to me, believe that I really mean it, that I am suffering, and that it is different from my having a preference.
- If you are finding that you know less about autism or ADHD than you thought, please continue to research, learn, and ask questions so we can work together better.

- If you think my brain, my boundaries, or my needs are strange, find it in your heart and in your vision for our field to make room for me anyway.

You may even want to ask yourself, whether you are disabled or not: What feels like access intimacy for you? You deserve this feeling as much as anybody.

Access intimacy addresses a person-to-person engagement with disability justice. Much more is needed to truly transform the work we do, and the points of entry into that work. Next, I offer some succinct strategies for fostering disability justice in your writing centers and then, lastly, in our field.

Transforming Your Center
- Include questions about access needs on your intake form.
- Provide training strategies that can accommodate neurodiverse potential tutors.
- Have flexible scheduling.
- Normalize stimming, fidgeting, movement, and self-care.
- Work with your campus disabilities office to foster partnerships and collaboration.
- Include disability when teaching tutors about intersectionality and writing.
- Write a public "Accessibility Statement" (Moroski-Rigney and Appleton Pine 2020) framing your commitment to anti-ableism.
- Hire disabled tutors and disabled administrators.
- Use accessible software, marketing materials, and spaces.
- Do an accessibility audit of your website, your programming, your training course, your materials.

Transforming Our Field
- Ensure conferences are accessible, including all print and digital materials.
- Provide accessibility measures for sound, sight, and mobility impairments at events.
- Consider invisible disabilities when thinking through space, formatting, table arrangements, and so on.
- Publish scholarship *written by disabled scholars* that fosters inquiry on disability and disability justice.
- Create Accessibility Committees in major field organizations.
- Write Accessibility Statements in major field organizations.
- Research and center the needs of disabled writing center practitioners.

These are just ideas, some of which are easy and some of which are hard. But each of these moves represents a way to bring disabled colleagues in from the margins—by publicly committing to better understanding their needs, by centering their voices, by fostering cultures both in your writing center and in our field that consider disability justice a vital component of equity.

It's funny: the same way my brain doesn't know how to start at the beginning, it also doesn't know how to end at the ending. For me, everything is recursive, turning into and around itself, becoming prismatic. While this style of thinking hinders traditionally held perceptions of efficiency, I think there's something remarkably hopeful about never quite feeling the work is done, over, or obsolete. I return to it; I return to myself. I hope you will too. The work of fostering access requires listening, hearing, reflecting, and beginning again, and beginning again, and beginning again.

There is no instruction manual on the "right" way to do this work or what, exactly, the work might look like—there is nothing I can directly prescribe. There is only your willingness to move toward the margin, take my hand, and welcome me home.

Notes

1. I will use the words "neurodivergent" or "neurodiverse" throughout this article to describe individuals, me included, whose neurology is nonstandard. I prefer the term "neurodiverse" to "disabled," because I think it prompts a different rhetorical point of entry into thinking of how the brain works and for whom. Rather than framing a nontypical brain as a disabled or limited brain, I would prefer to frame the nontypical brain as diverse, different.
    "The term 'Neurodiversity' was originally developed by stakeholders . . . to advocate for conservation of all species, since a high level of biodiversity is considered desirable and necessary for a thriving ecosystem. Neurodiversity advocates adapted this principle to argue that society would benefit from recognizing and developing the strengths of autism or dyslexia (for example) instead of pathologizing their weaknesses" (Nancy Doyle 2020, 108–125, quote from 109).
2. When I describe executive function in writing center work, I am referring to the management of daily minutiae, the moving pieces of administrative duties and teaching tasks, the unpredictable and multifaceted world of working with students, and all the other aspects of writing center work that are constantly in flux and demanding of attention, management, and memory recall. "Executive function, defined as the ability to hold in mind information in working memory, to inhibit fast and unthinking responses to stimulation, and to flexibly shift the focus of one's mental frame, is more or less the foundation for the intentional, volitional self-directed control of behavior. The cognitive skills that make up this construct help us to limit impulsive responses, to regulate emotions, and to avoid bad decisions that might bring short-term gain but longer-term problems" (Clancy Blair 2016, 3–7, quote from 3).
3. Being able to pull your brain from one task to another is task-switching. This includes being able to start or stop a task easily, zone into meetings or new conversations (or out of them, as need may be), or respond appropriately to unexpected situations—like

drop-in consultations or a student in crisis: "Task switching refers to a multitasking situation where two or more tasks are presented sequentially without temporal overlap" (e.g., Monsell 2003; Kiesel et al., 2010). Wendt Strobach and Janczyk Strobach (2018, 108).

4. Masking is how, as an autistic person, I put on the face I need the world to see: masking is an often-inadvertent coping strategy in which a person does their best to respond to the world around them or to social situations in the way they believe they're expected to respond, rather than how they feel inside. You might be thinking "Doesn't everyone do that?" Sure. To a degree. But autistic folks are less able to generate organic, socially "readable" responses to overstimulating situations. Masking helps give us the appearance of organic social response.

   "Masking encompasses the aspects of camouflaging that focus on hiding one's ASC characteristics . . . through suppressing, hiding, or otherwise controlling behaviours associated with ASC that were seen as inappropriate in the situation. The extent to which this happened could vary depending on who the person was with; camouflaging tended to occur less often with close friends and family members, although some respondents described camouflaging at all times" (Laura Hull 2017, 2519–2534, quote from 2525).

5. "Women with autism are able to apply the systemic nature of their autistic brain . . . to the study and replication of people skills in order to imitate and participate socially. However, the mechanical (rather than intuitive) basis of these strategies means that at times of stress, it may be impossible for them to be maintained" (Sarah Hendrickx and Julie Gould 2021, 33).

6. Autistic Burnout is an experience through which an autistic person has become so overstimulated or overwhelmed for long enough that all their sensory and affective systems shut down temporarily. People, this is very different than just being stressed. When I am burned out, I become selectively mute—speaking is possible but feels excruciating, sometimes for days at a time unless I manage to keep masking. Burnout can include a total loss of appetite or interest in daily life, can seem like dissociating, can prevent a person from carrying out tasks necessary to their own survival. And Autistic Burnout is not solely caused by, say, a crisis. Too many meetings in a day, too long under fluorescent lights, too much noise—any sort of overstimulation can cause this deeply painful emotional and physiological state for an autistic person. For me, it feels like my brain is short circuiting—which doesn't always require, say, a hurricane, sometimes it's just a loose wire. Still, power's out. "Autistic adults described the primary characteristics of autistic burnout as chronic exhaustion, loss of skills, and reduced tolerance to stimulus. They described burnout as happening because of life stressors that added to the cumulative load they experienced, and barriers to support that created an inability to obtain relief from the load" (Dora M. Raymaker 2020, 2, 132–143, quote from 132).

7. "Moreover, the university can never be viewed as the space responsible for causing disability. Disability had to exist prior to, has to remain external to, and has to be remedied according to the arm's length accommodations of a blameless and secure academic institution" (Dolmage 2017, 56).

8. Price pushes against this: "I am not arguing that mentally disabled persons can measure up to current 'standards' of academic discourse. I am arguing that academic discourse needs to measure up to us" (2017, 9).

9. In short, *affect management* means "fixing my face" to make my insides match my outsides. They don't, always, organically. I can be listening to a story with great curiosity and interest but look bored to death. Remembering to align my face and my feelings takes a lot of work and is particularly exhausting in long-form face-to-face interactions.

References

American Association of University Professors. 1999. "On Collegiality as a Criterion for Faculty Evaluation." AAUP. Rev. 2016. Accessed July 5, 2021. https://www.aaup.org/report/collegiality-criterion-faculty-evaluation.

Blair, Clancy. 2016. "Developmental Science and Executive Function." *Current Directions in Psychological Science* 25 (1): 3–7. https://doi.org/10.1177/0963721415622634.

Bloom, Lynn Z. 2005. "Collegiality, the Game." *Symplokē* 13 (1/2): 207–218. http://www.jstor.org/stable/40550628.

Doyle, Nancy. 2020. "Neurodiversity at Work: A Biopsychosocial Model and the Impact on Working Adults." *British Medical Bulletin* 135 (1): 108–125. https://doi.org/10.1093/bmb/ldaa021.

Dolmage, Jay. 2017. *Academic Ableism*. Ann Arbor: University of Michigan Press.

Elston, M. Melissa. 2015. "Psychological Disability and the Director's Chair: Interrogating the Relationship between Positionality and Pedagogy," *Praxis: A Writing Center Journal* 13 (1). http://www.praxisuwc.com/elston-131.

Evans, Broido, and Wilke Brown. 2017. *Disability in Higher Education: A Social Justice Approach*. San Francisco, CA: Jossey-Bass Press.

Grutsch McKinney, Jackie. 2005. "Leaving Home Sweet Home: Towards Critical Readings of Writing Center Spaces." *Writing Center Journal* 25 (2): 6–20. http://www.jstor.org/stable/43442220.

Hendrickx, Sarah, and Julie Gould. 2021. *Women and Girls with Autism Spectrum Disorder: Understanding Life Experiences from Early Childhood to Old Age*. Philadelphia: Jessica Kinglsey Publishers.

Hitt, Allison Harper. 2021. *Rhetorics of Overcoming: Rewriting Narratives of Disability and Accessibility in Writing Studies*. Urbana, IL: National Council of Teachers of English.

Hull, Laura et al. 2017. "'Putting on My Best Normal': Social Camouflaging in Adults with Autism Spectrum Conditions." *Journal of Autism and Developmental Disorders* 47 (8): 2519–2534. https://doi.org/10.1007/s10803-017-3166-5.

Mingus, Mia. 2011. "Access Intimacy, the Missing Link." Leaving Evidence, WordPress blog, May, 6:40 a.m. https://leavingevidence.wordpress.com/2011/05/05/access-intimacy-the-missing-link/.

Moroski-Rigney, K., and Appleton Pine, A. 2020. "What About Access? Writing an Accessibility Statement for Your Writing Center." *Peer Review* 4 (2). http://thepeerreview-iwca.org/issues/issue-4-2/what-about-access-writing-an-accessibility-statement-for-your-writing-center/.

Prendergast, Catherine. 2001. "On the Rhetorics of Mental Disability." In *Embodied Rhetorics: Disability in Language and Culture*, edited by Wilson and Lewiecki-Wilson, 45–60. Carbondale: Southern Illinois University Press.

Price, Margaret. 2011. *Mad at School*. Ann Arbor: University of Michigan Press.

Raymaker, Dora M., et al. 2020. "'Having All of Your Internal Resources Exhausted Beyond Measure and Being Left with No Clean-Up Crew': Defining Autistic Burnout." *Autism in Adulthood: Challenges and Management* 2 (2): 132–143. https://doi.org/10.1089/aut.2019.0079.

10
Please! Stop Doing More with Less

ELENA GARCIA

Like many other writing center employees, I learned early on that writing centers are misunderstood, relegated to basements and margins (Boquet and Lerner 2008). Amy Getty (2003) describes her experience at one with no funding, space, or support. Neal Lerner (2006) describes "haves" and "have-nots," or how some positions are reasonable and well supported while others are not. Decades of struggling to be seen as a legitimate discipline (Driscoll and Perdue 2012) have left a legacy that both creates and sustains the marginalization of writing centers and the administrators who oversee them. The precarity of our place in the academy has encouraged us to, essentially, martyr ourselves by doing more work without the aid of more support—doing more with less.

Now, let's compare this to the "grand narrative": the concept that writing centers are comfortable, iconoclastic, safe, and brave(r) spaces for everyone, including writing center administrators (WCAs). However, when I look at the list of twenty-five tasks that Jackie Grutsch McKinney (2013) shares in *Peripheral Visions for Writing Centers*, I am struck by their overwhelming immensity. Not only is the work to create such spaces substantial, but it's also incredibly varied: WCAs hire and educate tutors, mentor for conferences, write reports, schedule, field questions, do strategic planning and assessment, and do all the little things that keep a center running—and this doesn't even include teaching work. The reality of all this work remains hidden within academic institutions, despite the fact that our discipline is full of "anecdotal scholarship that tends to underscore only the difficulties of directing a writing center" (Caswell, Grutsch McKinney, and Jackson 2016, 6). For me, it seems that the "comfortable" writing center is instead a space where work demands often exceed the scope of both the compensation received and, more important, my own physical capabilities, similar to the ways Salcedo and Moroski-Rigney describe in chapters 8 and 9 respectively. It took my body turning against me to see the "periphery" that Grutsch McKinney (2013) describes. Many WCAs will do whatever is necessary to keep their centers going. Their care, passion, and hard work are commendable, but doing more with less is an ableist practice. I am using this narrative to share my new sense of marginalization.

The Price Is Too High

I'd always been an energetic person who loved working with people and engaging in exciting research. Higher education, and writing centers in particular, seemed the perfect place to find a career. I saw the hours being put in by the WCAs I worked under, and I felt I had the kind of energy to put in the extra hours like they did. Anything for my center!

However, around 2011, I started feeling muscle and joint pain. In 2014 I learned that I have a chronic pain and fatigue condition called fibromyalgia (FM). It's a tough condition to figure out and diagnose because there's no test for detection. A lack of a clear medical diagnosis made me fear that my colleagues and supervisors wouldn't understand the limitations of my body, which Shalene Werth (2014) identifies as a common difficulty.

Fibromyalgia takes a toll on the entire body since it affects the nervous system. For me, pain is widespread, muscles get tight and knotted up, I get worn out easily, my eyes get tired, and much more. The symptoms wax and wane, leading to a massive inconsistency in how I feel. One day I can sit in my office for hours, ticking items off my to-do list, and the next I might be completely disabled with pain. Some days I'm clearheaded while other days bring the dreaded "fibro-fog," a state where my thinking and memory loses clarity—to the point of having trouble communicating my thoughts. As someone who works with and loves language, it's this last issue that troubles me most.

Coming to Terms with FM

When I first started experiencing these symptoms, my initial impulse was to hide my limitations. Nicole Brown, an FM sufferer, states that "the decision about whether or not to hide a condition is . . . an act of self-preservation, information control and impression management" (Brown and Leigh 2020, 62). I wanted to preserve the image of the academic I thought I would be and thought that admitting my limitations would be a sign of incompetence or, worse, laziness. For me, the cost of working extra hard, day after day, is very high; it can take days for me to recover from overtime work. Moroski-Rigney (chapter 9 in this collection) explains this cost as "metaphorical debt," or the price paid to work within existing WCA expectations.

In academic year (AY) 2021–2022, I went back on the job market primarily because I wanted to live closer to my family. When I saw postings for WCA positions, I first felt excitement and then let down when I thought that I likely couldn't meet the hiring expectations. I had to carefully read through the long lists of job requirements, trying to discern the labor necessary to complete those tasks. I did not apply to many WCA positions because I felt certain that with my FM I couldn't do what the jobs demanded.

I know for a fact that I can't put in the kind of time (> forty-hour weeks) that seems to have become expected of many WCAs. For the sake of my career, I can struggle my way through forty-hour workweeks, but I suffer for it. I love working in writing centers, but I have accepted that I can't keep up with their demands. Institutions push WCAs to put in more time, to compensate for a lack of resources, and WCAs—through love, fear, or both—do the work. They sacrifice for their centers, becoming martyrs, but not all of us can do that. When sacrifice and martyrdom become the norm and the expectation, those of us who can't be martyrs are marginalized, perhaps being seen as incompetent, or lazy. It turns out that the price, that impact on my body, is too high for me to pay. It has been incredibly difficult to admit, especially to myself.

Then, when I would decide to apply for WCA positions, I worried about indicating my disability because "academia powerfully mandates able-bodiedness and able-mindedness, as well as other forms of social and communicative hyperability" (Dolmage 2017, 7). I am not able-bodied. I am not always able-minded. I cannot push myself to do increasingly more, because then I wouldn't be able to work at all—my body would shut down. But, as Moroski-Rigney states in chapter 9 in this collection, "the academy cares very little about if [academics with disabilities] are here or what we need—only whether or not we can do the job and do the job the way the university imagines it." Would "outing" myself on applications negatively impact my chances, despite the Americans with Disabilities Act, because I would indicate an inability to do the job as they might envision?

Please! Stop Doing More with Less

I know that many WCAs struggle against our history of labor; it feels like we've always had to make our centers work with limited resources. Many WCAs compensate for that limitation with their own time and energy, often feeling that pressure because of their precarious positions—I can certainly understand that. Academia is obsessed with hyperability (Dolmage 2017, 7) that, when combined with an absent critical conversation regarding WCAs with disabilities (Rinaldi 2015; Moroski-Rigney, chapter 9 this collection), makes it difficult to announce, let alone research and write about, our own disabilities. I'm fretting right now making my health conditions so publicly known. I worry that a potential collaborator or employer might come across this chapter, read it, and then decide that they would much rather hire someone who is willing and able to meet excessive demands.

As a discipline, we have been complicit in creating a legacy of martyrdom. The precarity of many WCAs (many do not have the security of tenure) means that, individually within our institutions, we tend to keep our mouths shut. I have been part of disciplinary conference presentations and conversations where troubling stories are shared about just how far some are being asked to stretch. In my experience, the idea of saying NO to doing more and more with less and less is met with clear indications that fear of losing a job or fear of a center being closed has led many a WCA to insist that saying no is simply not possible. There are some WCA jobs I would simply not be able to manage, not because I am intellectually incapable but because I simply couldn't work those hours. My disability has pushed me to the margins of a discipline that I love, a discipline that I could be part of if only the expectations didn't exceed what is reasonable and fair, if only I wasn't asked to do so much with so little.

References

Boquet, Elizabeth H., and Neal Lerner. 2008. "After 'The Idea of a Writing Center.'" *College English* 71 (2): 170–189. https://digitalcommons.fairfield.edu/cgi/view content.cgi?httpsredir=1&article=1001&context=english-facultypubs.

Brown, Nicole, and Jennifer Leigh, eds. 2020. *Ableism in Academia: Theorising Experiences of Disabilities and Chronic Illnesses in Higher Education.* London: UCL Press. https://doi.org/10.2307/j.ctv13xprjr.

Caswell, Nicole, Jackie Grutsch McKinney, and Rebecca Jackson. 2016. *The Working Lives of New Writing Center Directors.* Logan: Utah State University Press. https://upcolorado.com/utah-state-university-press/item/2981-the-working-lives-of-new-writing-center-directors.

Driscoll, Dana Lynn, and Sherry Wynn Perdue. 2012. "Theory, Lore, and More: An Analysis of RAD Research." In *Writing Center Journal, 1980–2009. Writing Center Journal* 32 (2): 11–39.

Dolmage, Jay T. 2017. *Academic Ableism: Disability and Higher Education.* Ann Arbor: University of Michigan Press.

Getty, Amy. 2003. "The Short and Sputtering Life of a Small Community College Writing Center: A Cautionary Tale." *Writing Lab Newsletter* 27 (9): 10–12.

Grutsch McKinney, Jackie. 2013. *Peripheral Visions for Writing Centers.* Logan: Utah State University Press.

Lerner, Neal. 2006. "Time Warp: Historical Representations of Writing Center Directors." In *Writing Center Director's Resource Book*, edited by Christina Murphy and Byron L. Stay, 3–11. New York: Routledge.

Rinaldi, Kerri. 2015. "Disability in the Center: A New Approach (That's Not so New)." *Praxis: A Writing Center Journal* 13 (1): 9–14. http://www.praxisuwc.com/rinaldi-131.

Werth, Shalene. 2014. "Working with Chronic Illness: The Modes of Working." *Labour and Industry: A Journal of the Social and Economic Relations of Work* 24 (3): 235–248. https://doi.org/10.1080/10301763.2014.961682.

11
Sign of the Cross

A Case Study of a First-Gen Latina's Experience of Marginalization at an Evangelical Christian University

DEBORAH ESCALANTE

> You are neither here nor there, but everywhere. You carry your cultura in your veins and academia in your heart. You have not forgotten where you come from, but you have earned and maybe even forced your way into spaces not meant for you. You are poderosa like that.
> —Prisca Dorcas Mojica Rodríguez, *For Brown Girls with Sharp Edges and Tender Hearts*

She Se Puede

When I applied for the writing center assistant director position at Azusa Pacific University (APU) in October 2017, I had some reservations about whether I would fit the demographics that the majority of their administration, faculty, and staff held, which was conservative, evangelical Christian, and White.[1] I convinced myself, however, that I wasn't *that* different—as the proud daughter of Mexican immigrants, raised with Catholic beliefs, I landed somewhere along the blurry intersection of their conservative Christian morals and my Catholic values. Only one month before I applied, APU had earned its designation as a Hispanic Serving Institution (HSI), with an approximate 30 percent Hispanic undergraduate and graduate student body (Azusa Pacific University 2020). Although I considered myself more of an inclusive liberal than a religious conservative, I figured that, if hired, I would not only represent who was lacking in APU's administration but also represent who was lacking in colleges and universities across the nation: a bilingual and bicultural Mexican-American woman with two graduate-level degrees (an MA in English and MFA in creative writing). According to an Education Trust analysis of the US Census Bureau's American Community Survey, only 5.9 percent of Latina women had earned a graduate degree as of 2018 (Anthony Jr., Nichols, and Del Pilar 2021); thus, I could only imagine what percentage of Latinas held roles as directors or administrators at colleges or universities, and what fraction of that worked as either a writing center director or an assistant director. If my being the only Latina in my graduate cohort was any indication,[2] I imagined the number would be extremely low.

When I applied to APU, I didn't fully comprehend how the intersections of race/ethnicity, gender, and cultural upbringing would affect me at a predominantly White administration and faculty institution. I had no idea how systemic and institutional racism represent real hurdles for underrepresented minorities, and even more so for those who work in writing center spaces, which are often marginalized and devalued (Hamel-Brown, Del Russo, and Fields 2017). It wasn't until I became a writing center assistant director and then director—and eventually resigned as such—that I realized my experiences at APU could serve as a case study for other writing center directors and administrators. In this chapter, I will examine how navigating a marginalized space as a marginalized person can heighten the sense of "otherness" (which can be compounded by managing disabilities and health issues) and offer suggestions on how to intentionally cross into areas of support for minority directors and leaders.

Jefa Moves

Prior to working at APU in October 2017, I had worked as a translation director for a federal contractor, an institutional research and assessment specialist for Brandman University, an adjunct professor teaching several lingual composition and literature courses for Ameritas College, and as a lead department coordinator for the English and Foreign Languages (EFL) Department at CSU Pomona. Throughout these work experiences, I successfully managed teams, trained employees, taught students, and created writing workshops. My bilingualism was considered a significant asset in all of my prior professional positions. Since most of my colleagues identified as Black, Indigenous, and people of color (BIPOC), bicultural, or bilingual, I always felt comfortable in a multicultural environment. Since I had years of training, teaching, and administrative experience, I wanted to take the next step and seek the opportunity and ability to diversify staff and conduct outreach to my community: *mi gente*.[3]

I had previously applied to APU in July 2017 as a writing center director and was eventually asked to interview. I considered my first video interview successful; however, I was notified I didn't get the position one week later. Despite the rejection, I was grateful for the opportunity to interview and sent an email to thank the assistant provost. Fast-forward to a few months later, and the newly hired writing center director emailed me asking if I wanted to apply for the assistant director position. The new writing center director was a White, evangelical Christian woman whose demographic reinforced the stereotype of the White, female director as a fairly accurate one, as indicated by writing center scholars Sarah Banschbach Valles, Rebecca Day Babcock, and Karen Keaton Jackson (2017) in their report entitled "Writing Center Administrators and Diversity: A Survey." I applied, interviewed face-to-face, and was offered the job. I was thrilled to represent a significant portion of the university's student body and excited to learn from an experienced writing center director, who seemed progressive in wanting to implement diversity and inclusivity in the department.

My first several months were mostly positive, although I chose to ignore some red flags, like the high staff turnover rate and the fact that every previous writing center director and assistant director had resigned after only one year. Instead, I focused on the writing center's mission and goals. The current writing center director took on a mentor role; perhaps it was due to her having a master's degree in linguistics or her decades of experience working with multilingual individuals, but she seemed to have a heightened awareness of my experiences as a Gen 1.5, first-gen college, bilingual Latina. She often encouraged me to share my experiences and background with the writing coaches and students we served.

I felt welcomed by the more than thirty professional and student coaches[4] working across the two main campuses and satellite campuses, and they were interested in learning more about me. I was transparent about coming from a Spanish-speaking home and learning English at around five years old. I never felt that sharing my background with them was a hindrance; on the contrary, I had insight into streamlining writing resources and writing workshops to engage multilingual speakers and identify confusing or vague content in handouts. Because I considered my bilingualism an advantage and never held a deficit view of myself, I never imagined that I could potentially be perceived as inadequate or incompetent in standard academic American English.

Despite my writing center director being mostly progressive, she succumbed to cultural insensitivity at times. One time, she expressed her aggravation regarding the constant greeting and saying goodbye habits of a self-identifying Latino graduate student who regularly came to appointments. She told me he didn't have to say hello or goodbye to her every single time he came in and that she found him incredibly annoying. I explained to her that in Latina/o/x culture, people who do not greet or say goodbye when entering spaces are considered rude or disrespectful. I didn't have to assume how the Latino graduate student interpreted her dismissiveness—he told me directly. When he dropped by my office one day, he said it was refreshing to see a Latina in a directorial role and that he appreciated my friendliness. He added that he always felt welcomed in the writing center by me, unlike how he felt with the director. She was, in his words, not welcoming and always gave him a sour face. As he told me this, he scrunched up his face with a look of annoyance to reflect his interpretation of her body language. As we continued chatting, I wondered how many Latina/o/x students felt unwelcomed by faculty and administrators in different spaces across the university, either through body language, words, or behaviors. I greeted and said goodbye to the writing center director every day too. Was I annoying her as well? Did my other colleagues feel the same way about me? My greetings and farewells had never been something I questioned in my previous places of employment. These kinds of cultural nuances add to the difficulty of minorities feeling like they fit in.

After a few months, the first of several significant administrative changes occurred that would impact my future at APU. The first change was that the Office of the Provost would promote the writing center director to writing program administrator, which involved overseeing all undergraduate writing courses. This potential change meant that the assistant provost wanted to discuss the possibility of promoting me to writing center director. Ultimately, I was promoted to writing center director in May 2018, six months after I first started working at APU.

Poder Structures

In Romeo García's (2017) article "Unmaking Gringo Centers," he discusses how topics of race and power in writing center scholarship often default to a White/Black paradigm to pursue antiracist agendas (29). This paradigm, however, doesn't consider the conditions, needs, or interests of other racial/ethnic groups, such as Mexican American student writers (32). García thus suggests writing center scholars "make and remake writing centers in productive and meaningful ways" (32)—and when I began my new role in the writing center, I didn't waste any time remaking mine. I worked with a graphic designer to remake our marketing materials to include images of BIPOC in authoritative tutor roles instead of as tutees. I encouraged international students to apply as coaches, thus diversifying the staff more than in previous years. I streamlined five resource website platforms into a singular Squarespace site to function as a "one-stop" online hub to improve student accessibility. Since I could finally update content via our new site, I added coaches' biographies so that students knew we employed coaches from varying ages, backgrounds, majors, races, ethnicities, and interests. In short, I wanted students to feel they could enter our space without feeling "othered." Visibility and representation matter significantly in student support spaces.

The first year in my new role, I thrived—and so did the writing center. I supported my team of professional coaches by creating a space where they could articulate their concerns and I could apply their feedback to improve our services. I also wanted to explore race, diversity, and language topics in the writing center by having professional coaches read articles by BIPOC writing center scholars and discuss them in our staff meetings. García emphasizes that "directors play a critical role in this type of transformative learning and praxis . . . and should be the one to initiate these professional development sessions and monthly meetings dedicated to such topics" (2017, 50). Following the recommendations of García to make and remake writing centers in meaningful ways, my objective was to promote listening "as a form of understanding and action" (50–51). One of my professional coaches, a Latino man, informed me that a few years prior, the writing center director, a White woman, had attempted to engage in these conversations with coaches, but arguments ensued. He suggested that having a Latina moderating these conversations might help them run more smoothly.

In August 2018, a few months into my director role, I hired an assistant director who had a similar vision as me regarding marketing strategies and coach training, and a commitment to diversity, equity, and inclusivity. Only one week after he settled in, we received some troubling news during the fall 2018 convocation: APU had hit a major financial crisis, resulting in a $10 million deficit. Unfortunately, this massive mismanagement of funds primarily affected faculty and staff by cutting department budgets, eliminating retirement contributions, implementing hiring freezes, and forcing early retirements and layoffs. In other words, the university would be significantly impacted in terms of budgets and what would eventually result in endless departmental restructures (reorgs) for the writing center. This included a 25 percent budget cut during my first year; a 40 percent budget cut during my second year; and, ultimately, no actual budget by my last year. Writing center spaces are frequently marginalized in and of themselves, but these changes would push me to the edge in terms of roles, spaces, and support.

As writing center directors, we wear many different hats to meet the demands of managing a department. Between three full-time individuals (a writing center director, an assistant director, and a writing center coordinator), we were still set up for success despite a 25 percent budget cut. We effectively scheduled six campuses, managed thirty employees, and held 10,000 appointments between academic year (AY) 2018 and AY 2019, the highest ever in APU Writing Center history. I had a wonderfully supportive team of staff and coaches, and we worked productively within our marginalized space. Despite ongoing financial setbacks, the writing center thrived.

By the end of my first year as writing center director, in 2019, the assistant provost casually mentioned the possibility of moving my assistant director to another department due to the financial crisis, but nothing was set. Two months later, I traveled to México for a family emergency. As I was checking into the hotel lobby, the assistant provost called to tell me that upon my return, the writing center would report to an entirely new umbrella, the Academic Success Center (ASC), and that I would have a new supervisor. I had no idea what this change meant for my department or me. I told her that I was in a noisy lobby with awful cell reception, so we agreed to end the call and discuss it further when I returned to work.

The following week, I returned to the office and asked the writing center coordinator where my assistant director was. With a disconcerted look, she informed me that the writing center no longer had an assistant director. I was completely dumbfounded. I subsequently discovered that during my five-day absence, the Office of the Provost had gathered several departments together, including the writing center and tutoring center staff—both of whose directors were noticeably absent—and announced the shift of reporting and structure to them. I was appalled at the lack of consideration and professionalism.

I called the assistant provost, and she insisted that she had told me my assistant director was moving to another department when she called me in México. In a slightly indignant tone, she added that she didn't know I would need to leave the country when senior administrators decided to share the news with the departments. It was like she was implying I should blame myself for my poor timing or need for international travel, even though a significant restructure like that doesn't typically happen within five days. It didn't seem to matter that I could have been informed a few days before—if not a few weeks—to prepare my team.

New Umbrellas, Same Sistemas

A week later, I met my new supervisor, the newly appointed Academic Success Center (ASC) executive director. He introduced me to the other departments under ASC, which included only undergraduate services. The reorg didn't make sense to me—our writing center supported a large percentage of graduate students, and it was challenging to balance their needs when being compartmentalized with undergraduate support services. In addition, my new supervisor held a PhD in mathematics, and although friendly and approachable, he admitted he wasn't familiar with a writing center or its demands. I wasn't given any guidance on restructuring my department with the loss of a full-time assistant director. I felt stuck in transition: a marginalized person trying to navigate a marginalized space.

As mentioned beforehand, despite an approximate 25 percent budget cut, the writing center held over 10,000 appointments in AY 2018–2019, the highest number since its inception, which meant my team had done an excellent job marketing our services. However, with the move to ASC in summer 2019, I had to restructure the writing center with a now 40 percent cut to the budget, which meant I was limited in hiring enough coaches to meet our new student demand. I couldn't hire an assistant director, which was the first time the writing center didn't have one, so I delegated some tasks to professional coaches and the writing center coordinator. The new structure wasn't optimal, but I didn't have many other options to stay within the new budget.

Several months after the reorganization, the university president retired, and the provost and associate provost stepped down from their positions. The assistant provost, writing program administrator, and my former assistant director all resigned that same summer. I was left feeling a lot more alone and with a lot less support. I was also notified that the writing center would be physically moved away from our location in the library and to a former men's dorm in an isolated corner on campus. Not only had the writing center shifted space in terms of reporting structure, but it would physically transition to an undefined, undetermined, marginalized space until further notice.

Due to increased demand and fewer coaches, I regularly worked over forty hours each week to keep up with administrative, staff, and student demands. I was also privately seeing specialists to control my health conditions, but my health deteriorated quickly due to high stress. My physician placed me on medical leave the last two weeks of December 2019 while a new administration was underway, including a new university president, interim provost, and assistant provost. During my medical leave, I contemplated whether I could continue working at an institution where I had experienced constant instability, exclusion, and marginalization.

On many occasions throughout my time at APU, I experienced microaggressions and cultural insensitivity from various administrators, faculty, and staff regarding my ethnicity and cultural traditions—far too many for this chapter—and they became more prominent as time went on. I think most individuals who committed the microaggressions and cultural insensitivity were unaware of them, but I cannot dismiss them as unintentional. Words are intentional, and so are thoughts—and, in articulating those thoughts, I couldn't help but ponder the bias behind them.

Most of these interactions involved faculty and university leaders, like a colleague who entered my office and visibly shuddered at the sight of my Día de los Muertos office decorations, saying she found my skulls "creepy." She didn't ask me about the skulls or why I displayed them. Another time, two Latina colleagues and I were jokingly referred to as "spicy Latinas" by a supervisor because we articulated our discomfort and refusal to complete a task that we considered unethical. During my medical leave, my coordinator informed me that the associate provost expressed her annoyance to the entire ASC team about my absence and for having to scramble to find someone to interpret from English to Spanish for a commencement event—even though I was never once approached or asked to use my interpreting skills from anyone at any time. It seemed that because I was the only fluent Spanish speaker on the ASC team, I would be told to offer such services whenever an administrator deemed fit. On another occasion, a White academic administrator would begin emails to Latina staff members using the term "Yo!"—a greeting I doubt she used when speaking to the president or provost.

I also encountered challenges when I wanted to support other underrepresented and marginalized groups at the university. The International Writing Centers Association (IWCA) Diversity Initiative (2006) states that writing centers should serve all students and members of underrepresented groups inclusively, including "people of color, lesbian, gay, bisexual, and transgender people with a range of abilities, economic needs, and linguistic expression." Yet, this set of goals is nearly impossible to accomplish at an evangelical Christian university. I was admonished twice by both assistant provosts on separate occasions: the first time, I wanted to promote inclusivity and a safe space for lesbian, gay, bisexual, transgender, queer/questioning, plus (others) (LGBTQ+) students when the university couldn't decide whether to be inclusive or exclusive of them (Reyes-Velarde 2018). I had casually mentioned my idea to my former director, who reported my idea to the assistant provost. Essentially, I was instructed not to rock the boat. The second time, I wanted to be inclusive of our Muslim and Jewish students' holidays by offering well wishes in an acknowledgment post on the writing center's social media page. I attempted to follow the proper channels by emailing the director of diversity, equity, and inclusion for guidance. My supervisor, the ASC executive director, told me conversations were held behind closed doors without his or my involvement. In a sheepish tone, he notified me that his superiors wanted me to stop and "stay in my lane." I questioned how I could continue to work at a place that went against my inclusive values.

I share these examples because these are common experiences of minorities in workplaces where the administrators are White and Christian. I've mentioned only a few examples of the types of microaggressions and cultural insensitivity I encountered at the university—there are countless more, including blatant racism against other minority groups, which deserve more than a summary due to their disturbing nature—but these encounters were common and happened more frequently than I had ever experienced at any other place of employment. In chapter 13 of this collection, Jordan describes "personal vignettes of racial marginalization in and near the sites of my WCA work" and later explains how she was reminded that she had not left behind the "identity negotiations" she faced as a founding director at a small predominantly White seminary. Like Jordan, I was navigating through mainstream perceptions of my ethnic and gendered embodiment, or "identity negotiations," which felt exhausting amid the other emotional, physical, and spiritual demands of directing an increasingly marginalized department. Yet, I wanted to expand others' viewpoints as one of the very few Latina/o/x directors at the university, and I thought I could help bridge cultural differences between faculty and administrators and the Hispanic/Latina/o/x students they served. At that time, I simply didn't comprehend the cumulative effect of the microaggressions and exclusionary tactics or that they were a glimpse into the questionable administrative practices that were to come.

When I returned to work from medical leave in January 2020, APU had an entirely new administration: a university president (White male), an interim provost (Sri Lankan American male), and an assistant provost (White woman). I also had a new and confusing reporting structure: the new assistant provost and the executive director of ASC would both be my supervisors from that point forward.

The new assistant provost requested to meet with all ASC staff members and listen to our experiences in one-on-one meetings. I met with her and summarized my experiences with the previous administration (more than I mention in this chapter) while she took notes and shot me bewildered looks. When I finished, she said I had experienced gaslighting and systemic abuse from the previous administration due to their exclusionary tactics and lack of communication. I was shocked. No one in a position of power at the university had ever acknowledged any unethical practices. The assistant provost emphasized that she was my "friend," my ally. She assured me that she and the new interim provost would evaluate current structures and that they intended to "put the right people in the right positions." In the meantime, she would move the writing center away from ASC and merge it with the tutoring center. This transition meant yet another reorganization and another push toward constant changes, instability, and directing from the margins.

The new administration emphasized that they would consider each individual's ideas, but I never saw that happen. The COVID-19 pandemic in March 2020 further exacerbated the marginalization of spaces, and, like many other departments and universities, the writing center moved to an online-only space. Since we offered online appointments pre-pandemic, we pivoted quickly. Still, the shift to an online-only space resulted in the assistant provost deciding to vet and approve all directors' written documents, resulting in long and inconvenient turnaround times. Despite meeting all demands, requirements, and deadlines, the new administration began to micromanage every aspect of directors' jobs.

By summer 2020, the assistant provost's demeanor had changed. She became curt for reasons unbeknownst to me and cut my colleagues off repeatedly during meetings. I eventually realized she was the most harmful type of individual to lead a marginalized person and department: a performative ally. She was someone who pretended to empathize with marginalized groups but had an agenda behind "putting the right people in the right places."

That summer, the assistant provost notified me that in addition to directing the department with a decreased budget and teaching a course, I needed to participate in additional reorganization requests and "affinity groups" (discussion groups for departments they planned to merge), the latter of which sucked valuable time from my schedule. The increasing barriers to manage my department effectively, with no control over my workload, led to increased feelings of anxiety and powerlessness. I became increasingly stressed and frustrated, and my health began deteriorating.

Perhaps my mental and spiritual unease transitioned into physical malaise because I became extremely ill. My physician scheduled me for invasive surgery in August 2020, and my recovery time and medical leave would last six weeks. I notified my supervisors immediately, submitted all required paperwork, and left the writing center organized as best I could. Upon my return, I was expected to begin teaching four weeks into the semester, despite not knowing which course I would be assigned.

Two days before my scheduled surgery, I received a letter from the new provost, the same individual who had served as the interim provost. The letter detailed that my one-year contract could be terminated immediately following a sixty-day notice, without cause, and the letter served as that notice. It added that I would transition from a faculty designation into an exempt staff position but that I was still expected to teach one course each year. In addition, this meant my employment when I returned from medical leave would be "at will." The provost ended the letter by thanking me for my service to God's kingdom. Although I had intended to work at a place that valued God first, I felt like God was nowhere to be found in terms of that place.

Calladita No More

When I returned to work six weeks later, I discovered that my team had lost access to the scheduling systems because the Office of the Provost had canceled my department credit card while I was out on medical leave. Since the writing center's scheduling software was on autopay, and my supervisors never notified me before my leave that my card would be canceled, I returned to unpaid bills to rectify. In addition, I was instructed to cancel an internal scheduling system (Humanity) even though it allowed me to easily publish 500 coach shifts per month, manage sick/vacation time, and approve payroll. The rationale behind these decisions was due to continued university budget cuts. My ability to effectively manage my department had already dwindled, but these new setbacks seemed oddly intentional to me, as though setting me up to fail. The course I was scheduled to teach was canceled due to low enrollment, and I was relieved—it's not that I didn't want to teach; I just wanted time to heal from my surgery and adequately prepare for the course.

Most significant, the provost and assistant provost wanted the tutoring center and writing center administrative staff to merge, consolidate duties, and create a restructured organizational chart. They also emphasized that all APU directors should be faculty members with terminal degrees. I technically had a terminal degree (MFA), but I was no longer faculty due to the recent contract change; I was staff but expected to teach. The assistant provost indicated that out of our two respective coordinators, only one would keep the position, and the same could happen between the assistant director of the tutoring center and me regarding the director role as well. In other words, the four of us were asked to permanently remove two positions and state which of us two should fulfill the remaining roles—it was like a twisted academic version of Hunger Games where the competitors decided who would move on and who would not.

During a follow-up meeting with the assistant provost, I articulated the concerns about writing ourselves out of our positions. When I pointed out our respective demographics,[5] she became flustered, stumbling over her words to avoid using "discrimination" in the conversation. I was emotionally, physically, and mentally exhausted at that point. Putting the right people in the right places meant continuing the university tradition of promoting and demoting without transparency. I received excellent scores and feedback about my leadership skills in my "2020 Associate Deans and Academic Administrators Assessment Report" conducted by the university, and I had a proven track record of successfully managing the budget and implementing strategic initiatives. It became clear to me that they wanted me out for reasons not relating to my documented abilities. I requested a meeting with the provost and assistant provost, much to their expressed annoyance.

During our virtual meeting in November 2020, I asked the provost if he planned for all directors moving forward to be faculty with a PhD. He confirmed that, traditionally, the desired qualification and classification for the writing center director position was faculty; faculty lines are generally PhD-driven; and it was "highly likely" the writing center director would be a faculty member with a PhD. I had heard—and endured—enough. I notified them I would be submitting my resignation with my final date but that I would stay on board for another two months to minimize the impact to the writing center. Despite the agreement that I would email my resignation in one week, within that time frame, the assistant provost notified me that my verbal resignation was considered effective. She ended the email by stating that my last day would be in two and a half weeks. What ensued were carefully worded emails with boilerplate language from the assistant provost and HR, where I felt carefully monitored during my last few weeks. I never gave any indication that I would be uncooperative or unprofessional, and there was no reason to believe that I would behave as such based on the care and concern I had for the writing center. The assistant provost even insisted on inspecting my emails announcing my resignation to my staff and colleagues.

Shortly after my resignation, the university posted a new writing center director job announcement, which sought an individual with a PhD in rhetoric/composition to teach two courses each semester and direct all writing center campuses. When I checked PhD degree attainment for rhetoric/composition in the United States, I found that in 2019, a total of 191 doctorate degrees were awarded in rhetoric/composition; out of individuals who earned those degrees, 153 identified as White and 9 identified as Hispanic/Latino (National Center for Science and Engineering Statistics 2019). According to a survey by Valles et al. (2017) on writing center administrators and diversity, less than 2 percent of writing center directors were Hispanic/Latino and only 5 percent of those who obtained PhDs in rhetoric and composition were Hispanic/Latinos. By requiring a PhD in rhetoric/composition, APU would be inevitably hiring a White female over anyone with my ethnic background. Once again, this was simply another barrier that precluded my placement as a writing center director and for other minorities seeking this role.

Sign of the Cross

What began as wanting the ability to diversify the hiring and training of professional and student writing coaches and conduct outreach to my community ended with a labyrinth of barriers that I could no longer find my way around. When I say that I wanted to conduct outreach to my gente, I meant that figuratively and literally. For the past seventeen years, I have lived near the border between Glendora and Azusa. Azusa is a suburb of Los Angeles, with over 60 percent of its residents identifying as Hispanic (DataUSA n.d.). It was—and still is—my community. As mentioned previously, APU earned its designation as an HSI in 2017 with approximately 30 percent of its *students* identifying as Hispanic (Azusa Pacific University 2020). I emphasize students because although an institution is designated as an HSI or Minority Serving Institution (MSI), this does not necessarily mean that its faculty, supervisors, or administrators are representative of their student body, and this disparity should be acknowledged and questioned. Many institutions highlight their diversity, ethnicity, and inclusion departments and training programs, but are they transparent about their administrators, faculty, and staff demographics? If an institution's administrators and faculty do not represent the diverse student demographics they publicize and claim, where exactly is the representation?

I have sat in many diversity-training sessions and often wondered if the moderators had only read about diversity, equity, and inclusion topics or if they had ever actually held conversations with underrepresented individuals. In *For Brown Girls with Sharp Edges and Tender Hearts* (2021), Dorcas Mojica Rodríguez writes that academics "love to learn about cultures, people, communities they have never experienced, and then with that knowledge they love to tell people what to do" (3). How many academics—and writing center directors, specifically—ask *students* to open forums or exchanges to share what they have been through? How many have taken their students' knowledge and experiences to ask them how they can improve their own writing centers? As writing center administrators and directors, how many of these individuals ask their supervisees or colleagues those same questions? Beyond the IWCA Diversity Initiative, I think there are more ways for the IWCA to redefine spaces and make them more welcoming. Rather than offer prescriptive strategies, I ask the IWCA to remember the I in "International": inquire, invite, and invest.

INQUIRE

Inquire more about minority leaders' lived experiences and actively listen. More important, provide minority leaders with a voice or outlet to share their lived marginalized experiences, much like I have been offered here. Ask yourself if you are actively seeking honest feedback from underrepresented groups in your writing centers, including from your students and staff. Ask yourselves if you need to create more forums, panels, and calls for papers and edited books to provide underrepresented minorities and groups involved in writing center work with outlets to share their experiences and offer suggestions for improvement. If you do, then inquire if any minority leaders would be willing to mentor individuals and groups through the emotional difficulties of sharing these lived experiences.

INVITE
Invite individuals involved in writing center work to lead panel presentations, special interest groups, and open forums, but be transparent with the expectations, time commitments, and energy it will involve. My daughter's school principal recently asked me to participate in the parent committee for the Ethnic Studies course and related work to implement AB101 (a high school ethnic studies graduation requirement). Although interested, I had to ask how many other parents would serve on the committee, the frequency of meetings, and so forth to determine if the effort and time put forth would be collaborative or independent. Writing this chapter was emotionally demanding, especially when recalling harmful experiences. Once again, you may want to assign a mentor to help minority leaders navigate through these experiences.

INVEST
Invest in new writing center leaders and continue developing proposals in collaboration with the IWCA Finance and Scholarship committee to provide scholars of color opportunities to present at conferences and conduct research (International Writing Centers Association 2006). I also suggest dedicating specific funding for minority writing center directors to attend the IWCA Summer Institute with a full travel grant.[6] The sessions on tutor training, scheduling platforms, budget systems, and other administrative aspects proved invaluable to my eventual success as a first-year writing center director. One topic that I did not encounter during the Summer Institute was how to navigate marginalization as a minority leader, so invest in space for minority leaders to share their experiences and seek guidance. More important, invest *time*—specifically, *respond* to writing center surveys about diversity to help gather statistics and make productive changes.

As I conclude this chapter, I know I made the right decision resigning as the writing center director at APU and regaining the autonomy of my life narrative. I currently have steady work as a freelance writing consultant and translator, and I also teach part-time for an analytic linguist training program. I have flexibility in my schedule, which allows me to dedicate more time to my family, all of whom provided me with unwavering love and support throughout my time at APU. Admittedly, I'm unsure whether I want to continue working in higher education, because I do believe academia is unwelcoming to people of color. That said, I can't help but feel sentimental as I glance above my desk at a framed picture of a Victor Hugo quote that reads, "A writer is a world trapped inside a person." This gift arrived a week ago from a former international student coach, and it was a complete—and heartwarming—surprise. When I sent a message to thank her, she said that working with me was one of the best experiences she had and that I had no idea how much I had inspired her. She then added that I "inspired some of us." If all of the experiences I encountered at APU led to even one student of color, "one of us," to feel inspired, then I consider my time there well spent.

Notes

1. In a Washington Post article by historian Nell Irvin Painter (2020) entitled, "Why 'White' Should Be Capitalized, Too," she discusses her reservations with the "new formula" of capitalizing B for "Black" while using lowercase w for "white" and lowercase b for "brown." Painter contends that in terms of racial identity, "white Americans" have had the choice of "being something vague, something unraced and separate from race," and allowed the comfort of racial invisibility or absence; a capitalized "White," however, challenges that freedom by unmasking "Whiteness" with its power and privilege. For this and other reasons, I capitalize "White" throughout my chapter.
2. I identify as a Mexican American woman or as a Latina. When referring to the Hispanic/Latino community as a collective, I utilize the term "Latina/o/x" to include women, men, gender nonconforming individuals, and nonbinary individuals. For the purpose of citing research or other academic designations in this chapter, I use the term "Hispanic" if the original name or source defines the subject as such.
3. In For Brown Girls with Sharp Edges and Tender Hearts (2020), Prisca Dorcas Mojica Rodríguez explains that she does not italicize her Spanish because to do so would denote Spanish as foreign, which is not the case. She "has been in conversations, attended classes, and read books" where she was "outside an assumed circle of common knowledge" and had to discover that "privileged information" for herself (2). Dorcas Mojica Rodríguez thus asks her readers to fully sit in the experience of being an outsider (2020, 2); that is, experience what it is like to feel marginalized. I implore my readers to do the same, so I do not italicize any Spanish in my chapter.
4. The APU Writing Center refers to professional writing consultants/tutors as "professional coaches" and student writing consultants/tutors as "student coaches."
5. During this time, the assistant director of the tutoring center was an Asian American man (there was no director). The tutoring coordinator, writing center coordinator, and I were first-gen college Latinas; technically, we all held different terminal degrees, but none of us had a PhD.

6. I was grateful to receive an IWCA Summer Institute grant in 2018, but my travel expenses were not fully covered. The APU Office of the Provost agreed to fund the remaining balance of my travel expenses since I had been selected for the grant; otherwise, I would likely not have attended.

References

Anthony, Marshall, Jr., Andrew Howard Nichols, and Wil Del Pilar. 2021. "A Look at Degree Attainment among Hispanic Women and Men and How COVID-19 Could Deepen Racial and Gender Divides." The Education Trust. https://edtrust.org/resource/a-look-at-degree-attainment-among-hispanic-women-and-men-and-how-covid-19-could-deepen-racial-and-gender-divides/.

Azusa Pacific University. 2020. "HSI Forum: Strengthening Our Designation as a Hispanic Serving Institution." Last modified 2020. https://www.apu.edu/posts/27584/.

DataUSA. n.d. "Azusa, CA Census Place." Accessed February 5, 2022. https://datausa.io/profile/geo/azusa-ca#demographics.

Dorcas Mojica Rodríguez, Prisca. 2021. *For Brown Girls with Sharp Edges and Tender Hearts*. New York: Seal Press.

García, Romeo. 2017. "Unmaking Gringo-Centers." *Writing Center Journal* 1 (36): 29–60.

Hamel-Brown, Christine, Celeste Del Russo, and Amanda Fields. 2017. "Activist Mapping: (Re)framing Narratives about Writing Center Space." In *Making Space: Writing Instruction, Infrastructure, and Multiliteracies*, edited by James P. Purdy and Dànielle N. DeVoss. Ann Arbor: University of Michigan Press. https://www.digitalrhetoriccollaborative.org/makingspace/ch9.html.

International Writing Centers Association. 2006. "IWCA Diversity Initiative." https://docs.google.com/document/d/1zpGvZuZY6MX7oNEFtTDYhSWlp5MdcBXp4ssnV8hq718/edit.

National Center for Science and Engineering Statistics. 2019. "Doctorate Recipients, by Subfield of Study, Citizenship Status, Ethnicity, and Race: 2019. Table 22." Accessed July 29, 2021. https://ncses.nsf.gov/pubs/nsf21308/data-tables.

Painter, Nell Irvin. 2020. "Why 'White' Should Be Capitalized, Too." https://www.washingtonpost.com/opinions/2020/07/22/why-white-should-be-capitalized/.

Reyes-Velarde, Alejandra. 2018. "Ban on Same-Sex Couples Roils Small Christian College: 'This Isn't Something Sinful, God.'" https://www.latimes.com/local/lanow/la-me-ln-azusa-Pacific-university-lgbtq-ban-20181005-story.html.

Valles, Sarah Banschbach, Rebecca Day Babcock, and Karen Keaton Jackson. 2017. "Writing Center Administrators and Diversity: A Survey." *The Peer Review* 1 (1). http://thepeerreview-iwca.org/issues/issue-1/writing-center-administrators-and-diversity-a-survey/.

12
Is the Writing Center Safe Yet?

Narrative Vignettes of Women's Bodily Security in Our "Cozy Homes"

SARAH FISCHER

A survey conducted by Stop Street Harassment found that 81 percent of women have experienced sexual harassment and 38 percent of women have experienced it in the workplace (Chatterjee 2018). Anna Sicari has reflected on women's lack of safety in writing centers specifically.[1] She narrates her own gendered oppressions as a woman writing center professional, drawing on the "cozy homes" writing center grand narrative (WCGN) Grutsch McKinney describes as misguided: "I think many women tutors and writing center professionals can think of many times in which the writing center was anything but cozy" (Sicari 2018, 74). Sicari encourages us to work toward institutional change by "push[ing] back" on this narrative by sharing our "moments of being harassed, undermined, or ignored by students, faculty and administrators" in the writing center (2018, 74). Like Sicari and many other women, I too have encountered this un-coziness and believe the insistence on this aspect of the WCGN contributed to my experiences of marginalization.

I will describe some of my un-cozy writing center moments to explain how I, a woman with PTSD, have contended with these ideas in my writing center at a large public midwestern university. I will highlight three rules (or WCGNs) my center follows that, coupled with my identity, have led to a space that was

https://doi.org/10.7330/9781646426119.c012

not cozy or comfortable: (1) tutors should sit next to tutees; (2) tutees should choose their own seats; (3) tutors should record online tutorials. With these narrative vignettes, I aim to disrupt the cozy home grand narrative that fails to account for the unique realities of women, including women like me, who are survivors of sexual violation. In spaces as physically intimate as writing centers, women's bodies—and women's comfort inside their bodies—remain at risk if our stories are not heard.

Searching for Safety

WCGN #1: SITTING SIDE-BY-SIDE

My writing center is tucked away in a corner of the library, not demarcated by walls; what separates us from the rest of the library is a retractable belt barrier. Most of our center is visible to the entire floor, but a few tables are blocked by bookshelves. During a training session themed around power and privilege, our director reminded us to sit side-by-side with the students we are tutoring. She told us that this arrangement would help emphasize the peer-to-peer relationship that writing centers work to foster (Pemberton and Carino 2003). It is an easy way to build rapport, she said, implicitly reaffirming the narrative of the writing center as a cozy home—a space where community-building and bonding should happen.

Among the nodding heads, I felt a surge of nervousness run through me. I raised my shaky voice and said, "I prefer to begin the session by sitting across from the student first, and then after I read their paper, I ask if it's okay if I sit side-by-side." With my own stories and those from the #MeToo movement in mind, I added, "I don't know if everyone feels comfortable sitting that close to a stranger they just met." There was a quiet but palpable understanding. Aside from myself and our director, everyone in the meeting was a man. Their realization that close proximity with a stranger may feel uncomfortable, or even dangerous, was one that I, as a woman, had realized long before becoming a writing center tutor.

When the meeting ended, a peer thanked me for my input. Later that day, I heard him ask a student if he could sit next to her before moving his chair. With my comment, I implied that our efforts to make the space a cozy home were misguided; these efforts made the space a not-so-cozy home for some, like me and other women.

WCGN #2: CHOOSING SEATS

When writers visit our center, the receptionist tells them they may sit wherever they would like. Fellow tutors and I have discussed the positive impact this procedure has on writers; it shows them that they have the agency to make their own decisions, a hallmark of writing center praxis for decades (North 1984). One evening, I was working with a student on his personal statement for law school. He selected a table made private from the rest of the library by the bookshelves.

As the session progressed, the student inched closer to me, passionately explaining his writing. With each paragraph, his chair moved closer—his *body* moved closer. His hands grazed my hands. His kneecaps brushed my kneecaps. I knew the bookshelves kept our session too private for my comfort, and I awkwardly scooted backward. I found myself more focused on my safety than on tutoring. Reflecting on this session, I do not believe he had any inappropriate motives with his increased physical proximity. First, I think his maleness likely afforded him the privilege not to think about his body and its closeness to mine. Second, I think because the space is treated as a cozy home, he felt comfortable engaging this way; he may have even thought his proximity was contributing to the coziness of the space. However, because people have different ideas of cozy, a concept that Garcia unpacks in chapter 10 in this collection by noting how her physical disability affects the labor she can perform, writing centers should not be treated as cozy homes unless they are comfortable—and safe—for all.

WCGN #3: RECORDING ONLINE SESSIONS

In response to the pandemic, we shifted to Zoom, complicating the notion of the writing center as a physical space let alone a cozy home. Our administrative team worked hard to adjust to virtual tutoring, outlining procedures for each session. One procedure included recording each session, if the writer gave us permission, then deleting it if there were no issues requiring follow-up. Since there was no site manager present, the recording would protect us; we should feel safe knowing that we could send a copy to our director if anything inappropriate happened. With online tutoring, as with the pandemic in general, came a rise in conversations about safety, which, perhaps counterintuitively, led to more issues.

One afternoon, in preparing for a session, I noticed in previous reports that several coworkers had documented that the tutee—specified as a man—was "aggressive" and "verbally combative." I prepared myself for a potentially difficult session, in which gendered dynamics would be inevitable. When the session began, I introduced myself and asked if I could record the meeting. For the first time in my online tutoring experience, I was met with an aggressive "Why?" While I knew the answer was "for our safety," I was scared to tell him that; if I said that I needed to record the tutorial in case something went wrong, would he be offended? Combative? Would I provoke aggression? I hesitated to answer, and he followed up in an agitated tone: "Why do you guys need to record these things? What do you think I'm going to *do* to you?" I fumbled out an answer about standard procedures, and the session progressed without any major challenges, but his words reverberated in my mind. Thinking of what this man could do to me terrified me and triggered me. The options were infinite, and they were haunting. I spent the remainder of the session more focused on calming my fight-or-flight response than I did on helping him with his paper. Ultimately, the director contacted this student explaining the purposes of our procedures, and I was never assigned to work with him again.

The new procedures challenged the idea of the writing center as a cozy home; they overtly acknowledged that the writing center may not be cozy, or even safe, for everyone. However, they were met with resistance, demonstrating just how accustomed to this narrative we have become and how difficult it may be to disrupt it.

Concluding Comments

The narrative of the writing center as a cozy home, though providing comfort for some,[2] has created a lack of safety for others. While these vignettes have focused on my own experiences, I believe women—especially women who have experienced sexual violation—place their bodies at risk when they enter a writing center space that is viewed as a "cozy home." In writing centers, which are comprised predominantly of women (Sicari 2018), it is time we value women's lived experiences and bodies by acknowledging that many spaces are not cozy and should not be treated as such. The writing center should not be cozy. It should be safe.

To work toward a safe center, some practices can change. First, one-size-fits-all rules for seating arrangements should be swapped with individual decisions, and tutors and tutees alike should ask for permission before engaging in close contact.[3] Second, face-to-face tutoring should happen in public, visible places, with others around to monitor these sessions and function as safeguards for inappropriate, and potentially unsafe, closeness—even if this means assigning seats. Third, when challenging the cozy home narrative, we can be prepared for pushback; we can plan how to respond in ways that remind others of a commitment not to coziness but to safety. Above all, to work toward a safe writing center, we must hold space for women tutors, and all marginalized folks, to voice when they feel un-cozy.

Notes

1. A brief note about the language of "safety": writing center praxis that seeks equity "reject[s] the idea of 'writing center as safe space,' a concept that stems from our field's long history with accepting the metaphor of writing center as home, even though our spaces are not, and never have been, homelike or safe for all" (Martini and Webster 2017). After all, "tutors feeling 'safe,' which Brian Arao and Kristi Clemens (2013) note is often conflated with 'comfort,' (135) can '[contribute] to the replication of dominance and subordination, rather than a dismantling thereof' (140)" (qtd. in Martini and Webster). In my tutoring, however, I am not searching for safety as comfort; I am not seeking a writing place or tutoring style that allows me to lean back in my chair, slip my shoes off, and get ready for a day of binge-watching reality TV; I am pursuing a writing center that does not leave me feeling triggered.
2. Such as the man from vignette #1, who chose a table that allowed for cozy privacy, and the man from vignette #2, who was able to sit so closely because he felt comfortable in the cozy space.
3. Fortunately, the pandemic may already be normalizing these kinds of permissions.

References

Chatterjee, Rhitu. 2018. "A New Survey Finds 81 Percent of Women Have Experienced Sexual Harassment." NPR, February 21. https://www.npr.org/sections/thetwo-way/2018/02/21/587671849/a-new-survey-finds-eighty-percent-of-women-have-experienced-sexual-harassment.

Martini, Rebecca Hallman, and Travis Webster. 2017. "Writing Centers as Brave/r Spaces: A Special Issue Introduction." *Peer Review* 1 (2). https://thepeerreview-iwca.org/issues/braver-spaces/writing-centers-as-braver-spaces-a-special-issue-introduction/.

North, Stephen M. 1984. "The Idea of a Writing Center." *College English* 46 (5). https://doi.org/10.2307/377047.

Pemberton, Michael A., and Peter Carino. 2003. "Power and Authority in Peer Tutoring." In *The Center Will Hold: Critical Perspectives on Writing Center Scholarship*, edited by Michael A. Pemberton and Joyce Kincaid, 96–113. Logan: Utah State University Press.

Sicari, Anna. 2018. "Everyday Truths: Reflections from a Woman Writing Center Professional." In *Out in the Center: Public Controversies and Private Struggles*, edited by Harry Denny, Robert Mundy, Liliana M. Naydan, Richard Sévère, and Anna Sicari, 70–75. Logan: Utah State University Press.

13
Womanist Way-Making in Writing Center Administration

Reflections on Marginalization, Misogynoir, and Resistance

ZANDRA JORDAN

When I became a writing center director, I was aware that I was joining an often-marginalized group. Like writing programs that contend with misperceptions of their labor as peripheral to the "real" work of academic departments, writing centers have historically been treated as ancillary and therefore subject to both physical locations and institutional ideologies and structures that for better or worse render their contributions invisible or expendable. Writing center directors, especially those who do not hold faculty appointments, are doubly vulnerable to the devaluing of their expertise and concomitant struggles around equitable pay, research support, and unpaid labor. In addition to these concerns, race is a compounding factor for Black, Indigenous, and people of color (BIPOC) leading writing programs, for they may contend not only with the marginalization of the field but also with belonging to a marginalized group (Carter-Tod 2020).

Drawing on misogynoir and womanist ethics, I describe some of the marginalization that I have encountered and strategies employed as a Black female, non-tenure-track, writing center director in two contexts, as founding director of a center at a small private, predominantly white theological institution offering master's and doctoral degrees, and as director of a center at a large private, historically white research institution serving undergraduate and graduate students across the disciplines. *Misogynoir*, a term coined and theorized respectively by Black feminist/womanist scholars Moya Bailey and Trudy, "describes the uniquely co-constitutive racialized and sexist violence that befalls Black women as a result of their simultaneous and interlocking oppression at the intersection of racial and gender marginalization" (Bailey 2021, 1). Stereotypical images of Black womanhood in "US visual and digital culture," such as "the Jezebel, mammy, Sapphire, and later the 'welfare queen' or even the 'strong Black woman' archetype" (Bailey 2021, 1–2), circulate in popular culture with harmful material effects on the "interpersonal, social, and institutional" lives of Black women (Bailey and Trudy 2018, 763), including their "livelihoods and health" (Bailey 2021, 2). Womanist ethics provides a counterresponse to misogynoir, an epistemological and moral standpoint for resisting racial and gender oppression. Pioneered by Katie G. Cannon (1985) and other trailblazing Black women theologians, womanist ethics is a revolutionary paradigm for interpreting Scripture and worldly systems that refutes the denigration of Black women's bodies and epistemologies while promoting freedom for all peoples (Cannon 1988; Riggs 2011). Gleaning liberatory principles from Black women's lives and literature, womanist ethics offers principles for thriving as we build a more just world.

While writing center scholarship frequently presumes a white, female middle-aged director as its audience and the student or tutee as the Other—as Sarah Banschbach Valles, Rebecca Day Babcock, and Karen Keaton Jackson (2017) have noted—this chapter provides a counternarrative of a Black female writing center administrator (WCA) negotiating misogynoir through racial and gender marginalization and institutional hegemony. Misogynoir speaks to the abuse I experienced when senior administrators sought to exploit my labor and questioned the morality of my independent consultant work. It also aptly describes the erasure that ensued when I was unseen or misidentified both inside and outside of the workplace, which challenged my sense of belonging and ability to maintain joy in the everyday. In the sections that follow I describe some of the misogynoir that I have encountered in institutional and community settings while moving into WCA roles and the womanist principle of way-making that is helping me negotiate these challenges.

"Making a Way out of No Way": Black Women's Homeplace Versus the Cozy Grand Narrative

What kind of way-making is needed for Black women navigating the historically white and female terrain of writing center administration? In my experience, becoming a WCA brought more than the usual adjustments that come with taking on a new role; my acclimation and success have also required an ethic for negotiating racialized and gendered attitudes about Black women and their labor. The womanist principle of way-making—a deeply rooted, faith-based belief that there is a God-inspired way forward, a way through white hegemony—has helped me challenge the usurpation of my labor and the narratives that reinscribe Black women's marginality. Forged across generations of God-fearing Black women, way-making is passed down as daughters glean life-sustaining truths from grandmothers and mothers whose lives testify to God's overcoming power.

In my grandmother's and mother's kitchens, I have heard countless stories of God "making a way out of no way," of sugar biscuits and vegetables sustaining a family of eight that could only afford to eat meat on Sundays. Of a domestic and a farmer, by the grace of God, helping four of their children become first-generation college graduates and one a major in the United States Air Force, despite the obstacles that poverty and racism posed. I add my own Divine way-making stories to these, sharing publicly what is often reserved for the safe homeplaces of our own making, in hopes that other WCAs of color will glean survival strategies from my experiences.

Let us begin, then, with personal vignettes of racial and gender marginalization in and near the sites of my WCA work. In the first, I am in the writing center kitchen refilling my water bottle when I notice the countertop in disarray and decide to straighten things up. A white male student enters in search of coffee and finds me rearranging tea boxes and Keurig coffee pods, wiping up breadcrumbs, and restocking paper goods. I greet him warmly, direct him to the coffee, ask about his day, and proceed to tell him about tutoring and why he should book an appointment. Then he asks a perfectly logical question, especially since I had yet to mention my role—"So, what do you do here?" When I tell him that I direct the center, his eyes widen in surprise. Whether he was shocked to find the director tidying the kitchen, amazed to find a Black woman at the helm, or just astonished at his good fortune in meeting the director is difficult to discern. Yet, given the activity in which I had been engaged as well as our institutional context, where only 3 percent of senior staff are Black, I could not help but wonder if I had initially appeared to him to be "the help."

An incident several days prior likely contributed to my wondering. While standing at a crosswalk a few miles from the university, a white, male, same-sex couple approached me. I was making my way home from work, having stepped off the train just minutes before, when without so much as a "hello," the couple with a baby in arms looked at me and declared, "We need a nanny." Stunned, I managed to reply, "I don't know any," and walked away as they turned toward a nearby Latino staff employee whom I recognized from campus and repeated the microaggression.

In retrospect, while I rarely saw other Black people in the area, I had seen a few Latinas who appeared to work as domestics. They pushed white children in strollers up and down sidewalks and carried cleaning supplies in and out of homes. I donned a backpack and slacks, but these cultural markers went unnoticed. Having claimed their own freedom from heteronormativity, the same-sex couple still relied upon a colonial worldview in which BIPOC were presumed to be or to know domestics. Likewise, while the university boasts a diverse student body,[1] 67 percent of faculty are white in comparison to 2 percent who are Black, and 4 percent of staff roles are held by Blacks. In this context, I am overwhelmingly in the minority and more likely to be the help than the head of the center.

I begin with these stories to illustrate the ubiquity of racialized and gendered attitudes toward Black women and their compounding effects. Whether inside or outside of the academy, these encounters pervade my experience and in my WCA work contradict grand narratives of writing centers as "cozy homes" (Grutsch McKinney 2013, 20). In the preceding vignettes, I had recently assumed directorship of an established center at a large elite institution and was quickly reminded that I had not left behind the identity negotiations that I faced as founding director of a writing center at a small predominantly white seminary. In both contexts, I have contended with mainstream perceptions of my racialized and gendered embodiment, negotiations always felt but not always spoken, that complicated the welcoming ethos to which both centers aspired. Despite the cozy decor and liberal supply of coffee and tea that invite visitors to make themselves at home, I have found it difficult at times to claim a sense of home inside and outside of the academy even as I work hard to create it for others.

Writing center practitioners have warned against using the metaphor of home uncritically. "Homes are culturally marked," Jackie Grutsch McKinney

(2013) reminds us, and while they conjure feelings of acceptance and comfort for some, those associations are not true for all and may even contradict some of the challenging work we want writers to embrace, such as interrogating choices, engaging new ideas, and considering new approaches (25–26). Furthermore, as home has traditionally been deemed the domain of women, in contrast to the male-dominant business world, relying on this metaphor could have an unintended impact for female directors, rendering their labor as "unintellectual in the eyes of some" or constructing them as the nurturing "mother" (26).

While nurture is not inherently problematic, there is an additional concern for marginalized bodies that makes me even more wary of the cozy grand writing center narrative. When we depict writing centers as cozy homes, who does the Black female director become? Given the proliferation of anti-blackness and misogynoir in and out of the academy, she might unwittingly become the mammy, a racist image of Black women supposedly content to serve white families and nanny white children in homes that would never be their own. Carmen Kynard (2019) speaks to the "mammification" of Black women's labor in the academy and the commonplace exploitation of their administrative work (35). "The racial authority of Black women's work as university faculty and staff," Kynard explains, "is hypermediated by [the] historic role of the mammy" (34). Her labor is expected to be in service of whiteness and more generally in service of others rather than herself as an autonomous human being.

The enduring impact of the mammy on perceptions of Black women's bodies and labor was made palpable for me during a tutorial at the small theological institution where I founded the writing center. A white female seminarian tasked with describing her image of God wrote a characterization of the Divine as a large comforting Black woman who provided all her needs. To explain the problematic nature of that description, I could not rely upon a writing center ethos of home and comfort that might reinforce her internalization of Black women as mammies but drew instead upon a womanist ethic of truth telling and world building in courageous collaboration with others. Womanism, inspired by Alice Walker's (1983) coining of the term and the revolutionary paradigm presented in her four-part poetic definition, centers Black women's flourishing in opposition to white supremacy. Taking seriously Black women's experiences with tripartite oppression, womanism derives liberatory strategies from the gardens of Black mothers and grandmothers—the principles revealed in their everyday resistance to white oppression and refusal to be diminished. We learn from their tireless way-making in a world convinced of their inferiority how to build despite systems committed to our demise and to leave blueprints for our daughters to follow. Such way-making narratives, bell hooks (1990) explains, are often shared outside the "culture of white supremacy" in the "homeplace" that Black women create for their own family and community—a space where "all Black people could strive to be subjects, not objects, where we could be affirmed in our minds and hearts, despite poverty, hardship, and deprivations, where we could restore to ourselves the dignity denied us on the outside in the public world" (42).

My own recollections of homeplace include frequent visits to my maternal grandmother's house, where I heard stories about her upbringing. My grandmother was raised in a God-fearing home in a rural, racially bifurcated town with few opportunities for Black families. Her family attended church bimonthly when the itinerant Baptist minister came to town and the Black Methodist church held services. Outside of her religious education, she excelled in school but was unable to continue beyond the seventh grade because there was no local high school for Black children. She and her counterparts were largely expected to go to work in the cotton and corn fields unless they could board with Black relatives who lived in towns with a Black high school. If given the opportunity, she might have become a teacher like my mother, aunts, and most of their friends, indeed like me. But with few alternatives, my grandmother laundered clothes in white homes and cooked meals at the local hospital. With God's help, she made a way for her family the best way she could. Our hands bore the signs of our different social conditions. When I nestled against her, she often held my hands and remarked on their softness and even tone. In comparison, her hands were rough and discolored from a life of hard domestic labor, a life that she shared with my grandfather, a farmer who passed before I had the privilege of meeting him.

Mine is a familiar story that Black feminists and womanists have told before me about mothers and grandmothers with "leathery" hands (Pierce 2021, 33) who "worked outside the home serving white folks, cleaning their houses, washing their clothes, tending their children . . . [doing] whatever they could to make ends meet" (hooks 1990, 42). The experience of going to their grandmothers' houses and listening to their stories produced an epistemology for way-making, which in womanism refers to "an ethic of survival and quality of life among Black women" (Baker-Fletcher and Baker-Fletcher 1997, 156–157) emanating from their relationship with God who helps them to "make a way out of no way" (Coleman 2008, 33). It recognizes Divine revelation of "a way forward, a way toward life" and "justice," as well as "human agency" in walking out a "new vision" for the "future" (33–34). I carry this spirit of futuristic world-building with me into writing center administration, striving for a more just world as I lead the center's programs. This way-making ethic enabled me to encourage the white female seminarian to interrogate her image of God—its resemblance to a racist stereotype of Black womanhood and the implications for her work in the world if she left it unexamined.

Building from the Ground Up: Marginalization and Way-Making in the Absence of Homeplace

In my first WCA role, I was tasked with establishing a writing center at a small theological institution providing master's and doctoral degrees to aspiring clergy and theologians. A compositionist and ordained gospel minister with several years of experience teaching undergraduate writing, coordinating writing programs, and supporting congregations, I had recently completed a Master of Divinity and saw the position as an ideal way to combine my passions for rhetoric and homiletics. The role was part-time and did not provide medical benefits or a retirement plan, but I was told that it would likely become full-time after a pilot phase and accepted the position on that promise and a strong conviction that it was the "way forward" God was providing. To make ends meet, I continued independently to coach dissertation writers and to edit manuscripts.

My first month on the job was devoted to setting up the physical space, hiring tutors, and laying out the center's infrastructure. The center would be housed in an unfurnished, unused wing of the seminary library with a few empty rooms and a foyer left behind after a building remodel. I quickly went about designing the space: searching basement storage rooms for usable furniture and supplies and demarcating spaces for tutoring, workshops, and events. I ordered a couch, cushioned chairs, a rug to make the common area more inviting, and training materials for the tutors that I would soon hire, mostly doctoral students in religion or theology looking for part-time employment while they completed their degrees.

Library and writing center partnerships have been instrumental in helping students better understand the relationship between information literacy and research-based writing (Cooke and Bledsoe 2008; Albanese and Fena 2021), so I initially considered the center's placement in the library advantageous. But the reporting structure ultimately created a barrier between me and senior administration that contributed to my marginalization. I reported to the library dean, whom I found to be supportive but misguided in setting my hourly wage. I later learned that the dean chose not to give me the full amount that administration earmarked, because they thought it unfair that I receive a higher hourly wage than another library employee with managerial responsibilities. This seemed to me to be more of a structural issue caused by the reporting line, rather than intentional racial discrimination. The effect, however, was discriminatory, as I was charged with establishing an entirely new program where none had formerly existed and given only a few hours weekly to do so, while other library employees were full-time and engaged in well-established roles. A better decision would have been to advocate for equitable pay for staff rather than denying me full compensation.

The problems I faced are all too familiar to Black women writing program administrators (WPAs) as well as others in contingent or part-time roles who must, as Aja Gorham notes in chapter 5, "patch" together a living. Denial of fair or equitable compensation for work performed (Carter-Tod 2020, 203); making requests through white coworkers, in my case a supervisor, to manipulate our labor (Kynard 2019, 39); and undervaluing our work and credentials (Perryman-Clark and Craig 2019, 3–4) convey disrespect for Black women's personhood, knowledge, and authority. In my case, these traumas were exacerbated by my employment status as a part-time, non-tenure-track director. While the dean relied upon my expertise—I was trusted to develop the center as I saw fit—I felt vulnerable to institutional abuse.

Shortly after my hire, the dean informed me that administrators wanted me to edit the seminary's new devotional, which included student and faculty contributions. When I pointed out that editing the devotional exceeded my job description and inquired about a separate consulting fee, my supervisor agreed to ask on my behalf but advised me to accept regardless, because refusal would be politically detrimental. This warning indicated that I was vulnerable to reprisal, and while the dean did relay my request, they did not challenge the system that presumed ownership of my labor and the right to withhold fair compensation.

I considered declining outright but feared retaliation and therefore accepted the project with conditions: a separate consulting fee and copyeditor's credit. Although administrators agreed to this arrangement, the feeling of coercion lingered. Rather than asking what I charge for editorial services, administrators determined what I would receive. Given my part-time status, I had no recourse. Once the task was completed, the devotionals were printed without the requested editor's credit, though I cannot say for certain if the omission was intentional. A sticker listing me as the copyeditor was affixed to the backside of the copies that I received.

As I developed the center, my hours were increased, but they remained below the threshold required for full-time status, exempting the institution from providing health benefits and retirement savings. As an act of survival, I continued to supplement my income through writing, coaching, and consulting. While I understood this choice as womanist way-making, emblematic of the survivalist strategies of Black women forebears who used what they had to make ends meet, a senior administrator interpreted my assertion of autonomy as unethical.

One of my writing clients, whom I will call Natalie, first made me aware of the senior administrator's claims. Natalie and I originally met as students at another institution. When I was hired to establish the writing center, Natalie let me know that she was also employed at the seminary and enrolled in one of its doctoral programs. I had been working there around five months when Natalie asked me to be her personal writing coach. I initially declined and encouraged Natalie to see me at the center, where I could work with her free of charge, but she insisted that she needed more contact and support than thirty-minute tutorials provided. She wanted a personal writing coach to help her turn previously written papers into cohesive dissertation chapters, to develop an individualized writing plan based upon her goals and schedule and to hold her accountable for sticking to it, to provide editorial revisions and feedback on her ideas, and to offer strategies for persevering when writing became difficult. Natalie was right. This level of ongoing, in-depth support surpassed my role at the seminary and the paid hours allotted for the work. What she wanted was worth paying for, she said, and I agreed.

We had been working together for a few weeks, always off-campus and outside of the center's regular hours, when she called to share an upsetting conversation. A senior administrator contacted her directly with allegations that I was charging students for my services and asked for her corroboration. I have no idea who spread this false report, but Natalie was having none of it. She lambasted the administrator for questioning my integrity, noting that she was the one who solicited my services and insisted on compensating me for work that exceeded my role at the seminary. She boldly added that since the institution refused to give me a livable wage, it should not be surprising that I needed to take on additional work.

I appreciated Natalie for defending me but also wanted to speak on my own behalf. As with the devotional, I was never contacted directly. Rather, the administrator took their suspicions to others, which I felt maligned my character. When I mentioned it to my supervisor, they revealed that the senior administrator had also spoken to them, calling my independent consultant work a "red flag." My supervisor explained to the administrator that it was common practice at the seminary for students to hire staff as personal writing coaches, a fact that my unknown accuser failed to disclose. This trend likely emerged in response to the high demand for English as a Second Language (ESL) support prior to the establishment of the writing center and the hiring of an ESL instructor. I was also unaware of the practice, but even if I had known I would not have solicited students as clients. I only agreed to work with Natalie because of our prior relationship and the clear distinctions between the center's services and what she requested.

Given the student's strong rebuke and my supervisor's acknowledgment, the complaint and investigation were dropped, but the matter was not closed for me. Despite hearing nothing more about it from anyone, I carried the weight of knowing others had presumed me guilty of wrongdoing and once again denied my ability as an autonomous being to have ethical purposes for my own labor. In the long history of co-opting and stereotyping Black women's bodies and labor, this is not an overreaction. From the mammy, to the Jezebel, to the "welfare queen" and the "angry Black woman" stereotype, Black women have been stigmatized as incapable of acting ethically on their own behalf and therefore as needing surveillance and restraint.

Despite the prevalence of misogynoir, I remained certain that there was divinely appointed way-making for me at the seminary. Until the next opportunity arrived, I was determined to carry out a transformational vision for the center. In delineating its mission and pedagogical approach; designing physical and digital spaces; hiring, training, and supervising staff; creating and facilitating workshops; providing faculty support and, along with the staff, holding hundreds of tutorials, I strove to advance a liberatory model of writing center work. In all of its doing, the center could be a space for challenging oppressive ideologies and cultivating emancipatory worldviews.

The most representative example of this effort is the two-part Courageous Communicators Series that I designed. In the fall, I invited students and faculty to join me at the human rights center downtown for a social justice write-in. Nineteen students of different ethnicities, genders, orientations, denominations, and degree programs participated in the event, representing in their diversity the hope of a beautifully complex global community that can come together in service of shared goals. As students moved through the exhibit halls, journals in hand, writing center staff and seminary faculty prompted them periodically to pause, reflect, and record their theological musings. The write-in concluded with lunch and dialogue on the human rights center lawn and encouragement for students to continue thinking, composing, and speaking theologically about social justice issues.

One of the write-in participants who took up my charge produced a particularly noteworthy response. Drawing upon her visual literacy, she re-created the all-white faculty portraits hanging prominently in the seminary's dining hall with faculty and staff of color. The photo exhibit invites the seminary community to think deeply about its "history" and "future," as it considers the stories that "visual imagery" tells about "community" and "difference." I was honored to be included in the exhibition. My photo remake and the accompanying statement about my founding of the writing center were posted in a campus office, one of the few lasting acknowledgments of my contributions to the seminary.

The student's photo exhibition created space for honest dialogue about racial justice at the institution, leading to a student-led rally and work groups in which the entire campus community was invited to participate. At the rally, students, faculty, and staff voiced their truths about racial prejudice—what they had experienced as an instigator or a recipient—and agreed to transformative action. The ideas from the rally then became the talking points for working groups designed to promote institutional change.

While I cannot take credit for the student work that gave rise to these events, the venue for the write-in was intentional, as was the focus on social justice. I wanted to help students and faculty expand their conceptions of the literacies that students need in an increasingly diverse and technological world. I hoped that seeing the human rights center's multimodal social justice exhibits and having space to journal and dialogue about their rhetorical impact would plant seeds that students would carry forward in work of their own choosing. The write-in participants did that in courageous ways.

The second part of the series, a two-day oratory training and preaching palooza, built upon the social justice write-in. I invited expert homileticians from differing sociocultural backgrounds to speak during a luncheon about their methods for sermon development and delivery. Following the luncheon, I facilitated an interactive workshop on voice, embodiment, and delivery, inviting participants to consider how styles of delivery, including the physical and oral representation of abstract ideas, can animate the sermon. Through rounds of writing, peer review, and practice, the participants then formed a supportive writing community for developing justice-minded sermons.

Shortly after the series, I was informed by my supervisor that the funding needed to make my position full-time was unavailable, so I accepted another job offer. I have no doubt the library dean's approved budget did not include a full-time WCA; however, after I left, the institution had no problem finding the money and other perks for a young white alumna whose preparation was incomparable to my own. She did not have a terminal degree or formal pedagogical experience and writing training, nor had she invested what I had to establish the center. To make matters worse, I had unwittingly mentored this young woman when she expressed her interest in writing centers. Having enjoyed helping some of her international peers with their papers, she was curious about writing center work and asked for my professional insight. I spoke with her about writing center pedagogy, obtained funds for her to accompany me to a local writing conference, and encouraged her to pursue professionalization in the field. As it turned out, she did not need professionalization to become a WCA. Despite her comparative lack of experience, she received everything that I was denied and more: full-time status with benefits and even an offer to pay for her to go back to school to obtain formal training in writing pedagogy. What can this possibly convey to me other than disdain for Black womanhood and devaluation of my credentials, expertise, and labor? Misogynoir and structural inequality made it possible for a qualified Black woman to be denied full-time status and benefits, while an underqualified white woman received it all with little effort.

"You Made It!": Womanist Leadership and World-Building from the Margins

For my next administrative role, I moved to a predominantly white city, where I initially experienced an invisibleness that I had not fully anticipated. People did not "see" me. They looked down to avoid making eye contact with me on the street. They stepped in front of me in the produce aisle as if I were not standing there. But the bank teller where I went to open an account saw me right off. An Indian American woman in her thirties, the teller's welcoming eyes met mine when I walked in. As she went about the procedures for creating my account, she asked what brought me to the area. I explained that I would be directing a center at the university, and her eyes lit up with pride. "You made it!" she exclaimed and proceeded to share her own aspirations for career advancement. I appreciated this moment of celebration and solidarity with another woman of color but knew that my "making it" was not as utopic as it seemed.

Undoubtedly, my current role is a vast improvement upon my last. I am the full-time director of the center, which is situated in the university's writing program, and have the support of an administrative team that includes an associate director and other office staff. Together, we manage the center's daily operations and thousands of tutorials annually. As director, I also serve on the senior leadership team overseeing the undergraduate writing requirement and faculty support for writing in the major, among other initiatives. Therefore, I have joined a program of credentialed and supportive writing professionals who understand the value of our work at the university. Even so, marginality remains a reality of my professional experience. As a program without departmental status largely reliant upon lecturers and staff, the writing program and the center that it manages sit on the margins, despite our central location on the main campus.

Additionally, as a Black WPA and the first director of color in the center's twenty-year history, I have experienced both enthusiastic support and clear disdain. While students, supervisors, and others have affirmed my leadership, I have also contended with passive-aggressive behavior and even verbal attack from white coworkers when attempts to circumvent my administrative decisions were thwarted. Such misogynoirist encounters, coupled with reports of campus racism and national anti-BIPOC violence, inspired me to elevate the center's commitment to antiracist and racially just pedagogies. I believe that writing centers can influence the campus culture and beyond and have therefore made antiracism a core, explicit tenet of tutoring practice, racial justice an ongoing theme of tutor professional development, and social justice a hallmark of the center's campus programming. In these ways, I continue to engage in womanist way-making and world-building—the unapologetic cultivation of an emancipatory future in which BIPOC and other marginalized bodies are equally valued, and cross-cultural dialogue and collaboration are normative.

On a programmatic level, walking out these commitments requires deliberate, sustained action over time. Significantly, I am not building from scratch as I had at my previous institution. Having inherited an established and thriving center that my predecessors built with care, I am adding to the foundation already laid the womanist ethic guiding my commitment to antiracist, racially just tutor training and other programming.

I began by familiarizing myself with existing protocols and getting to know the tutors and staff whom my predecessors handpicked and trained. Then, in my first year, I facilitated a workshop on racial literacy for lecturers in the university writing program who also tutored at the center and co-led a workshop on rhetorical grammar for writing and oral communication tutors. I began talking to the tutors about reciprocal risk-taking in the one-to-one tutorial, how we could open ourselves to courageous engagement with difference. When I was invited by professors and campus programs to inform historically marginalized groups about center resources, I underscored that the center was for everyone, expressed my desire for a tutoring staff that better reflected the diversity of the student body, and asked for their help in accomplishing that goal. When it was time to enroll a new cohort of peer and graduate writing tutors in the required training seminar, I shared my belief that the one-to-one tutorial was a space where we could contribute to building a more just world and introduced new materials on racial literacy, and the privileging of white discourses and historic degradation of non-white Englishes in the academy (Jordan 2020).

While we have not arrived, for there is still much to accomplish, our commitment to antiracism and racial justice is gaining notice at the university. Through tutor trainings on racial bias and antiracist praxis, Diversion, Equity, and Inclusion (DEI) pedagogy workshops, and special events, such as a write-in/speak-in "In Conversation with Amanda Gorman's Inaugural Poem" and an expressive arts workshop on Black women's womanist preaching, we are becoming a center that is known for its radically inclusive and racially just ethos. Of this year's aspiring undergraduate writing tutors, 85 percent self-identify as people of color, including Asian, American Indian or Alaska Native, Black or African American, Hispanic or Latino, Middle Eastern, and Native Hawaiian or Pacific Islander. Comparatively, while tutors were not previously invited to share their racial identity, during my first year I could count on one hand the undergraduate writing tutors whose phenotypical presentation was non-white. Given the racial makeup of the student body (see note 1), students of color were underrepresented among tutoring staff.

To advance and make visible the center's efforts toward antiracism and racial justice, I present at professional conferences and publish. Divisional leadership and programmatic supervisors make professional development funds available for staff, and I use these funds to support my scholarly engagement in the field, but the nature of my role makes professional engagement challenging. Conference attendance and participation are recognized as professional development that supports my work, but unlike tenure-stream faculty who have nonteaching days and sabbaticals, I do not have protected time for research and writing. When I write, then, it feels like survivalist work, like the supplemental independent writing consulting that I did on my own time while directing the seminary writing center. This work, we know, does not necessarily yield monetary compensation, but it does help promote the profile of Black women WPAs navigating marginality and misogynoir, drawing attention to our way-making, and inviting new narratives about the field—who does this work, under what conditions, and with what epistemological impact. A final vignette underscores the point.

Recently, while picking up lunch off-campus, I passed a white woman sitting on a pallet positioned at the edge of a parking lot with her worldly possessions sprawled around her. She asked where I was headed and when I would be returning. Upon learning that I worked at the university, she exclaimed with astonishment, "What the f*ck do you do there!" "I direct a writing center," I said. Puzzled, she replied, "Well, you're just a little brown" and proceeded to name places on campus I should be sure to visit if I had not already. She clearly knew a lot about the institution, enough to know that historically I was "just a little [too] brown" to be directing a writing program there. Womanist way-making in writing center administration works to disrupt marginalization and normative expectations around Black women's embodiment and labor so that we know and value their contributions and learn from their narratives ways to build a more equitable future.

Note

1. In fall 2020, 29 percent of all undergraduates were white, 25 percent Asian, 17 percent Hispanic or Latino, 11 percent international, 7 percent Black or African American, 1 percent American Indian or Alaskan Native, and <1 percent Native Hawaiian or Pacific Islander (Stanford Facts 2021). The number of White undergraduates has decreased by 6 percent since fall 2016 (Stanford Facts 2017).

References

Albanese, Jennifer, and Christine Fena. 2021. "Bridging Boundaries: Perceived Roles of Librarians and Writing Center Tutors in Supporting Student Research Writing." *WLN* 45 (9–10): 18–25.

Bailey, Moya. 2021. *Misogynoir Transformed: Black Women's Digital Resistance*. New York: New York University Press.

Bailey, Moya, and Trudy. 2018. "On Misogynoir: Citation, Erasure, and Plagiarism." *Feminist Media Studies* 18 (4): 762–768.

Baker-Fletcher, Karen, and Garth KASIMU Baker-Fletcher. 1997. *My Sister, My Brother: Womanist and Xodus God-Talk*. Bishop Henry McNeal Turner / Sojourner Truth Series in Black Religion, no. 12. Maryknoll, NY: Orbis Books.

Cannon, Katie G. 1985. "The Emergence of Black Feminist Consciousness." In *Feminist Interpretation of the Bible*, edited by Letty M. Russell, 30–40. Louisville, KY: Westminster John Knox Press.

Cannon, Katie G. 1988. *Black Womanist Ethics*. Scholars Press.

Carter-Tod, Sheila. 2020. "Administering while Black: Negotiating the Emotional Labor of an African American Female WPA." In *The Things We Carry: Strategies for Recognizing and Negotiating Emotional Labor in Writing Program* Administration, edited by Courtney Adams Wooten et al., 197–214. Logan: Utah State University Press.

Coleman, Monica. 2008. *Making a Way Out of No Way*. Minneapolis: Fortress Press.

Cooke, Rachel, and Carol Bledsoe. 2008. "Writing Centers and Libraries: One-Stop Shopping for Better Term Papers." *Reference Librarian*, 49 (2): 119–127.

Grutsch McKinney, Jackie. 2013. *Peripheral Visions for Writing Centers*. Logan: Utah State University Press.

hooks, bell. 1990. "Homeplace (A Site of Resistance)." In *Yearning: Race, Gender, and Cultural Politics*, by bell hooks, 41–49. Boston: South End Press.

Jordan, Zandra L. 2020. "Womanist Curate, Cultural Rhetorics Curation, and Antiracist, Racially, Just Writing Center Administration." *Peer Review* 4 (2). http://thepeerreview-iwca.org/issues/issue-4-2/womanist-curate-cultural-rhetorics-curation-and-antiracist-racially-just-writing-center-administration/.

Kynard, Carmen. 2019. "Administering While Black: Black Women's Labor in the Academy and the 'Position of the Unthought.'" In *Black Perspectives in Writing Program Administration: From the Margins to the Center*, edited by Staci M. Perryman-Clark and Collin Lamont Craig, Conference on College Composition and Communication, 28–50. Urbana, IL: NCTE.

Perryman-Clark, Staci, and Lamont Craig. 2019. *Black Perspectives in Writing Program Administration*. Studies in Writing and Rhetoric. Conference on College Composition and Communication. Urbana, IL: NCTE.

Pierce, Yolanda. 2021. *In My Grandmother's House: Black Women, Faith, and the Stories We Inherit*. Minneapolis: Broadleaf Books.

Riggs, Marcia. 2011. "Living as Religious Ethical Mediators: A Vocation for People of Faith in the Twenty-First Century." In *Womanist Theological Ethics: A Reader*, edited by Katie Geneva Canon, Emilie M. Townes, and Angela D. Sims, 247–253. Louisville, KY: Westminster John Knox Press.

Stanford Facts 2021. Stanford University. https://facts.stanford.edu/wp-content/uploads/sites/20/2021/02/Stanford-FactBook-2021-v7.6-FINAL.pdf.

Stanford Facts 2017. Stanford University. https://www.scribd.com/document/371079886/StanfordFacts-2017.

Valles, Sarah Banschbach, Rebecca Day Babcock, and Karen Keaton Jackson. 2017. "Writing Center Administrators and Diversity: A Survey." *The Peer Review* 1 (1). https://thepeerreview-iwca.org/issues/issue-1/writing-center-administrators-and-diversity-a-survey/.

Walker, Alice. 1983. *In Search of Our Mothers' Gardens: Womanist Prose*. New York: Harcourt Brace Jovanovich.

RESPONSE TO SECTION THREE
Embodied Marginalization

RACHEL AZIMA

As I write my way into this response, I find myself wondering: what role does my own bodymind play in responding to these chapters? Should I mention I am chronically ill and have never disclosed this to my workplace? That I am biracial and often racially illegible to others? That in recent years I have become certain I am neurodivergent but haven't sought any diagnoses? Disclosure—as Garcia (chapter 10), Moroski-Rigney (chapter 9), and Salcedo (chapter 8), in particular, note in this section—is complex and fraught. I suppose it's not strictly necessary for me to divulge the details of my own subject position, but it feels as though I should. Not merely to honor the candor of these authors, though certainly for that reason, but also in recognition of the important argument they make: that we engage in writing center (and other) work through our racially marked, and variously abled and disabled bodies, and that to privilege only the mind leaves the picture incomplete at best and replicates destructive practices at worst.

These authors all uncover deep fault lines in the "cozy homes" grand narrative: as Jordan puts it in chapter 13, "I have found it difficult at times to claim a sense of home inside and outside of the academy even as I work hard to create it for others." Jordan calls attention to how oppressive this narrative is when combined with misogynoir. Fischer (chapter 12) highlights how policies that ignore consultants' possible experiences with sexual assault can make the writing center not only "un-cozy" but also a hostile and an unsafe work environment. These authors also invite us to question other writing center orthodoxies, such as prohibitions against tutors writing things down (Salcedo, chapter 8) and the primacy of the social (Moroski-Rigney, chapter 9). These choices come with costs, and these costs are not borne evenly. Collectively, these authors indicate how we must question our taken-for-granted practices, in light of varying embodied experiences and histories.

The issue of disclosure runs through all these chapters—whether or not they discuss disclosure directly, all reveal the personal, which can be both stressful and cathartic. Crucially, Jordan and Moroski-Rigney (chapter 9) emphasize the importance of being able to tell their own stories—not to be the subjects of others' narratives. Reading all these chapters together highlights the benefits and hazards of disclosure within professional settings while also bringing into relief the flow of information we can't control; for instance, how others perceive us racially or ethnically and to what extent that shapes how they interact with us. Jordan and Escalante (chapter 11) make visible the harms of daily microaggressions, demonstrating how inhabiting Othered racial identities in historically White spaces—which writing centers typically are—adds to the already overwhelming burdens of writing center administrative work.

These burdens represent another central theme, as these authors press us to ask: What labor is acceptable to undertake and what is not? What does equity look like? How can we demand it? Garcia cautions us against tacitly agreeing to the common model of writing center overwork; Escalante reveals the serious and all-encompassing costs of engaging in this disproportionate labor. Moroski-Rigney encourages us to look for other ways in which this labor can happen. While some of these issues are endemic to writing centers, others extend to the institutions within which we perform our labor. Together, these authors poke at the unstable underpinnings of academia itself, which has long served as a prime example of Western attempts to separate body and mind. These authors expose the urgent need for integrated practices that recognize all thoughts and experiences are embodied and that we ignore this fact to our own detriment. Writing centers already push against the pressures of the neoliberal university—What, on its face, is less efficient than one-to-one work?—and part of this resistance should mean giving sustained attention to the embodied experiences of those who work in writing centers, not merely those who visit.

Above all, reading these chapters together makes visible the need for these (and all) conversations to be *intersectional*.[1] While all experience is of course embodied, the more marginal one's embodied identity, the more embodiment gets foregrounded. People who are multiply marginalized not only find themselves in further disempowered positions, but they/we are never allowed to forget how others perceive their embodiment. Yet it's important not to let embodiment stay invisible where supposedly neutral bodies, those perceived as the norm, are concerned (read: White and able-bodied). It's time for other folks to recognize the degree to which inhabiting a normative body deeply shapes their experiences—just as much as for those deemed non-normative. And none of these questions around race and disability or any other embodied marginalization can be understood separately from one another. Whether it is university budget cuts or COVID-19 mortality rates, we don't all bear structural and other burdens equally. These authors help us recognize these oppressions in a writing center context and the various harms they cause, and they reveal how imperative it is for us to reexamine all our practices, from the personal and individual (how much work we take on, what we disclose) to the local (what practices we engage in at our centers) to the institutional and structural (What demands can we push back on? What can we advocate for together?). And we must be vigilant in our attention to where intersecting identities make ourselves and our colleagues even more vulnerable. I think about the growing push toward unionization in the US as this publication is coming together, and what is true for us also in writing centers: no one is coming to save us. We must save ourselves, and we can only do this together: by working to truly understand one another's stories, recognizing where we are privileged and where we aren't, and engaging in support and advocacy wherever we can.

Note

1. There is obviously a great deal to be said about intersectionality, more than I can sum up here. Sami Schalk's *Bodyminds Reimagined: (Dis)ability, Race, and Gender in Black Women's Speculative Fiction* (2018) and activist Imani Barbarin's work around race and disability strike me as particularly relevant.

References

Barbarin, Imani. Crutches and Spice. Accessed December 21, 2023. https://crutches andspice.com/.

Schalk, Sami. 2018. *Bodyminds Reimagined: (Dis)ability, Race, and Gender in Black Women's Speculative Fiction*. Durham, NC: Duke University Press.

AFTERWORD

Imagining—and Enacting—Inclusive Writing Center (Scholarly) Practices

ELIZABETH KLEINFELD, SOHUI LEE, AND JULIE PREBEL

It is a truism that writing centers are differently situated on college and university campuses and, by this logic, that the experiences of writing center practitioners may range more divergently than has been recorded in writing center scholarship. While we, the editors of this collection, have familiar positions as tenured faculty directors of writing centers in comprehensive universities or a liberal arts college, our individual experiences as writing center practitioners involved difficult navigation through marginal spaces. It led to long conversations that inspired us to research and study who was published in *WLN: A Journal of Writing Center Scholarship* (Kleinfeld, Lee, and Prebel 2021a) and then to design this collection. The following are the short summaries of our experiences.

ELIZABETH'S STORY: Elizabeth stumbled into writing center work as an adjunct instructor at a community college in the 1990s because it offered additional hours. Even after securing a tenured position as faculty at a community college, she found herself repeatedly marginalized by the writing center community. One time when someone she was talking to at a conference noticed her institutional affiliation on her nametag, they said with surprise, "Oh, you're from a community college! What are you doing here?" Her community college affiliation was typically greeted with condolences or the assumption that she had nothing to contribute to conversations about research. Later, in a tenured position at a four-year university, she felt pressure to hide her disability and "pass" as able-bodied. Finally rejecting that notion—with the protection of tenure and the security of being promoted to full professor—she added information about her disability to her email signature and was amazed at how many people responded to her emails with disclosures of their own disabilities and struggles to "pass."

SOHUI'S STORY: The first Asian American faculty writing center director in the California State University system, Sohui remembers how her mother worried when she said she wanted to teach English: Would white students respect her? How could an Asian American woman teach English? While studying for her PhD at Boston University (BU) in the mid-1990s, she remembers being the only Asian student in her class. Looking up BU's English Department demographics in the *Guide to American Graduate Schools*, she noted she was a number, the "one" Asian or minority listed on the page. When she transitioned from English literature to composition and then writing center studies, the feelings of racial isolation only increased (there were even fewer Asian Americans in writing center studies than English or composition studies). While participants in the International Writing Centers Association (IWCA) conferences have become more diverse over the years, Sohui remembers the discomfort of sitting in a session on English as a Second Language (ESL) where the panelists were Anglo-American professionals speaking about how to empathize with multilingual writers. The assumptions that writing center professionals were white and native speakers of English were not completely misplaced: the majority of the attendees were indeed both. However, as a non-white professional for whom English was a second language (after Korean), she found that these assumptions made her wonder about the tunnel vision we might have as writing center administrators (WCAs)—how do our assumptions, for instance, overlook the multilingual individuals who work as writing center tutors and administrators?

JULIE'S STORY: Julie's pathway to directing a writing center started when she was a student who benefited from visiting writing centers. As a first-generation college student, Julie found the experience of being in college unfamiliar and at times alienating. The writing center at the community college where she began her education helped her build confidence as a student and a writer and inspired her to transfer to a four-year university that led eventually to a PhD program. While she worked in undergraduate and graduate writing centers, often as a source of needed income, Julie found herself somewhat unprepared and untrained for the challenges of administering one. When she took over a college writing center that needed rebuilding and rebranding (from hiring/staffing and tutor training to creating/managing budgets and developing programming), she experienced another version of the imposter syndrome she had throughout college: Did she really belong here? It took years before she felt she could contribute, even in small ways, to the conversations about writing center work at national conferences or in scholarly journals.

Although areas of marginalization we've experienced—such as disability, white habitus, and first-generation imposter syndrome—have been explored in writing center scholarship for some time, the current wave of scholarly interest in marginalized voices folds in new and challenging ideas for consideration. Recent articles by Sue Mendelsohn and Clarissa Walker (2021), Talisha Haltiwanger Morrison (2021), and Andrea Scott (2021) attest to the continued interest and expansion of this arena for research. In particular, the March 2023 issue of *WLN*'s inclusion of an article by Paula Rawlins and Amanda Arp on fat studies testifies to this focus on experiences of marginalization. Our collection of thirteen narrative essays and research articles examine the structural and material barriers experienced by writing center practitioners; the North American bias of dominant writing center discourse and its impact on writing center practitioners outside the United States; and, finally, the embodied marginalization influenced by intersectional experiences of disabilities, race, gender, and sexuality. Three responses to the essays and articles suggest implications of these discussions and direct readers to further lines of inquiry.

We believe the chapters and responses of this collection provide plenty of rich food for thought and reflection on our practices and scholarship as a discipline. This collection highlights many assumptions about what things writing centers should do, how they should do them, and from where they should do them that are part of writing center grand narratives. At the same time, as we edited the collection, we found ourselves recognizing ways we ourselves are complicit in marginalization because we have also imbibed, unconsciously, various parts of writing center grand narratives. Elizabeth, for example, realized as she read the discussion in chapter 4 by Shareen Grogan, Pam Bromley, and Denise Stephenson that she had overlooked the fact that while her peer tutors have access to travel funds through the university student activities office, professional tutors on her staff did not have access to travel funds. With knowledge gained from chapters by Sarah Fischer (chapter 12), Deborah Escalante (chapter 11), and Zandra Jordan (chapter 13), Julie found herself rethinking—and ultimately revising—her center's approach to supporting tutors when they experience racial microaggressions or express feeling uncomfortable when working with students who do not respect their boundaries. The chapters on globalization and marginalization by Nancy Henaku (chapter 6) and Abigail Villagrán Mora (chapter 7) helped Sohui become more aware of how writing center literature assumed its default reading audiences to be North American writers; the chapters led her to discuss assumed audiences in literature studied in tutor training courses as well as to acknowledge the global audience assumed in published scholarship.

Here, we would like to extend an invitation for all readers to reflect on the work of this collection, both as it pertains to the writing center you work in and the scholarship you engage with. The following questions we share grow out of the pieces in this collection that we think can help all of us reflect. Because institutions, writing centers, and the positions of WCAs vary so widely, not all questions will apply to every reader, but we envision these as starting points for further consideration.

1. What did your graduate training privilege in its attention to writing centers? How might this have impacted your own values and unseen spots about writing center work and scholarship?

2. Are there practices or processes in your writing center that seem to raise tensions with someone? What do you know about why? What more could you learn? What other perspectives could the situation be seen from?

3. Do some staff positions have more or less or different access to resources, such as scheduling priority, hours, funding for conference attendance, books, professional development, health insurance, pay, service opportunities, or research experiences? How might these differences impact staff relations? Are there ways you can address the differences?

4. What do you believe is necessary for collaboration between tutors and students? Do others on your staff or campus have different ideas? Is there overlap?

5. Do you know how students' experiences are impacted by staffing in your writing center? What more could you learn?

6. Are there stories you tell yourself about your position that may not be serving you right now?
7. What are your assumptions about what writing centers should do, how they should do them, and where they should do them from? For each assumption, can you think of another reasonable perspective?
8. What are some ways the space and practices of your writing center convey what a "good writer" looks like, how their body functions, or what their writing process looks like?
9. Who is underrepresented in your writing center's staff or your scholarship?
10. How have you done more with less? What strategies might be available to you to resist this impulse?
11. Do you know what kinds of microaggressions your staff has experienced? What kinds have you experienced?
12. Do you know how safe and comfortable your staff feels in the writing center space? Do you feel safe and comfortable in the writing center space? What can you do to increase feelings of safety and comfort for yourself and your staff?
13. What role does your own body-mind play in your responses to these questions?
14. What stories about your writing center experience have you not told? Where are the gaps between your writing center work and the stories told about writing center work in the scholarship? In what ways do you feel you "don't belong" in writing centers?
15. If you've worked in multiple writing centers, what are the assumptions and values you've brought with you from other writing centers that may no longer be serving you in your current writing center?

Undoubtedly, your answers to these questions will be individualized to the unique context of your centers and institutions, and in terms of your perspectives, experiences, identities, and histories working in academe.

For readers who work as editors and wish to practice the kind of activist editing methodology illustrated in the making of this collection, we share our own experiences and recommend the following five actions for redesigning a manuscript selection process that is intentionally inclusive:

- Design a survey that collects relevant demographic information of authors who submit manuscripts (racial/ethnic background, roles, abilities, national affiliations, etc.).

- Track the progress of manuscripts by underrepresented authors and identify where authors are facing barriers. Use this method to explore how authors might be offered more support in these areas, if possible.
- When evaluating manuscripts for fit, consider prioritizing underrepresented perspectives over general writing quality, especially if editors plan on providing extensive feedback and guidance.
- Design a feedback process that builds in multiple rounds of both synchronous feedback through video conference and asynchronous feedback. In our experience, multiple rounds of feedback improve author-editor communication and establish trust.
- When the selection process is complete, editors should be cognizant of who is being published and collect data on how well various demographic groups are being represented in the publishing effort. This data collection will help editors track how their process is working and whether they are achieving their objectives.

Finally, we would like to share our findings on how our professional organizations and scholarly journals might disrupt current marginalizing practices. While we reviewed chapter submissions for this collection, we facilitated a roundtable discussion at the 2021 IWCA Conference titled "Imagining an Anti-Racist, Decolonial, and Anti-Ableist Writing Center Studies Publishing Model" (Kleinfeld, Lee, and Prebel 2021b). As part of the roundtable activity, the attendees worked with us to brainstorm ideas for disrupting the existing publishing conventions in writing center studies. Some of the key takeaways from this discussion include suggestions for transforming how we (as individuals and an organization) "do" publishing. Participants at the IWCA panel raised four significant changes to how writing center studies should operate:

1. Change the structures of our professional organizations to promote and not restrict wider participation and leadership. For example, if leadership requires so much time that someone without access to institutional support such as course releases wouldn't be able to do it, then only people from certain types of institutions will ever lead our organizations. If the majority of writing center administrators are in nonfaculty positions, we need to create leadership opportunities they can participate in.
2. Be deliberate in soliciting scholarship from, amplifying the work of, and engaging emerging scholars who are underrepresented in the field. This may mean promoting calls for papers (CFPs) differently or issuing direct invitations more often and open CFPs less often. We can also demystify

the publishing process and proactively support first-time authors.
3. Problematize our publishing standards by questioning conventions and best practices. While anonymous peer review, for instance, is common in scholarly publishing, we can question who is served by it and who is not. Editors can resist the conventions by exploring activist editing methodologies such as the one used for this collection.
4. Remember that writing centers and writing center professionals outside of the US matter, and actively support their work. Decenter the American experience of writing centers in our thinking and research. Collaborate with writing center practitioners in other countries.

The participant discussion, along with putting together this collection and interacting closely with its authors, underscore the importance of questioning how writing center scholarship is vetted, created, and distributed.

In working on this collection, Elizabeth, Sohui, and Julie have come to realize that writing center practitioners who are active in the field cannot wait for institutions, organizations, and journals to make changes. We must realize that *we are* the institutions, organizations, and journals. The suggestions for change generated at the IWCA roundtable highlight the agency we have as WCAs, as scholars and editors, as IWCA members and officers. We need to recognize the hierarchies and value judgments that are deeply embedded in our institutions, discipline, journals, and our own views—views that are rendered invisible and natural until they are outed by alternate perspectives and voices. Likewise, the act of publishing should be an intentional act to be inclusive. By employing an activist editing approach, we will be doing more than providing opportunities for voices to be heard—we will expand our understanding of our practices, invigorate our scholarship, and draw more diverse talent that will transform our field.

References

Kleinfeld, Elizabeth, Sohui Lee, and Julie Prebel. 2021a. "Whose Voices Are Heard? A Demographic Comparison of Authors Published in *WLN* 2005–2017 and Writers Interested in Publishing." *WLN: A Journal of Writing Center Scholarship* 45 (7–8). https://wac.colostate.edu/docs/wln/v45/45.7-8.pdf.

Kleinfeld, Elizabeth, Sohui Lee, and Julie Prebel. 2021b. "Imagining an Anti-Racist, Decolonial, and Anti-ableist Writing Center Studies Publishing Model." International Writing Centers Association (IWCA) Conference, October 20–23.

Mendelsohn, Sue, and Clarissa Walker. 2021. "Agents of Change: African American Contributions to Writing Centers." *Writing Center Journal* 39 (1/2): 21–54.

Morrison, Talisha Haltiwanger. 2021. "A Balancing Act: Black Women Experiencing and Negotiating Racial Tension in the Center." *Writing Center Journal* 39 (1/2). https://doi.org/10.7771/2832-9414.1957.

Rawlins, Paula, and Amanda Arp. 2023. "Taking Up Space and Time: How Writing Center Administrators Can Better Support Fat (and All) Tutors." *WLN: A Journal of Writing Center Scholarship* 47 (3). https://wac.colostate.edu/docs/wln/v47/47-3.pdf.

Scott, Andrea. 2021. "A Radical and Sustainable Vision for Inclusivity: Internationalizing the Writing Center. A Guide for Developing a Multilingual Writing Center (2020)." *WLN: A Journal of Writing Center Scholarship* 46 (1–2). https://wac.colostate.edu/docs/wln/v46/46.1-2.pdf.

Index

Page numbers followed by *f* indicate a figure; page numbers followed by *n* indicate an endnote; and page numbers followed by *t* indicate a table.

able-bodiedness/able-mindedness, 174, 215
ableism, 152, 156, 159, 160, 161, 168, 173
Academic Resource Center, 53
Academic Success Center (ASC), 170*n*4, 182, 183, 184, 185, 186
academy, invisible disabilities and, 155, 157–61
access: labor and, 11; pain of, 166; student, 40
accessibility, 152, 156, 168
access intimacy, 166–69
accommodation, 152, 157, 159, 167
accountability, 21, 99, 207
activist editing, 9, 12–17, 225
Activist Editing Methodology, 223, 225
ADA. *See* Americans with Disabilities Act
ADHD. *See* attention deficit hyperactivity disorder
Adichie, Chimamanda Ngozi, 128
adjuncts, 21, 95; composition, 57, 88; course reduction for, 58; term, 69–70*n*2
administration, 14, 44, 109, 116, 161, 210; duties, 63–64; relationships with, 65, 94; understanding of, 34; writing center, 37
Administrative-Problem: Solving for Writing Programs and Writing Centers (Myers Breslin), 37
administrators, 49, 119; daily labor of, 45; disabled, 161, 168; graduate student, 39, 40;

meeting of, 123*t*; tenure-track, 104; warning to, 45
affect management, 164, 170*n*9
affirmative action, 97
African Popular Culture, 117
ageism, 52
agency, 141, 196, 204; fostering, 131, 142; lack of, 60
American Association of University Professors (AAUP), 163
American Community Survey, 178
Americans with Disabilities Act (ADA), 150, 152, 175
Antelope Valley College (AVC) Learning Center, 66, 67, 68, 69
antiblackness, proliferation of, 203
antiracism, 5, 7, 12, 111, 112, 114
"Anti-Racist Scholarly Reviewing Practices," 12
APU. *See* Azusa Pacific University
Arao, Brian, 198*n*1
Arp, Amanda, 221
ASC. *See* Academic Success Center
ASD. *See* autism spectrum disorder
Ashesi University, 117, 120
Ashesi Writing Center (AWC), 117, 119, 121, 122
Asperger's syndrome, 164

attention deficit hyperactivity disorder (ADHD), 23, 155, 167
Author Survey, 10
autism, 155, 170n4, 170n6; professional socializing and, 162–165; women with, 170n5
autism spectrum disorder (ASD), 23, 155
Autistic Burnout, 158, 163, 164, 170n6
autoethnography, 110, 111
autonomy, 42, 54, 160, 141, 158, 191
AVC. *See* Antelope Valley College
AWC. *See* Ashesi Writing Center
Azima, Rachel, 16, 25
Azusa Pacific University (APU), 177, 178, 179, 180, 184, 186, 188, 191, 192; as HSI, 190
Azusa Pacific University (APU) Writing Center, 182, 192n4

Babcock, Rebecca Day, 10, 14, 150, 152, 179, 200
Bailey, Moya, 200
Barbarin, Imani, 217n1
Before and after the Tutorial: Writing Centers and Institutional Relationships (Mauriello, Macauley, and Koch), 37
Bempah, Daniel Kwaku, 119
best practices, 26, 27, 46, 141–42
bias, 13, 26, 184, 221; lore, 3; racial, 212; systemic, 98
BIPOC, 19, 178–79, 181, 199, 202
Black Methodist church, 204
Black people, 192n1, 202, 203–4; marginalization of, 7
Black women: family/community for, 204; mammification of, 203; quality of life among, 204; racist image of, 203; strategies for, 207
Blewett, Kelly, 12, 14
Bloom, Lynn Z., 163
BodyMind, 154, 159, 215
Boquet, Elizabeth, 4, 72, 149
Botvin, Joshua, 20, 37, 55, 57–58, 67, 70n4, 104, 105; advice narrative and, 38
brain, disabilities and, 154–55
Brannon, Lil, 35
Bromley, Pam, 21, 81, 89, 104, 212
Brooklyn Project, 73
Brooks-Gillies, Marilee, 111
Brown, Nicole, 174
Brown, Shan-Estelle, 75
Brown, Wilkie, 160, 161
Brueggemann, Brenda Jo, 151
Bruffee, Kenneth, 73, 75
Buck, Elisabeth, 49, 50, 221; narratives of, 51–55; role of, 59; WRC and, 61

Buck, Elisabeth H., 10–11, 20, 37, 67, 104, 105; access and, 11; advice narrative and, 38 budgets, 40, 44; concerns over, 34; controlling, 43; discovering, 38–39; managerial tasks for, 46; setting, 41
burnout, 91, 95, 96, 97, 98, 106, 165–66. *See also* Autistic Burnout
Burns, Deborah, 74
Butler, Judith, 36

California State University, 178, 220
calls for papers (CFPs), 224–225
Camarillo, Eric, 112
Cameron, 93–94, 95, 96, 97
Cannon, Katie G., 200
Carino, Peter, 74
Carroll, Meg, 4
case studies, 9, 24, 134; approach, 131–32; purpose of, 132–33
Caswell, Nikki, 34, 37, 44, 49, 50, 57, 61
Cheatle, Joseph, 78
Clark, Irene L., 73, 74
Clemens, Kristi, 198n1
Cockayne, Daniel, 11
coding, 134, 136f
collaboration, 15, 19, 21, 67, 72, 73, 75, 79, 112, 129, 137, 138–49, 151, 162, 163; campus, 158; cross-cultural, 211; importance of, 138; peer, 83; student, 222; tutor, 222
College Reading and Learning Association, 53
"Collegiality, the Game" (Bloom), 163
communication, 117, 119, 122, 174; adaptations, 153; oral, 211; personal, 16; strengthened, 16
community: building, 195; campus, 209; Hispanic/Latino, 192; learning, 131, 132, 140; research and, 163; writing center, 16, 162, 209
community of practice (CoP), 130, 131, 132, 133, 135, 142; cultivation/knowledge management and, 140–41; endemic learning and, 141; learning community and, 140; learning culture of, 134; perception of, 138–40
compensation, 98, 173, 213; fair/equitable, 206
composition studies, 4, 36, 90, 105, 127, 178
Composition Studies, 12
Condon, Frankie, 4, 7, 8
Connecting Writing Centers Across Borders, 145
contingency, 58, 63, 90, 96–97, 99, 101, 105; impact of, 89; professional tutors and, 93–95
conversations, 18, 220; intersectional, 217; professional, 149
CoP. *See* community of practice
Corbett, Steven, 74, 75
Cortez Community College, 91

Cortez Community College Writing Center, 88, 91, 93, 94, 98, 99
counterstories, 8, 45, 46; interdisciplinary, 110; methodology of, 22; transnational, 109, 110, 112, 113, 116
Courageous Communicators Series, 208, 209–10
COVID-19 pandemic, 19, 34, 40, 42, 63, 91, 100, 142, 186, 217
critical discourse studies, 115
critical race studies, 23
Critical Race Theory (CRT), 110
culture, 18, 72, 111, 119, 152, 165, 178, 184, 186; academic, 164; campus, 211; departmental, 120; higher education, 142; learning, 22, 128, 129, 130, 132, 134, 140, 141, 142; workplace, 160; writing center, 123, 160
curriculum, 20, 34; expectations of, 145

"Dangers of a Single Story, The" (Adichie), 128
Dangling Modifier, 6
data analysis, 100, 135–37
data collection, 9, 100, 134–35, 224
de Certeau, Michel, 36
de Herder, William, 114
decolonialism, 110, 112, 124
demographics, 15, 177
Denny, Harry, 5, 12, 36, 69, 80, 81
Derrida, Jacques, 36
Devet, Bonnie, 79
directorship, 51, 185, 210–11; elements of, 64; full-time, 103; tenure-line, 105
disabilities, 15, 150, 165, 221; ableism and, 152; academics with, 155, 174–75; brain and, 154–55; disclosing, 157, 160; hearing, 149; hidden, 151, 158; invisible, 155, 156, 157–61, 168; managing, 178; mental, 157, 158, 159; narratives on, 152; physical/learning, 151; psychological, 159
Disability in Higher Education (Evans and Brown), 160
disability justice, 24, 166, 169; fostering, 155, 168
disabled people, 11, 24, 160–61, 167, 215; financial price for, 165; higher education and, 160; representing, 169; tales of, 159; unemployment and, 160
disciplinary practices, 8, 11, 35, 111
disciplinary responses, re-assessing, 43–45
discourse, 109, 166; academic, 80, 150, 153; writing center, 6, 15, 76, 82, 99, 156
discrimination, 7, 188, 206
Diversion, Equity, and Inclusion (DEI), 212
diversity, 9, 11, 190; engaging, 111; lack of, 14

Diversity Initiative (IWCA), 185, 190
Dixon, Elise, 20, 33, 41–43, 50, 67
Dolmage, Jay, 23, 156, 158
Driscoll, Dana, 36

Eckstein, Grant, 74
Edie, 93, 94, 97
editing process, 14, 16, 118
"Editorial Philosophy and Vision" (Sicari, Denny, and Garcia), 12
education, 40; higher, 4, 62, 90, 97, 98, 99, 128, 160, 173, 192; literacy, 116; quality, 89; tutor, 128, 129, 130, 132, 140, 146
Education Trust, 178
efficiency, perceptions of, 160, 169
Elston, M. Melissa, 159
embodiment, 23, 156, 209, 217; Black women's, 213; disclosure of, 25; gendered, 185, 202
emotional exhaustion, 50, 91, 95, 96–97
employment, 43; full-time, 99; security, 51, 162; status, 206; student, 39, 40, 46; tentative, 58–59; tenure-track, 51
energy, 159; depletion, 155; physical/emotional, 96
engagement, 109, 159, 160; academic, 116, 119; community, 129; person-to-person, 168; transnational, 112
English: limited skills in, 115; non-native speakers of, 117–18; non-standard, 112; proficiency in, 115; standard, 112, 114, 146
English as Foreign Language (EFL), 118
English as a Second Language (ESL), 117, 208, 220
Eodice, Michele, 4
equity, 7, 25, 206
Escalante, Deborah, 24, 216, 222
ESL. *See* English as a Second Language
ethics, 98–99; misognynoir/womanist, 25; womanist, 25, 199, 200, 203, 212
ethnicity, 15–16, 17, 178, 184, 190, 191, 208, 223
Evans, Broido, 160, 161
executive function, 161, 165–66, 169n2
Expanding Circle, 115
experience, 34, 150, 216; Black women's, 203–4; educational, 89; international, 123; marginalization, 190; neurological, 161; patchwork, 88; pedagogical, 210; professional, 211; research, 222; student, 222; writing center, 21, 38, 139, 223

faculty director, 51, 52, 54, 60, 63
Faison, Wonderful, 5, 7, 8
Fat Studies, 221

feedback, 60, 114, 164, 190, 224; directive, 81; editorial, 16; providing, 16, 120; tutor, 73, 81; writing, 118
Fels, Dawn, 89
fibromyalgia (FM), 173, 174–75
Finance and Scholarship committee (IWCA), 191
financial issues, 39, 94, 95, 97, 98, 99, 182
Fischer, Sarah, 24, 215, 222
flexibility, 103, 156, 158
Floyd, George, 7
FM. *See* fibromyalgia
For Brown Girls with Sharp Edges and Tender Hearts (Mojica Rodriguez), 177, 190, 192*n*3
Foucault, Jean, 36
funding, 37, 53, 55, 62–63, 67, 90, 104, 113, 158, 191, 210, 222; finding, 46; issues, 46, 54; providing, 45; seeking, 38, 39

Garcia, Elena, 24, 151, 152, 215
García, Romeo, 12, 112, 181, 196
Gardner, Phillip, 80, 81
Geller, Anne, 4, 36, 69, 141
gender, 23, 178, 197, 202, 208, 221
Getty, Amy, 172
Ghana, 116, 119–20; ESL and, 117
Global North, 129
Global South, 112, 128, 129, 141, 146; tutor education in, 140; writing centers in, 131–32
globalization, 23, 121, 221, 222; capitalist, 129; marginalization and, 18, 22
Gorham, Aja, 21, 82, 103, 206
graduate teaching instructor (GTI), 113
grand narratives, 3–4, 6, 118, 128, 157, 172, 195; academe's, 51; challenging, 21; collective tunnel vision and, 72; disrupting, 4, 41, 83; enduring, 33; homeplace and, 201–5; investment in, 22–23; power and, 109, 146; studying, 9–10; tutors and, 83. *See also* writing center grand narratives
Greenfield, Laura, 4, 5, 44
Grimm, Nancy, 81
Grogan, Shareen, 21, 98, 104, 221
Grutsch McKinney, Jackie, 3, 34, 35, 37, 44, 49, 50, 57, 61, 67, 111, 124, 162, 166, 172, 173, 194–95; on tutoring, 72; on writing center work, 109
Guide to American Graduate School, 220

Hall, Mark, 130
Harbord, John, 18
Harper Hitt, Allison, 23
Harris, Mickey, 75

Harris, Muriel, 35, 120
Hashlamon, Y., 105
Haswell, Richard H., 8
health issues, 96, 178, 184, 207, 222
Healy, Dave, 73
hearing loss, 150, 151, 152
Heidegger, Martin, 36
Henaku, Nancy, 22, 23, 144, 222
hiring process, 39–41
Hispanic Serving Institutions (HSIs), 14, 177, 190
Historically Black Colleges and Universities (HBCUs), 8
history, 116, 119, 216
Hitt, Alison, 23, 156, 157, 158, 167
home: metaphor of, 202–3; writing centers and, 203
homeplace, grand narrative and, 201–5
hooks, bell, 36, 204
HSIs. *See* Hispanic Serving Institutions
Hugo, Victor, 192

"Idea of the Writing Center, The" (North), 120
identity, 5, 98, 131, 144, 150, 167, 202, 223; academic, 145; departmental, 120; differentiated, 129; disciplinary, 46; engaging, 111; intellectual, 37; intersectional, 217; linguistic, 145; other, 114; personal, 68, 145; professional, 37, 145; tutor, 21, 75; writing and, 36
"Identity and the Disabled Tutor" (Muceck), 151
"Imagining an Anti-Racist, Decolonial, and Anti-Ableist Writing Center Studies Publishing Model" (Kleinfeld, Lee, and Prebel), 224
imposter syndrome, 221
"In Conversation with Amanda Gorman's Inaugural Poem" (workshop), 212
"In the Name of Love" (Tokumatsu), 68
inclusion, 7, 9, 36, 156, 190
inequalities, 7; structural, 12, 210
Inoue, Asao, 111–12
institutional conditions, 14, 38, 50, 120
Institutional Review Board (IRB), 91, 100
interactions: face-to-face, 170*n*9; peer-to-peer, 75; tutor-student, 130
Interest Survey, 10
International Writing Centers Association (IWCA), 6, 26, 44–45, 68, 75, 220, 225; Diversity Initiative, 185, 190; funding for, 45; Summer Institutes of, 127, 191, 193*n*6
International Writing Centers Association (IWCA) Board, 84*n*4
International Writing Centers Association (IWCA) Conference, 224

"Interpreting Writing Center Tutorials with College-Level Deaf Students" (Babcock), 150
Intersections: Theory-Practice in the Writing Center (Mullin and Wallace), 37
interviews, 63, 134, 139; adjustments in, 92–93; data from, 136; protocol for, 100–101*t*; semi-structured, 134, 134*f*
IRB. *See* Institutional Review Board
Isaacs, Emily, 36
IWCA. *See* International Writing Centers Association

Jackson, Karen Keaton, 10, 14, 37, 44, 179, 200
Jackson, Rebecca, 34, 49, 50, 57
Jerome, 93, 95, 96, 97
Jewell, Megan Swihart, 78
Jordan, Zandra, 25, 185, 215, 216, 222

Kachru, Braj, 114
KC. *See* knowledge creation
KI. *See* knowledge initiative
Kleinfeld, Elizabeth, 219–20, 225
KM. *See* knowledge management
Knight, Melinda, 36
knowledge, 11, 36, 138–39, 206; analyzing, 141; collecting, 141; discipline-specific, 45; dominant, 123; explicit/tacit, 131; internalized/externalized, 131; professional, 110; theoretical/scholarly, 42; translation of, 140; tutoring, 140
knowledge creation (KC), 131, 132, 133, 135; CoP and, 138–40; described, 136; type of, 137–38
knowledge initiative (KI), 130, 132, 133, 134, 135, 137, 139, 141; constructing, 146; CoP and, 138; elements of, 136, 136*f*; sustaining, 22
knowledge management (KM), 131, 140, 141
knowledge preservation (KP), 131, 132, 133, 135; CoP and, 138–40; described, 136
knowledge sharing (KS), 131, 132, 133, 135, 139; CoP and, 138–40; described, 136
knowledgeability, 135, 137–38, 138–39, 140, 141
Koch, Robert T., Jr., 37
KP. *See* knowledge preservation
KS. *See* knowledge sharing
Kynard, Carmen, 203

labor, 98, 216; access and, 11; administrative, 37, 45, 46; Black woman, 208; contingent, 17, 62, 105; emotional, 44; essential, 37; experiences, 19; false perceptions of, 57; history of, 175; instability, 91; invisible, 6; non-faculty, 104; part-time, 105; professional, 90; queer, 6; shifts in, 50; underrepresented, 4; writing center, 49, 51, 52, 57
Laufer, Miriam E., 78
Lave, Jean, 36, 130, 138
LaVecchia, Christina, 12, 14
Lawrence, Sarah, 78
leadership, 117; divisional, 212; ecology of, 141; womanist, 210–13
learning, 83, 130; activities, 138; assistance, 67; benefit for, 142; fostering, 131; incremental, 35; individualized, 78; informal, 140–41; process, 98; specialist, 66; strategies, 141; student-centered, 75, 91, 97; transforming, 181; ways of, 156
learning environment, 129, 140
Leaving Evidence (Mingus), 166
"Leaving Home: Towards Critical Readings of Writing Center Spaces" (Grutsch McKinney), 162
Lee, Sohui, 16, 220, 222, 225
Legitimate Peripheral Participation (LPP), 138
Lerner, Neal, 57, 75
Lewanika, Thokozile, 130
LGBTQ+ students, safe space for, 185
Li, Weijia, 16, 17, 22–23
Linton, Simi, 150
literacy, 23, 116, 146; information, 205; practices, 4, 145; racial, 211, 212; visual, 209

McBride, Maureen, 120, 121
McCauley, William J., Jr., 37
McDermott, Richard, 131
Mahala, Daniel, 82
mammification, 203
marginalization, 3, 8, 9, 15, 17, 20, 23, 25, 39, 58, 61, 62, 72, 75, 128, 144, 145, 173, 178, 182, 183, 184, 187, 190, 198, 199, 210–13; Black, 7, 201; counteracting, 34; experiences of, 18–19, 26, 50, 194; gender, 201; globalization and, 18, 22; invisible disability and, 157–61; intellectual/disciplinary, 36; narratives of, 43; professional, 69; racial, 185, 201; research and theory and, 35–38; self-imposed, 37; structural, 17, 19, 20–21, 24, 104; systemic, 51; tales of, 67; way-making and, 205–10; writing center, 18, 33, 34, 40, 44, 46, 172
marginalized bodies, 203
marginalized voices, 3, 4, 27
Martinez, Aja, 8
Mauriello, Nicholas, 37
MCC. *See* Multiliteracy and Communication Center
memory impairments, 164, 173

Mendelsohn, Sue, 221
mental health, 62, 150, 151, 157, 159
Mentor Matching program, 45
mentorship, 21, 44–45, 164
metanarratives, 110, 111, 113, 121, 124
#MeToo movement, 195
Micciche, Laura, 12, 14
Michigan Tech Multiliteracies Center (MTMC), 113–14, 115, 117
Mick, Connie Snyder, 76
microaggressions, 24, 184, 185, 186, 222, 223
micromanagement style, 59, 186
Mingus, Mia, 152, 166
Minority Serving Institutions (MSIs), 14, 190
misogynoir, 199, 200, 203, 208, 210, 211
Moddelmog, Debra A., 151
Mojica Rodríguez, Prisca Dorca, 177, 190, 192n3
monolingualism, 145
Monty, Randal, 53, 98, 105
Moroski-Rigney, Karen, 23, 24, 154, 173, 174, 215, 216
Morris, Janine, 12, 14
Morrison, Talisha Haltiwanger, 221
Mossman, Mark, 150, 151–52
Mott, Carrie, 11
MSIs. See Minority Serving Institutions
MTMC. See Michigan Tech Multiliteracies Center
Muceck, Sarah A., 151
Mullin, Joan, 18
multilingualism, 115, 118, 122, 123, 145, 146
Multiliteracy and Communication Center (MCC), 50, 54, 55, 56, 61, 62, 63
Mundy, Robert, 5
Murphy, Susan Wolff, 81
Myers Zawacki, Terry, 78

Namubiru, Ester R., 16, 17, 22–23, 145
narratives, 8, 9–12, 15, 33, 49, 135, 145, 160, 195, 216; central, 134; "cozy home," 24; dominant, 123; lived-in, 153; marginalization, 144; research-based, 9; specific, 134; writing center, 123, 202. *See also* grand narratives; writing center grand narratives
Natalie, 207, 208
National Census of Writing (NCW), 76, 77, 89
National Institutes of Health (NIH), 150
Naydan, Liliana, 5
NCW. See National Census of Writing
Neaderhiser, Stephen, 80
neoliberalism, 104, 105, 118, 216
neurodiversity, 162, 163, 164, 165, 169; accommodating, 168; term, 169n1

Nier-Weber, Dani, 57, 58, 70n4, 89, 90
NIH. *See* National Institutes of Health
Noise from the Writing Center (Boquet), 149
Nordlof, John, 80, 81
Norman M. Eberly Multilingual Writing Center, 145
North, Stephen, 35, 120, 121
Northway, Kara, 81

Office of the Provost (APU), 180, 182, 187, 193n6
"On the Rhetorics of Mental Disability" (Prendergast), 157
Open Society University Network (OSUN) Writing Center, 121
Opoku, Gabriel, 119
"Other Invisible Hand: Adjunct Labor and Economies and Writing Center, The" (Nier-Weber), 57
otherness, 111, 118, 174, 200
"Our Publication Processes and Timelines" (University Press of Colorado), 12
"Outer Circle" (Kachru), 114, 115

Painter, Nell Irvin, 192n1
participant information, anonymization of, 92t
Paz, Enrique, 20, 33, 38–41, 50, 67
pedagogy, 78, 97, 146, 208; writing center, 127, 128, 132, 141, 210
peer, term, 73
peer collaboration theory, 76
peer review, 225; double-anonymous, 11, 12, 13, 13f
peer tutors, 71, 80; feedback on, 73; paying, 82; presumption of, 72–76; term, 79; undergraduate, 72–76, 78
Peer Writing Tutor Alumni Research Project, 73
peerness, 21, 72, 81, 82, 83
Pemberton, Michael, 78
people of color, 7; violence against, 116
Perdue, Sherry Wynn, 36
Peripheral Visions for Writing Centers (Grutsch McKinney), 3, 67, 109, 172
Piercy, Margaret, 69
positionality, 16, 50, 58, 114, 116, 159, 165
postcolonialism, 111, 112, 120
power: analytical, 73; coloniality of, 112; diffusion, 156; grand narratives and, 109, 146; layers of, 116; linguistic, 114–15; practice, 6, 36; landscapes of, 138, 140; writing center, 128, 196
Prebel, Julie, 16, 220–25
Prendergast, Catherine, 23, 157

Price, Margaret, 23, 159, 162, 163, 170n8; on mentally ill students, 150; on rhetoric, 156–57
Prim, Shih-Ni, 80
"Procrastination Night," 137
professional development, 20, 26, 58, 61, 67–68, 211, 212, 222
professional tutors, 71, 72, 81, 82, 88, 104; accountability for, 99; contingency and, 89, 93–95; downplaying, 83; employment of, 91; engaging, 97; ethical concerns of, 98–99; stability of, 83; studying, 91–92; working environment for, 90; writing centers and, 76–78
professionalism, 15, 35, 120, 122, 210
provost, 183, 187, 188
"Psychological Disability and the Director's Chair: Interrogating the Relationship between Positionality and Pedagogy" (Elston), 159
Public Speaking, 113
publication, 9, 11, 73, 224; barriers to, 8; data, 15; likelihood of, 12, 14; problematizing, 225; process, 12, 13; writing for, 105
Puebla, 127, 129, 133

queer people, 7
queer practitioners, narratives of, 7
"Queering the Writing Center" (Denny), 5
Queerly Centered: LGBTQA Writing Center Directors Navigate the Workplace (Webster), 6–7
questions, open-ended, 72, 134

race, 5, 8, 15–16, 17, 19, 75, 178, 199, 221, 223
racial isolation, 220
racial justice, 209
racialization, 8, 202
racism, 4, 5, 12, 178, 201, 203, 211
RAD. *See* replicable, aggregable, and data
radical work, 34, 43
Radical Writing Center Praxis (Greenfield), 44
Rafoth, Ben, 75
Ramsey, William, 80, 81
Rawlins, Paula, 221
relationships, 34, 165; peer-to-peer, 74, 195; professional, 133; staff, 222; symbiotic, 91; writing center, 116
replicable, aggregable, and data (RAD), 36, 37, 42–43; research, 8–9, 34, 45
research, 43, 73, 99, 129, 160, 168, 222; community and, 163; conducting, 105; cutting-edge, 42; future, 100; marginality and, 35–38; methods, 36, 78, 131–32; questions, 133; topics, 19; writing center, 36, 39, 116, 128

"Responding to the Whole Person" (McBride), 120, 121
responsibility, 105, 140, 159; individual, 161; structural, 22
revision process, 16, 26
Rey, 94, 95, 96, 97
rhetoric, 36, 105, 156, 189, 205, 211
Rhetorics of Overcoming: Rewriting Narratives of Disability and Accessibility in Writing Studies (Hitt), 156
Rider, Wendy, 20–21, 57, 89, 103
Rinaldi, Kerri, 16, 21–22
Romney, Abraham, 116
Rowan, Karen, 4, 5
Royster, Jacquelyn Jones, 11

safety: language of, 198n1; searching for, 195–97
Salcedo, Myra Tatum, 23, 173, 215
Salem, Lori, 80, 81, 180
Santa, Tracy, 18
Schalk, Sami, 217n1
scholarship, 58, 104, 152, 155; anecdotal, 173; empirical, 43; post/decolonial, 116; producing, 105; publishing, 168, 222; rhetorical, 43; soliciting, 224; writing center, 4, 5, 6, 7–8, 10, 11, 18, 24, 25, 26, 33, 35, 36, 78, 81, 144
Schonberg, Eliana, 81
selection process, 16, 17, 223, 224
self-determination, 99, 158
self-preservation, 51, 174
Senese, Marcelene, 130
service opportunities, 53, 222
Sévère, Richard, 5
Severino, Carol, 80
sexual harassment, 24, 194
sexual violation, 24, 195, 197, 216
sexuality, 23, 75, 221
Shamoon, Linda, 74
Shur-Sytsma, Mandy, 75
Sicari, Anna, 5, 12, 194
Siebers, Tobin, 150
Sieman, Catherine, 78
Sirc, Geoffrey, 36
Snyder, William M., 131
social environment, 162, 167
social interactions, 8, 140, 155
social justice, 3, 27, 36, 42–43, 46, 98, 112, 209
social media, 59, 162, 163
social service projects, 137, 138
socialization, 156, 163, 164
Socratic dialogue, 66
Southern California Writing Centers Association (SoCalWCA), 68

spaces, 139, 146, 167, 198; budgeting/maintaining, 20; collaborative, 162; marginalized, 183, 184; pedagogical, 146; physical, 38, 205; transnational, 115; white, 216; writing center, 182, 223
speech, 150; hearing and, 151
Squarespace, 181
Standard Edited American English (SEAE), 146
STEM, 78, 117
Stephenson, Denise, 21, 89, 104, 221
stereotypes, 23, 157; Black woman, 200, 208; racist, 205
stigmatization, 156, 157
Stop Street Harassment, 194
storytelling: counter, 110–13, 123, 124. *See also* transnational counter storytelling
strategies, 120, 223; creating, 33, 137–38
structural issues, 17, 19, 52, 54, 206
submissions, 14; disagreement on, 15; ranking, 15–16; reviewing, 8
Summer Institute (IWCA), 127, 191, 193n6

"Talking in the Middle" (Harris), 120
task-switching, 155, 156, 161, 165–166, 169n3, 170n3
Taylor, Breonna, 7
TCS. *See* transnational counter storytelling
technology, 11, 41, 78, 117; hearing, 150; media, 54
Texas Hispanic-Serving Institution, 151
theory, 37, 155; engaging with, 36; marginality and, 35–38; rethinking, 123
"Theory, Lore, and More" (Driscoll and Perdue), 36
theory and practice, 4, 116, 120; writing center, 18, 42, 100, 110, 121, 124
Thompson, Isabelle, 74, 81
"To Be of Use" (Piercy), 69
training, 20, 39, 60, 75, 120; administrative, 35; courses, 53; generalizability of, 43; materials, 59; programs, 120; staff, 34; structure, 39, 40; tutor, 67, 100, 165, 221, 222; writing center, 37, 40
transitions, 54–58
transnational counter storytelling (TCS), 110, 112
Trimbur, John, 73, 74
TRIO grant, 53, 54, 60
TRIO students, 54, 55, 56, 62–63
"Triumph over Structures That Disempower" (Hashlamon), 105
Trudy, 200
tutorials, 53, 89, 211; impact, 91; writing, 88
tutoring, 18, 40, 72, 83, 96, 114, 131, 137–38, 205; concepts of "good," 23; continuing, 93; deaf student, 152; face-to-face, 197; noninterventionist, 74; one-on-one, 145; peer, 21, 74, 81; practices, 120, 141; professional, 104; roles, 115; services, 133; types of, 136f; visual, 196; writing center, 72, 73, 82, 84n3, 114
tutors: administration relationships of, 94; compensation for, 98; development of, 211; experienced, 80, 81; faculty, 71–72, 76, 81; fatigue of, 96; feedback for, 81; former, 139, 140; global approach for, 121; graduate student, 75, 76, 77, 78, 81, 82, 84n3; hiring, 205; knowledge creation and, 137; nonundergraduate, 76, 78; peer, 128; relationship with, 133; study participation by, 133; term, 79; types of, 71, 77t, 79; undergraduate, 71, 72–76, 78, 79–80, 82, 114, 212; women, 194, 198; working environment for, 95–96; writing, 129, 131, 212; writing center, 114, 128, 195. *See also* peer tutors; professional tutors
"2020 Associate Deans and Academic Administrators Assessment Report," 188

Universidad Autonoma del Estado de Puebla, 132
Universidad Popular Autonoma de Estado de Puebla (UPAEP), 127, 132
University College Building, 41
University of Ghana, 117, 124n1
University Press of Colorado, 12
"Unmaking Gringo Centers" (García), 181
UPAEP. *See* Universidad Popular Autonoma de Estado de Puebla
US Census Bureau, 178

Valentine, Kathryn, 80, 81
Valles, Sarah Banschbach, 10, 14, 179, 189, 200
Villagrán Mora, Abigail, 22, 23, 112, 144, 146, 222
visual imagery, 209
visual learners, 149

WAC. *See* Writing Across the Curriculum
Walker, Alice, 203
Walker, Clarissa, 221
way-making, marginalization and, 205–10
WCAs. *See* writing center administrators
WCenter, 71, 77
WCGN. *See* writing center grand narrative
WCJ, 79, 80; review of, 81, 83
WCPs. *See* writing center professionals
Webster, Travis, 6

Wenger, Étienne, 36, 130, 131, 138
Werth, Shalene, 173
white privilege, 4, 114
white supremacy, 203
whiteness, 4, 5, 111–12
"Whose Voices Are Heard? A Demographic Comparison of Authors Published in WLN 2005–2017 and Writers and Interested in Publishing" (Kleinfeld, Lee, and Prebel), 10
"Why 'White' Should Be Capitalized" (Painter), 192n1
WLN: A Journal of Writing Center Scholarship, 145, 221. *See also Writing Lab Newsletter*
Wolfe, Janna, 80
womanhood, Black, 200, 205
Woolf, Virginia, 69
working environments, 24, 89, 95–96; unsafe, 90, 216
Working Lives of New Writing Center Directors (Caswell, Grutsch McKinney, and Jackson), 37, 44, 49
workshops, 56, 74, 119, 139, 205, 208, 209, 211; pedagogy, 212; training, 59, 60; writing, 178, 179
World Englishes, 115
WPAs. *See* writing program administrators
WRC. *See* Writing and Reading Center
writing, 83, 88, 131, 154–55, 207; centrality of, 82; genre of, 111; identity and, 36; personal, 208; quality of, 224; research-based, 205; rhetorical grammar for, 211; rhythm of, 149
Writing Across the Curriculum (WAC), 46, 119, 120
Writing and Reading Center (WRC), 50, 51, 52, 53, 54–55, 56, 58, 63; reputation of, 59; staff role of, 60–61; working at, 62
"Writing Center Administrators and Diversity: A Survey" (Valles, Babcock, and Jackson), 179
writing center administrators (WCAs), 6, 8, 17, 19, 23, 26, 37, 43, 172, 173, 174, 210; of color, 185, 201; courses for, 44; history of labor and, 175; marginalization and, 18; realities of, 50; role of, 200; work of, 42, 202, 205
writing center directors, 42, 43, 75, 77, 92, 158, 161, 178, 179, 180, 181, 182, 183, 191; assumptions about, 11; demographic finding of, 14; disabled, 160; full-time tenure-track, 13–14; job announcement for, 189; marginalization of, 20; success for, 165; tenure-track, 33; working as, 189, 199
Writing Center Director's Resource (Murphy and Stay), 37

writing center grand narrative (WCGN), 4, 17, 72, 81–82, 112, 118, 194–95, 221; samples of, 195–97
Writing Center Journal (WCJ), 12, 13, 18, 35, 72, 75, 78, 127
writing center practitioners, 10, 18, 23, 25, 26, 74, 160, 165, 166, 221; disabled, 155, 160; home metaphor and, 202–3; identity of, 6; neurodiverse, 161, 162; queer, 6; successful, 157
writing center professionals (WCPs), 19, 21, 34, 35, 38, 46, 69, 104, 225; academic legitimacy and, 36; contingent, 105; disabled, 156; experience of, 66–67; marginalization of, 12; part-time, 105; work of, 67
Writing Center Research Project (WCRP), 90
writing center work, 5, 35, 40, 53, 82, 89, 112, 114, 121, 145, 155, 156, 208–9, 216–17; administrative labor of, 6; culture of, 165; disability justice in, 166–69; diversity and, 14; experiences of, 123; grand narratives of, 4; linguistic implications of, 36; misperceptions of, 25; neurodivergent and, 161–62; power of, 43; practicalities of, 42; professional roles in, 17; rigors of, 43; structures of, 165
Writing Centers: Theory and Advancement (Olsen), 36–37
writing centers: assumptions about, 223; Global South, 131–32; globalization of, 22, 113; heteronormative origins of, 5; history of, 45, 64; impact of, 80–81; knowledge about, 127; mission of, 96; models for, 11; operating, 146; positions at, 21–22; racialized spaces of, 5; relationship to campus of, 49; situation of, 219; structures within, 99; understanding, 144; work in, 27, 33, 98
Writing Centers and Disability (Muceck), 151
Writing Centers and the New Racism: A Call for Sustainable Dialogue and Change (Greenfield and Rowan), 4
Writing Centers Research Project (WCRP), 76, 77
writing coaches, hiring/training, 189–90
Writing in the Disciplines (WID), 46
Writing Lab Newsletter (WLN), 10, 13, 14, 18, 35, 127, 221. *See also WLN*
writing plans, individualized, 207
writing program administrators (WPAs), 180, 184, 206, 211, 213

Yin, Robert K., 132
Young, Vershawn Ashanti, 4

Zaragoza Public Library, 137

About the Editors

Elizabeth Kleinfeld is professor of English and writing center director at Metropolitan State University of Denver. She teaches courses on disability studies, rhetoric, and composition theory and practice. Her pedagogy and research are informed by disability studies, feminism, and social justice theory. She has coauthored a textbook on multimodal and multigenre composition and has published articles on disability, inclusivity, writing center work, and student source citation practices. She has won awards for collaboration and accessible teaching. She blogs about disability at elizabethkleinfeld.com.

Sohui Lee is associate professor and the faculty director of the Writing and Multiliteracy Center at California State University Channel Islands (CSUCI). She gained writing center experience as assistant and associate director of Stanford's Hume Center of Writing and Speaking and helped start its multiliteracy programs. At CSUCI, she founded the Writing & Multiliteracy Center. Her research scholarship includes multiliteracy pedagogy, multimodal communication, and academic creativity. She is coeditor of *The Routledge Reader on Writing Center and New Media* (2013) and coauthor of *Design For Composition: Inspiration for Creative Visual and Multimodal Projects* (Parlor Press, Fall 2023). She also worked as associate editor at *WLN: A Journal of Writing Center Scholarship* (2017–2021) and published over thirty articles and chapters in peer-reviewed journals such as *Writing*

Center Journal (WCJ), WLN, Praxis, Southern Discourse in the Center (SJC), American Periodicals, Across the Disciplines (ATD), and *Computers and Composition.*

Julie Prebel is associate professor of American studies, writing center director, and director of the College Writing Program at Occidental College in Los Angeles. She teaches courses in American cultural studies, rhetorical studies, and writing. Her pedagogy and research are informed by feminist theory, gender and sexuality studies, theories of critical race and ethnicity, film and media studies, composition-rhetoric, and practices of equity and justice. She has published in top peer-reviewed journals in writing center and composition studies and presents her work widely at national conferences in those fields and in American studies.

www.ingramcontent.com/pod-product-compliance
Lightning Source LLC
Chambersburg PA
CBHW060557080526
44585CB00013B/597